Trauma-Informed Treatment and Prevention of Intimate Partner Violence

Trauma-Informed Treatment and Prevention of Intimate Partner Violence

Casey T. Taft, Christopher M. Murphy, and
Suzannah K. Creech

American Psychological Association • Washington, DC

Published by
American Psychological Association
750 First Street, NE
Washington, DC 20002
www.apa.org

To order
APA Order Department
P.O. Box 92984
Washington, DC 20090-2984
Tel: (800) 374-2721; Direct: (202) 336-5510
Fax: (202) 336-5502; TDD/TTY: (202) 336-6123
Online: www.apa.org/pubs/books
E-mail: order@apa.org

In the U.K., Europe, Africa, and the Middle East, copies may be ordered from
American Psychological Association
3 Henrietta Street
Covent Garden, London
WC2E 8LU England

Typeset in Goudy by Circle Graphics, Inc., Columbia, MD

Printer: Bang Printing, Brainerd, MN
Cover Designer: Naylor Design, Washington, DC

Library of Congress Cataloging-in-Publication Data

Names: Taft, Casey T., author. | Murphy, Christopher M. (Christopher Mark), author. | Creech, Suzannah K., author.
Title: Trauma-informed treatment and prevention of intimate partner violence / Casey T. Taft, Christopher M. Murphy, Suzannah K. Creech.
Description: First edition. | Washington, DC : American Psychological Association, 2016. | Includes bibliographical references and index.
Identifiers: LCCN 2015046297 | ISBN 9781433822315 | ISBN 1433822318
Subjects: LCSH: Abusive men—Rehabilitation. | Abusive women—Rehabilitation. | Psychic trauma—Treatment. | Intimate partner violence—Prevention.
Classification: LCC RC569.5.F3 T34 2016 | DDC 616.85/82—dc23 LC record available at http://lccn.loc.gov/2015046297

British Library Cataloguing-in-Publication Data
A CIP record is available from the British Library.

Printed in the United States of America
First Edition

http://dx.doi.org/10.1037/14918-000

CONTENTS

Trauma-Informed Treatment and Prevention of Intimate Partner Violence

INTRODUCTION

Trauma is life altering, and its effects are pervasive. It affects many life domains, and it may hinder the development of treatment relationships and help-seeking behaviors (Fallot & Harris, 2001). For services to be truly trauma informed, all aspects of service delivery must recognize and account for the impacts of trauma and the ways in which trauma may affect behavior change processes (Fallot & Harris, 2001). Our goal for this book is to provide a trauma-informed approach for understanding and intervening with individuals who engage in intimate partner violence (IPV). Although trauma-informed approaches are increasingly common in services for IPV survivors, in the chapters that follow we present evidence indicating that trauma-informed services are also very important in work with individuals who perpetrate IPV and represent an innovation over long-held approaches that tend to disregard or minimize the role of trauma.

http://dx.doi.org/10.1037/14918-001
Trauma-Informed Treatment and Prevention of Intimate Partner Violence, by C. T. Taft, C. M. Murphy, and S. K. Creech

There is seemingly universal acknowledgment that exposure to trauma and abuse contributes to aggression and other problem behaviors in children. Interventions designed to prevent these problem behaviors address the abused child's faulty ways of interpreting the world around them resulting from their experience of abuse (Dodge, Godwin, & The Conduct Problems Prevention Research Group, 2013). Although numerous books have addressed the topic of preventing aggression in trauma-exposed children (Crenshaw & Mordock, 2005; Gil, 2011; Goodyear-Brown, 2009; Levine & Kline, 2006), heretofore no such resource has focused on accounting for trauma in interventions for adults who engage in IPV. There is little reason to think that problem behaviors resulting from childhood trauma simply go away on their own when abused children reach adulthood, and an extensive research base indicates that both childhood and adult trauma are linked with abusive and violent behavior in intimate relationships.

This book is intended to assist clinicians in understanding the relationship between trauma exposure and IPV in adulthood and to provide the knowledge and skills to deliver effective trauma-informed intervention services to individuals who engage in IPV. As we discuss in the following sections, decades of research have demonstrated high rates of trauma exposure, most notably abuse in childhood, among individuals who engage in IPV. There is an increasing recognition that models of IPV that do not take trauma into consideration are incomplete and may impede the success of prevention and treatment of violent behavior. The notion that we must give greater weight to trauma has been highlighted recently, not only through work with returning military veterans who have experienced significant trauma and exhibit IPV but also by our own recent clinical studies that have demonstrated the effectiveness of trauma-focused interventions. As we will discuss, research also demonstrates that models of IPV that incorporate trauma are relevant for both military and civilian populations. There has been a movement in the general IPV intervention field to better train counselors on trauma and its impacts, although at the time this book is being written there is no singular resource that focuses on this important issue.

This book will benefit any provider who works with violent or partner-abusive individuals. This includes those who work with civilian and military populations who exhibit problems with IPV, forensic populations, and both men and women. We believe that no abusive client is without any prior trauma or other prior life event (or events) that has shaped the way he or she views others and that influences his or her behavior in interpersonal relationships. Thus, this book is not intended to be used only with a specific subgroup of traumatized individuals who engage in IPV; instead, it is meant to be used for work with anyone who has engaged in IPV or is at risk for engaging in IPV. Although the grouping of abusive individuals into subtypes has received considerable attention previously in the IPV literature (Holtzworth-Munroe & Stuart, 1994), these typologies have not lent themselves to effective treatment-matching strategies. Given the current state of knowledge in this area, we do not recommend dividing those who use IPV into different categories and providing different interventions, with the possible exception, as we discuss in Chapter 9, of couples therapy approaches, for safety reasons.

Training activities for individuals who provide services to persons who engage in IPV rarely focus on trauma, its impact on relationship functioning, or strategies to address its effects. This book constitutes an important resource for individual providers and program heads who would like to expand their training and clinical skill set in light of the increasing recognition of the salience of trauma in abusive behavior.

We believe this book is timely because the link between trauma and IPV is increasingly recognized in the IPV community and because even the most ardent supporters of models of IPV intervention that historically have not accounted for trauma are coming to realize that we cannot continue to ignore the elephant in the room. Trauma-informed intervention for those who engage in IPV is indeed an idea whose time has come; in fact, it is long overdue.

We want to make clear at the outset that taking a trauma-informed perspective does not minimize IPV, attempt to excuse it, or hold those who use IPV any less accountable. We can acknowledge the effects of one's prior trauma and other negative life experiences, and work to better understand the impact of these experiences on relationships and IPV behaviors, while working with clients to be accountable for their behavior. In fact, both elements are critical for successful IPV intervention, and those who engage in IPV will be far more likely to accept responsibility for their abusive behavior if they feel heard, and understood, by their provider.

DEFINING *INTIMATE PARTNER VIOLENCE*

IPV behaviors take many forms. Our focus is on physical and psychological IPV because these two forms of abuse have considerable topographical and functional overlap and are the primary targets for intervention. Furthermore, trauma and posttraumatic stress disorder (PTSD) seem to be particularly strongly linked to these forms of IPV, though not as strongly linked to sex abuse (Teten, Schumacher, Bailey, & Kent, 2009). Physical IPV is perhaps the more observable of the two forms and includes all forms of physical aggression, with abusive behaviors ranging in severity from pushing and grabbing to punching, kicking, or using a weapon on a partner.

Psychological IPV is typically less obvious than physical IPV, but research shows that it can have an equal or greater negative impact on the physical and psychological health of the recipient (Coker, Smith, McKeown, & King, 2000; O'Leary, Heyman, & Neidig, 1999). Furthermore, psychological IPV early in relationships often escalates to physical IPV later (Murphy & O'Leary, 1989). Murphy and Hoover (1999) described four groupings of psychologically abusive behaviors that are based on the functions that the abuse might serve:

- *Behaviors that make the other person afraid.* Examples include threats to harm the other person; threats to harm oneself; threats to harm friends or relatives; intimidating looks or gestures; destruction of objects or personal belongings; driving recklessly to frighten the other person; aggression towards walls, doors, furniture, and so on.
- *Behaviors that attack the partner's self-esteem.* Examples include put-downs, such as calling the other person stupid, crazy, ugly, or worthless; forcing the other person to do humiliating things; treating the other person like a child; and other such actions.
- *Behaviors that limit the other person's basic rights and freedoms.* Examples include trying to stop the other person from going places, trying to stop the other person from seeing certain friends or family members, trying to stop him or her from getting a job or going to school, controlling the family finances, making important family decisions without consulting the other person, acting like the other person is a servant, and similar behaviors.
- *Behaviors intended to punish the other person or make him or her feel insecure in the relationship.* Examples include refusing to have any discussion regarding a problem or relationship issue, withholding affection to get back at the other person, refusing to acknowledge a problem that the other person feels is important, leaving and angrily refusing to tell the other person where you are going, and so forth.

DEFINING *TRAUMA* AND *POSTTRAUMATIC STRESS DISORDER*

There are myriad terms with varying definitions and connotations in this area of mental health practice. For the present purposes, the common diagnostic definition of *traumatic stress* captures many of the life events and experiences that increase risk for IPV. As defined in the *Diagnostic and Statistical Manual of Mental Disorders* (fifth edition [*DSM–5*]; American Psychiatric Association, 2013), traumatic stress involves "exposure to actual or threatened death, serious injury, or sexual violence" (p. 271). Although trauma usually is conceptualized in terms of direct exposure to such events, the *DSM–5* diagnostic criterion also allows for exposure through witnessing such events in person, finding out that a traumatic event has occurred to a close family member or friend, or being exposed in a repeated or extreme fashion to the unpleasant details of a traumatic event (vicarious traumatization). The World Health Organization's (1992) *International Classification of Diseases, 10th Edition* (*ICD–10*), describes a *traumatic stressor* as exposure to a situation that is exceptionally threatening or catastrophic in nature and likely to cause pervasive distress. Examples include exposure to military combat, war, physical assault, sexual assault, being kidnapped or taken hostage, terrorist attacks, natural disasters, and motor vehicle accidents.

In understanding and treating IPV, it may be helpful to expand the definition of traumatic stress to include adverse experiences that can dramatically alter the development of interpersonal and emotional functioning but may not fit precisely within the diagnostic formulation of traumatic stress. Most notable are persistent experiences of emotional abuse, in which a child or adult is denigrated, humiliated, devalued, or intimidated; significant abandonment and detachment experiences; emotional neglect; and physical neglect. Even if not accompanied by trauma exposures consistent with the *DSM–5* or *ICD–10* definitions, such as physical or sexual abuse, these other adversities can alter one's core beliefs and emotions regarding safety, closeness, trust, power, and control. The results are often manifested as serious problems in intimate relationships.

Similar to the definition of traumatic stress, the common diagnostic formulation of PTSD has important implications for understanding and treating IPV, but it also provides an incomplete framework. Although the *ICD–10* includes PTSD under the stress-related disorders category, until the publication of *DSM–5*, which contains a separate category for traumatic stress disorders, PTSD was considered an anxiety disorder. This is not surprising given that the diagnostic definition of PTSD focuses primarily on the anxiety-related consequences of trauma exposure, specifically the tendency to be troubled by recollections and reminders of the trauma; avoidance of thoughts, feelings, memories, and situations associated with the trauma; and symptoms of anxious arousal, such as insomnia and hypervigilance. As we discuss throughout this book, these symptoms enhance sensitivity to danger and threat, thereby altering key aspects of social information processing that contribute to relationship problems and IPV.

Particularly relevant to our focus on IPV are changes to the *DSM–5* PTSD symptom cluster formerly known as *hyperarousal* and now renamed "alterations in arousal and reactivity that are associated with the traumatic event(s)," falling within Cluster E. One of the symptoms in this cluster has been changed from "irritability/anger" to "irritability or aggressive behavior."

The reasons cited for this change were to reduce overlap between this symptom and the new Criterion D ("Negative alterations in cognitions and mood that are associated with the traumatic event") symptom "persistent negative emotional state" and to reflect consistent findings, discussed throughout this book, that aggression is a common manifestation of PTSD (M. W. Miller, Wolf, & Keane, 2014). It is important to note, however, that irritability and outbursts of anger remain part of the hyperarousal symptom cluster in *ICD–10* and that aggression is not specifically included.

Acknowledgment of the link between PTSD and aggression in the revised *DSM–5* criteria appears to represent a positive development, but it also raises considerations in our work with trauma-exposed individuals who use IPV and those who experience the IPV. It is important that our clients and those who experience the abuse do not come to view IPV as an unavoidable psychological manifestation of trauma exposure. We caution partners in couples with whom we work to avoid the interpretation that the abusive behavior they experience is simply a component of PTSD and just goes along with the diagnosis. Similarly, we promote the view with our clients that they have learned to be aggressive and to view others in a negative way but that this can be unlearned despite one's PTSD status.

In addition to anxiety-based reactions that are central to the diagnosis of PTSD, traumatic stress and childhood adversities alter other aspects of emotion regulation and interpersonal functioning that are important in understanding and treating IPV. For example, among persons seen in community treatment agencies for engaging in IPV, more than 80% report traumatic stress exposures (Hoyt, Wray, Wiggins, Gerstle, & Maclean, 2012; Semiatin, 2012), yet only 13% to 28% meet the symptomatic criteria for a probable diagnosis of PTSD. In fact, many trauma-exposed individuals who use IPV report few or none of the classic anxiety-based symptoms of PTSD (Gutjahr, Portnoy, & Murphy, 2014). Thus, concepts that go beyond the diagnostic formulation of PTSD are necessary to understand the links between trauma and IPV, in particular with respect to the role of childhood trauma exposures.

It is interesting that laboratory studies have shown that the most common emotional reaction to exposure to trauma cues among those with PTSD involves anger rather than anxiety or other emotions (Pitman, Orr, Forgue, de Jong, & Claiborn, 1987; Taft, Street, Marshall, Dowdall, & Riggs, 2007), and anger tends to increase more sharply after such exposures than anxiety (Taft, Street, et al., 2007). Despite numerous studies showing a link between anger and use of IPV (Birkley & Eckhardt, 2015), as well as research indicating that anger statistically accounts for the relationship between PTSD and IPV (Taft, Street, et al., 2007), some professionals downplay the role of anger because they believe it diminishes personal responsibility for abusive behavior. We see no reason why one should be held less accountable for their abusive behavior if that person has problems with anger. It is far better to acknowledge rather than deny links between anger and IPV so that we can be more effective in our IPV intervention work.

Other diagnoses are informative here yet also limited in understanding how trauma exposure can lead to IPV. Most notable is that the emotional dysregulation and interpersonal turmoil associated with borderline personality disorder (BPD) appear to characterize a subgroup of individuals who engage in IPV (Holtzworth-Munroe, Meehan, Herron, Rehman, & Stuart, 2000). Although a history of childhood trauma is not a diagnostic element of BPD, it is highly prevalent among individuals with this condition (Newnham & Janca, 2014; Westphal et al., 2013), and it is thought to produce extreme emotion dysregulation and interpersonal dysfunction when combined with invalidation of emotional experiences by caregivers during development (Linehan, 1993). As with PTSD, however, it is important to note that only a modest proportion of those who engage in IPV meet the diagnostic criteria for BPD (<25% using a structured diagnostic interview; Hart, Dutton, & Newlove, 1993).

Some clinical scholars have conceptualized emotion dysregulation and interpersonal difficulties as core symptoms of complex trauma reactions, or *complex PTSD* (Cloitre, Miranda, Stovall-McClough, & Han, 2005). When linked to an extended pattern of childhood abuse exposure, however, the only thing that is truly "complex" about these symptoms is that they are not well captured by the traditional diagnosis of PTSD. Avoidance and suppression of negative emotions, perceived lack of control of one's emotional reactions, and periodic emotional outbursts are among the most common legacies of childhood trauma. These problems are often compounded by problematic coping, including the abuse of substances, as well as impulse control problems that can impair functioning in a variety of life areas.

STRUCTURE OF THIS BOOK

In Chapter 1, we describe a social information processing theory to explain how trauma exposure increases risk for IPV. This model is based on considerable prior research and theory and serves as the basis for clinical work to understand and address the links between trauma and IPV. In short, this model holds that the experience of trauma negatively affects how individuals process social information, which ultimately leads to a misappraisal of intimate relationship events, an overly hostile attribution bias, emotional avoidance and avoidant coping strategies, and reduced ability to generate and enact socially competent responses to normal challenges that emerge in relationships. We spell out the details of this model and provide a common-language, nontechnical review of research studies conducted by ourselves and others that support this model. A primary goal is to highlight the cognitive, emotional, and behavioral targets for intervention and prevention of violence from a trauma-informed perspective.

Chapters 2 and 3 focus on understanding the links between trauma and IPV in both military and civilian populations. Trauma and PTSD have been associated with use of IPV across both populations (Taft, Walling, Howard, & Monson, 2011), but the magnitude of the relationship differs, and different forms of trauma and life events may be especially relevant for one group versus the other. For example, military training and exposure to unique forms of trauma (traditional combat exposure, perceptions of threat in the war zone, and exposure to atrocities) present a unique set of factors to consider in understanding military IPV, whereas childhood trauma has received a greater emphasis in the civilian literature and perhaps has greater salience for understanding IPV. We also discuss the relevance of other models of aggressive behavior and the importance of examining combinations of risk factors in understanding IPV (Finkel, 2007), as well as the literature focusing specifically on women's use of IPV.

Chapters 4 and 5 focus on strategies and safety in IPV assessment and intervention. We discuss the concept of therapeutic assessment and how to incorporate motivational interviewing to directly assess and address IPV by clients. We discuss a trauma-informed, multimethod approach to assessing potential trauma, IPV, and other common co-occurring trauma-related disorders and problems, as well as motivational issues. Strategies for providing client feedback and assisting with goal setting are also covered. The critically important role of confidential partner assessment is discussed, as are issues related to ensuring safety of partners and the provision of appropriate mental health services and other resources. We also discuss available risk assessment measures and their use and the importance of forming relationships with the larger community of providers to help ensure safety for those who experience IPV.

In Chapter 6, we discuss process considerations in IPV intervention. We discuss *process factors*, or nonspecific factors, that exert a powerful impact on treatment outcomes regardless of the form of intervention we provide. This topic is particularly important for IPV intervention given that the field has largely downplayed the significance of process factors despite the fact that clients who use IPV often present to treatment with trauma histories and interpersonal features that make the development of a positive therapy process challenging. We review the literature on process factors, namely, the therapeutic alliance and motivational readiness for change, with respect to IPV intervention. We also discuss core themes that may underlie trauma and IPV, including guilt and shame, power and control conflicts, trust difficulties, and low self-esteem, and we address how to uncover and address these themes and their impact on the therapeutic process.

In Chapters 7 and 8, we address group interventions and techniques for facilitating a positive group atmosphere and effective IPV preventing and intervention. Group intervention is the standard format for IPV programs. We discuss the literature on the importance of group cohesion in IPV intervention and focus on why enhancing cohesion may be particularly important among trauma-exposed clients, who often have few sources of social support. With an emphasis on the work of Yalom (1995), we present specific techniques that providers can use to facilitate greater cohesion in IPV intervention. We then describe a specific example of a group IPV intervention, the Strength at Home Men's Program, which we developed and tested via pilot studies and a randomized controlled trial. We discuss session content for this intervention, provide (in the Appendixes) some handouts and materials that highlight trauma-informed elements of the program, and review the available research evidence that attests to its effectiveness.

We discuss couples interventions for preventing and treating IPV in trauma-exposed individuals in Chapters 9 and 10. We describe the controversy regarding the ethics and safety of treating IPV in the couples context as well as the evidence suggesting that dyadic intervention is most helpful for couples who display low-level situational couple violence. We also discuss how trauma may influence couple dynamics and hinder communication, emotional expression, and intimacy. Differences in treatment needs between single- and dual-trauma couples are described, as are advantages of addressing core themes in work with couples. We describe safety issues and steps to enhance safety in work with couples and review several dyadic interventions that may prevent or end IPV. We provide an example of a trauma-informed couples-based IPV group intervention program that we have developed and evaluated, the Strength at Home Couples' Program. We review session content and the evidence suggesting the effectiveness of the program.

Chapters 11 and 12 present individual therapy strategies and examples, a topic that has received relatively little attention in the clinical and research literatures. We discuss sequential treatment models in which individual sessions are delivered before or after a standard group intervention. For example, these interventions can involve pregroup preparation to enhance motivation, or they can be used postintervention to prevent relapse of problem behaviors or to address PTSD or other trauma-related problems that the group may not have fully addressed. Simultaneous models in which clients receive supportive individual intervention to address safety issues or imminent concerns while also engaging in group intervention for IPV also are discussed. We address individual treatment as an alternative to group intervention as well as the practical and clinical concerns worth considering when deciding on group versus individual approaches. We also detail case formulation strategies that allow for flexible selection and implementation of individually focused intervention strategies based on the client's needs.

In Chapter 13 we focus on adjunctive interventions that may be particularly indicated in a trauma-exposed population who uses IPV. We note the importance of examining the client's full diagnostic picture, which may include housing status, occupational status, literacy and education, parenting status, injury and physical health status, and psychiatric status. Whether the comorbid problems may impede IPV intervention is considered and then illustrated by how one of us handles substance abuse issues in a general IPV clinic. Finally, we consider adjunctive or concomitant interventions for some of the most common comorbid issues in persons who present for IPV intervention, including PTSD, depression, substance use problems, and traumatic brain injury.

We conclude the book with an Afterword in which we summarize the material covered in the chapters and offer our insights into what is needed to implement trauma-informed IPV intervention on a large scale. We discuss potential barriers to instituting trauma-informed IPV interventions, such as challenges in the coordination of care, state IPV intervention standards, a reliance on a system of court-mandated intervention, and an incorrect view that trauma-informed care means holding one's clients less responsible for their abusive behavior.

SUMMARY

Trauma and its impacts are often recognized and addressed among children, although when these traumatized children reach adulthood recognition of the effects of their trauma appears to fade among some treatment providers. In this book, we address how trauma in both childhood and adulthood may increase risk for IPV, discuss some potential reasons for this relationship with a focus on social information processing, present intervention strategies and examples for addressing trauma and IPV, and provide a summary of research findings demonstrating the efficacy of trauma-informed interventions for IPV in military veterans. This book is particularly needed at this time given the increasing recognition of the potential effects of trauma on relationships, and on IPV specifically, and the limitations of existing interventions that address such trauma.

I

FOUNDATIONS

1

SOCIAL INFORMATION PROCESSING MODEL OF TRAUMA AND INTIMATE PARTNER VIOLENCE

As is the case with individuals who exhibit a variety of problem behaviors, how one perceives and interprets his or her social world is of central importance to the treatment of clients who engage in intimate partner violence (IPV), and helping individuals to view others and their environment in a reasonable fashion is a key goal for therapy. With individuals who have histories of trauma, this process typically involves helping them to make more positive, and fewer negative, interpretations of their social world. Social information processing models are particularly relevant when discussing the impact of trauma on IPV and interventions designed to prevent and treat such violence. This perspective serves as the basis of our own IPV work, and throughout the remainder of the book we discuss how this model informs specific intervention strategies. At the core of the social information processing model is the concept that trauma affects how one interprets and otherwise processes information gathered from the social environment. Put

http://dx.doi.org/10.1037/14918-002
Trauma-Informed Treatment and Prevention of Intimate Partner Violence, by C. T. Taft, C. M. Murphy, and S. K. Creech

more specifically, trauma exposure can produce biases and deficits in social information processing that place individuals at risk for engaging in violence. Thus, it follows that developing a better understanding of how the client's processing of social information has been influenced by trauma exposures, and helping the client unlearn such biases and interpret various social situations in a more reasonable fashion, should lead to healthier relationships and a reduction in abusive behavior.

ORIGINS OF THE SOCIAL INFORMATION PROCESSING MODEL

Social information processing models derived from early work on social skills conducted by behaviorally oriented investigators (Twentyman & Zimering, 1979) who focused on understanding social skills and social competence among individuals with problems such as alcoholism (Chaney, O'Leary, & Marlatt, 1978) and sexual dysfunction (Lobitz & LoPiccolo, 1972). On the basis of this work, McFall (1982) developed an influential social information processing model of social skills that involves three sequential stages through which elements of social information are transformed into responses: (a) decoding skills, (b) decision skills, and (c) enactment skills. These responses may then be judged as "competent" or "incompetent" by the individual or significant others. In Figure 1.1, we illustrate a modified version of this model as it applies to trauma-exposed individuals at risk for IPV. Please note that this is a heuristic model and that some factors, such as substance use, can affect social information processing across multiple levels.

In the first processing sequence, which involves *decoding skills*, incoming information is received, perceived, and interpreted in relation to meaning structures, or schemas, available to the individual. As we discuss and illustrate later in this chapter, it is easy to see how core beliefs underlying trauma and relationship problems, such as guilt and shame, power and control conflicts, trust difficulties, and low self-esteem may influence one's decoding abilities in a given situation. Furthermore, compromised decoding skills may be caused by the inattention or distraction that often accompanies posttraumatic stress disorder (PTSD) and anger, traumatic brain injury, substance use, depression, and other problems associated with trauma.

In Chapters 7 through 13, which focus on clinical intervention, we describe several strategies to enhance the decoding of social information. As we discuss in those chapters, the self-monitoring of cognitions during anger episodes is an important tool to understand potentially biased and distorted negative thought patterns that may escalate difficult situations. The ultimate hope of intervention is that the self-monitoring and feedback learned will help the client uncover core beliefs or schemas that may be the result of

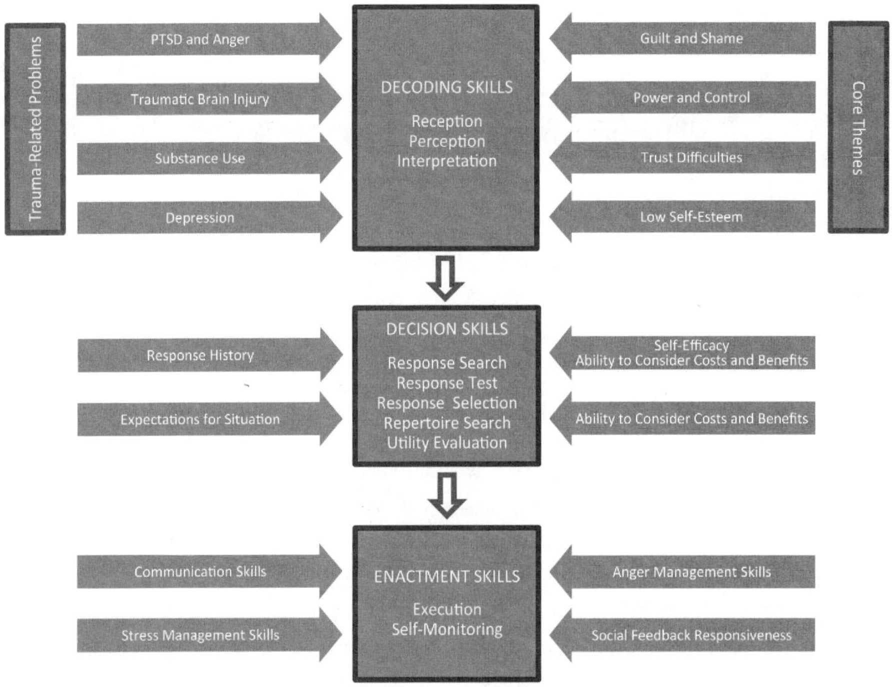

Figure 1.1. Trauma-informed social information processing model. PTSD = posttraumatic stress disorder.

trauma or other negative life events and that influence his or her decoding ability as well as processing along the other social information processing sequences. The recognition and understanding of other problems that may affect social information processing (e.g., PTSD, traumatic brain injury, substance use) are also important components of trauma-informed IPV intervention based on the social information processing model.

The second processing sequence is the *decision skills* stage, which involves generating possible responses to a given situation, evaluating the match of the response options to the situation, selecting the best response, searching one's own behavioral repertoire for appropriate responses, and weighing the usefulness of the selected response. The response choice is influenced by the individual's understanding of what is expected in the situation, appraisals of one's ability to carry out various responses, and potential costs and benefits of different response options.

The third and final sequence, *enactment skills*, involves carrying out the selected response, monitoring and evaluating its impact, and making any necessary mid-course adjustments to achieve the impact that was intended.

Here, skills learned in IPV intervention, such as those relating to communication, stress management, and anger management, are often put to the test, and the client's ability to be receptive to and benefit from social feedback are important determinants of future successful responses to conflictual situations.

Under most circumstances, social information processing sequences occur quickly and appear largely automatic to the individual. An essential component of IPV intervention guided by the social information processing model is to allow for a more deliberate and conscious processing of social information across difficult situations. Successful therapeutic work may often focus on walking the client through the different sequences just described. In addition to the decoding skills work we described, the provider often assists the client in generating and evaluating responses to conflict situations, determining the best available response, and working through issues related to self-efficacy to carry out effective responses. Of course, much IPV work focuses on processing and evaluating the impacts of chosen responses in order to learn from these events and respond more effectively in the future.

Amy Holtzworth-Munroe and colleagues (Holtzworth-Munroe & Anglin, 1991; Holtzworth-Munroe & Hutchinson, 1993) conducted a series of research studies in which they applied McFall's (1982) model to IPV (which we describe in more detail later in this chapter). In these applications, social information processing deficits interfere with the ability of partner-violent men to respond appropriately to relationship situations and scenarios. Holtzworth-Munroe (1992) posited that anger interferes with rational cognitive processing, resulting in a cascade of skills deficits that lead to IPV. This model has been highly influential, serving as a theoretical framework for cognitive–behavioral interventions designed to correct cognitive misappraisals and relationship skills deficits among those who engage in IPV (e.g., Murphy & Eckhardt, 2005).

SOCIAL INFORMATION PROCESSING DEFICITS AND AGGRESSIVE BEHAVIOR IN CHILDREN

The development of deficits in social information processing is believed to begin in childhood, and several studies conducted by Dodge and his colleagues have demonstrated that childhood exposure to trauma and abuse contributes to deficits that pose a risk for aggressive behavior (Dodge, Coie, & Lynam, 2006). For example, Dodge, Pettit, Bates, and Valente (1995) found that children who experienced physical abuse before age 5 were 4 to 5 times more likely to exhibit externalizing problems. Furthermore, social information processing deficits were shown to explain this relationship such that childhood abuse exposure predicted social information processing deficits, and these deficits in turn predicted aggressive behavior toward others. More specifically, abused children were more likely to assume that others had hostile intentions during ambiguous scenarios, and those who displayed this attribution style were more likely to exhibit aggression. Longitudinal evidence also indicates that social information processing deficits (specifically, response generation and evaluation abilities) help explain how exposure to interparental relationship conflict during childhood contributes to later aggressiveness in romantic relationships in young adulthood (Fite et al., 2008).

Theory and research on the role of social information processing in the development of children's aggression have led to interventions that target social information processing deficits and biases (Dodge, Godwin, & The Conduct Problems Prevention Research Group, 2013; Raver et al., 2011). For example, Dodge et al. (2013) evaluated whether improvements in children's social information processing abilities explained the effectiveness of the Fast Track prevention intervention. This program exposes high-risk kindergarten children to a multiyear intervention aimed at enhancing their social-cognitive skills via classroom teaching, parent training, tutoring and peer coaching, and small group activities. As the researchers hypothesized, the program had a positive impact on social cognition in Grades 1 through 5 that led to reductions in antisocial behavior and aggression; specifically, the intervention helped participants make more benign attributions in response to peer provocations, to generate more competent responses to social problems, and to view aggressive response options as more detrimental to the situation at hand.

RESEARCH FINDINGS FOR THE SOCIAL INFORMATION PROCESSING MODEL AND ADULT INTIMATE PARTNER VIOLENCE

As mentioned earlier, Holtzworth-Munroe and her colleagues have conducted a series of studies that demonstrated deficits in social problem solving and social skills among men who used IPV relative to nonviolent controls (Anglin & Holtzworth-Munroe, 1997; Clements, Holtzworth-Munroe, Schweinle, & Ickes, 2007; Holtzworth-Munroe & Anglin, 1991; Holtzworth-Munroe & Hutchinson, 1993; Marshall & Holtzworth-Munroe, 2010). To be specific, individuals who had engaged in IPV attributed more negative intentions to relationship partners in hypothetical conflict scenarios, were more angered by a range of partner behaviors, generated and selected more aggressive and less socially competent responses to challenging relationship events, and had more favorable expectations regarding the potential effects of aggressive responses to relationship conflicts.

Eckhardt and his colleagues have similarly demonstrated that men who had used IPV, in comparison with nonviolent men, display higher levels of irrational beliefs and cognitive distortions in response to hypothetical relationship events (Eckhardt, Barbour, & Davison, 1998; Eckhardt & Jamison, 2002; Eckhardt & Kassinove, 1998). These researchers used the Articulated Thoughts in Simulated Situations paradigm (ATSS; Davison, Robins, & Johnson, 1983), a methodology that assesses thoughts during anger arousal. The ATSS method is based on the expectation that anger-related thoughts are more easily accessed and reported when the individual is in an angry mood state and relevant relationship cues are present. This procedure is advantageous because automatic, affectively linked cognitions are often inaccessible in "cold" assessment contexts, such as responding to a standard questionnaire. With the ATSS procedure, participants listen to an audiotaped anger-inducing scenario and are instructed to imagine that they are participating in the scenario and to verbalize their thoughts and feelings when prompted. These verbalizations are then coded for a number of irrational beliefs, cognitive biases, and anger-control strategies.

In three separate investigations, Eckhardt and his colleagues have found that men who used IPV evidenced more irrational thoughts and cognitive biases, and fewer anger-control statements, during the ATSS procedure, in contrast to nonviolent men experiencing relationship distress (Eckhardt et al., 1998; Eckhardt & Jamison, 2002; Eckhardt & Kassinove, 1998). Evidence from these studies also suggests that men who had engaged in IPV experienced more hostile attributional biases. This body of research has assisted in elucidating specific cognitive biases and distortions that may serve as important targets for IPV intervention.

RISK FACTORS FOR SOCIAL INFORMATION PROCESSING DEFICITS

As we discussed in Chapters 2 and 3, a vast research base indicates that individuals who use IPV are particularly likely to report prior trauma experiences (e.g., childhood maltreatment, exposure to interparental violence, exposure to war zone stressors) and exhibit PTSD symptomatology (Rosenbaum & Leisring, 2003; Taft, Schumm, Marshall, Panuzio, & Holtzworth-Munroe, 2008; Taft, Street, Marshall, Dowdall, & Riggs, 2007). Research indicates that trauma and PTSD are associated with faulty social information processing, including a heightened perception of threat in ambiguous situations and a negative bias in interpreting others' behavior (Constans, 2005).

Earlier trauma theorists suggested that trauma may lead to aggressive behavior because of social information processing difficulties. For example, Chemtob and his colleagues (Chemtob, Novaco, Hamada, & Gross, 1997; Chemtob, Novaco, Hamada, Gross, & Smith, 1997; see also Novaco & Chemtob, 1998) have asserted that problems with anger and aggression among veterans with PTSD may occur because they enter into a "survival mode" of functioning. They have hypothesized that individuals with PTSD are more likely to perceive threats in their environment because of their prior experience of trauma and life threat, and these veterans become, in essence, physiologically and cognitively wired to misperceive social cues and thus inappropriately respond with aggression. As a result, a veteran may exhibit, across a range of nonthreatening situations, an increased fight-or-flight response and an overly hostile interpretation of events, an inclination toward confirming a potential threat, and a lower threshold for responding to the threat. When the survival mode is activated, these individuals are also less able to engage in appropriate self-monitoring or self-inhibition. As a result, the risk for violence and aggression is greatly increased.

Consistent with this "survival mode" model of social information processing among individuals who have been exposed to trauma, one would expect that PTSD hyperarousal symptoms, characterized by problems with anger, increased physiological arousal, and hypervigilance to potential trauma cues, would be strongly related to IPV. We have obtained research findings in military and civilian samples that highlight the role of hyperarousal symptoms and social information processing problems in the development of IPV (Taft et al., 2008; Taft, Street, et al., 2007; Taft, Weatherill, et al., 2015). We have also obtained evidence consistent with the notion that PTSD is associated with IPV through its influence on social information processing. In a community-based sample of 161 men (Taft et al., 2008), early trauma experiences were related to use of both physical and psychological IPV in adulthood because of their impact on both PTSD symptoms and social information processing deficits, assessed via responses to hypothetical relationship vignettes intended to assess decoding and decision-making skills.

We are currently conducting a series of laboratory-based studies funded by the Department of Veterans Affairs to investigate components of social information processing and their links to PTSD and IPV in returning military veterans. In collaboration with Eckhardt, and using the ATSS paradigm he has used in his studies, we have found, consistent with prior research, that among the PTSD symptom clusters hyperarousal symptoms are most strongly associated with anger expression and use of IPV (Taft, Weatherill, et al., 2015). Consistent with some prior research and the social information processing model (Schumacher, Feldbau-Kohn, Slep, & Heyman, 2001), hostile attribution biases are also a risk factor for IPV.

Amy Marshall and her colleagues have developed a line of research in which they are attempting to better understand how trauma and PTSD contribute to social information processing deficits and IPV. In a sample of 185 trauma-exposed undergraduates, Marshall, Robinson, and Azar (2011) found negative thoughts about oneself, negative thoughts about the world, and self-blame to be associated with use of both physical and psychological IPV. In addition, they obtained results suggesting that these negative thoughts contributed to interpreting social situations as more threatening, which in turn was associated with IPV, consistent with the social information processing model of IPV. In a related study, Sippel and Marshall (2011) studied a sample of 47 community participants and found that PTSD was related to shame-related cognitive processing and that such processing was related to use of IPV. In other words, persons with PTSD may be more likely to misperceive ambiguous partner behaviors as rejecting, and this may contribute to social information processing deficits and IPV. These findings extend the available literature by suggesting that PTSD contributes not only to perceived threats by others generally but also to perceived threats to interpersonal relationships that may contribute to IPV (see also Bell & Orcutt, 2009).

A number of other risk factors for IPV that can result from trauma, such as depression, alcohol use problems, and traumatic brain injury, may also elevate IPV risk through their impact on social information processing (see Heyman, Taft, Howard, Macdonald, & Collins, 2012). For example, trauma resulting from an assault experience may contribute to the use or abuse of alcohol. In turn, alcohol use can have negative influences on social information processing, enhancing negative interpretations of others' behavior (Clements & Schumacher, 2010) and biasing response selection by focusing attention on immediate cues to act aggressively and reducing awareness of the less obvious negative consequences of acting on violent impulses (Eckhardt, 2007; Murphy, 2013). Furthermore, it appears likely that the presence of more than one of these factors may increase risk in a multiplicative fashion (e.g., traumatic brain injury disinhibits aggressive behavior among those with preexisting social information processing deficits). Researchers are only now beginning to examine the potentially complex interrelationships among different risk factors for aggression (Elbogen et al., 2012; Taft et al., 2012).

CORE THEMES, SOCIAL INFORMATION PROCESSING, AND INTIMATE PARTNER VIOLENCE

The experience of trauma can have a profound effect on the way individuals view the world. There are several core themes, or schemas, affected by trauma that may affect how one processes social information and thus may underlie relationship functioning difficulties and IPV. Our work with individuals who commonly report trauma often focuses to a greater extent on these themes than on psychopathology, given that core issues or faulty ways of thinking and viewing the world are nearly universal for trauma-exposed individuals with anger problems and affect all areas of interpersonal functioning. Resick and colleagues (Monson et al., 2006; Resick & Schnicke, 1992) have identified core themes that represent important treatment targets for individuals who have been exposed to trauma. These, themes, which we discuss in the next few sections, may be particularly important to address in IPV interventions as well.

Trust

Trust in others is often disrupted following trauma. A trauma may have been caused by someone who was supposed to be trustworthy, such as a parent or relative, a supervisor at work, or a commanding officer in the military context. In other cases a trauma may have occurred because other people made poor decisions or mistakes. Trauma-exposed individuals may feel like they cannot trust anyone, or that all people are out to hurt or betray them. Social information processing is clearly relevant in this instance because the individual may be more likely to view others as having negative intentions and thus will interpret ambiguous situations in a more negative light. For example, individuals who have been the victim of interpersonal physical or sexual violence may come to assume that others will take advantage of them if they show vulnerability, and they will assume negative intentions on the part of the partner across situations as a sort of defensive self-preservation strategy. Such social information processing distortions may lead to assumptions that one's partner is not being faithful or otherwise has negative intentions when this is not in fact the case. Such hostile interpretations of the partner's behavior can contribute to controlling and abusive behavior in the relationship. The individual may describe his or her distorted beliefs in a seemingly logical, matter-of-fact manner, but when the situation is unpacked and discussed, and when more relevant factual information is brought to light, the social information processing distortions often become more evident. As we discuss in later chapters, it is critical that providers always be looking for examples of cognitive distortions related to trust and to help clients recognize and correct such distortions.

Self-Esteem and Other-Esteem

Trauma survivors may harshly judge themselves whenever they make a mistake, or unfairly blame themselves and experience guilt and shame for what happened to them. In the military context, self-esteem problems may develop when service members return home because they are no longer able to assist their fellow service members who remain on deployment and because they now feel less important in the civilian world, where they may have had to take a job with little meaning or low status relative to the role they performed in the military. Low self-esteem can lead to depression and insecurity in relationships, which increases the risk for abusive behavior when an individual misperceives "threats" to his or her relationship, or abandonment by his or her partner, by means of maladaptive social information processing processes.

Trauma can also influence *other-esteem*: how one views other people. Traumatic events involving other people may lead one to believe that others are inadequate, not deserving of respect, or easily deceived or exploited. Individuals may generalize such beliefs, leading to problems with anger, interpersonal coercion, control, or withdrawal from meaningful emotional investment in social relationships, increasing risk for IPV.

Power and Control

Clinicians and researchers have long asserted that men's violence toward women is influenced by beliefs related to power in relationships (e.g., Pence & Paymar, 1993). Traumatic experiences often involve reactions that include a profound sense of helplessness and uncontrollability during the event or events, which can lead to feelings of powerlessness that continue long after the trauma. Feelings of powerlessness contribute not only to PTSD (e.g., Finkelhor & Browne, 1985) but also to power struggles at home and ultimately may lead to IPV (Schwartz, Waldo, & Daniel, 2005). For example, a sexual assault victim may have felt powerless during the assault, and in an attempt to overcompensate and regain a sense of power and control, he or she may attempt to exert control over family members.

CASE EXAMPLE OF SOCIAL INFORMATION PROCESSING DEFICITS IN A RELATIONSHIP

A returning veteran, who has been trained to spot possible improvised explosive devices along the roadside, returns home to his wife and children. As his wife is leaving one morning, he asks her where she plans to go. She says she is going to run errands but is not sure exactly where she will be. He presses several more times for more details, and eventually he erupts into an angry outburst and demands to know where she plans on going with *his* children. He throws a remote control across the room and breaks it, scaring his family. He brings this example into a group therapy discussion and reveals that he wanted to know which route his wife would be traveling on so that he could suggest safer roads that did not have overpasses or go through bad neighborhoods. When she did not have an answer, he felt that she was not being careful enough. He also thought that she was being deceitful, which triggered memories of an experience of being lied to by his military commander while deployed in Iraq, which put him in harm's way. He reported feeling betrayed and hurt in the aftermath of this situation. During the group session he described feeling concerned that his wife was "sneaking around" on him or had something to hide. Upon further discussion of these thoughts, he realized that he likely had misread the situation at home in an overly negative manner. He then discussed the issue calmly with his wife in a group exercise and expressed his feelings about the situation. She explained that she did not know exactly where she was going because she was not sure how long it would take her to get the children settled in at day care and then meet with someone at the bank about refinancing options to lower their mortgage payments. She did not want to bring up the trip to the bank because talking about their troubled finances often irritated him, and she did not want to start his day off discussing stressful topics.

SUMMARY

In this chapter, we reviewed research and theory on social information processing models of IPV and other forms of aggression. These models have been developed and supported through research on both trauma-exposed children and adults. Although trauma-informed interventions have been successfully used to reduce risk for aggression in children, work in this area for adults lags far behind. We also discussed in this chapter how multiple factors, including PTSD symptoms and substance use, may increase risk for IPV because of their impact on social information processing abilities. Finally, we illustrated how trauma can affect core themes related to trust, self- and other-esteem, and power and control, which can affect social information processing abilities and increase the risk for relationship problems, conflict escalation, and IPV.

2

TRAUMA AND INTIMATE PARTNER VIOLENCE IN MILITARY VETERANS

Much of what we know about the relationship of trauma and posttraumatic stress disorder (PTSD) with intimate partner violence (IPV) has come from research and theory involving military veterans. In this chapter, we review the research and clinical literatures on military trauma and links to the use of IPV. Military trauma and other deployment-related experiences are unique in that they involve stressors that may include direct life threat for prolonged periods of time as well as sanctioned violence and military training to disinhibit violent behavior. On the other hand, military trauma may function similarly to civilian trauma in some respects, and work conducted with military samples may be helpful in understanding and treating trauma-related IPV in civilians. First we identify and discuss specific forms of military trauma that have been studied in relation to IPV and the associated research findings. We then address the specific role of PTSD symptomatology in understanding these associations.

http://dx.doi.org/10.1037/14918-003
Trauma-Informed Treatment and Prevention of Intimate Partner Violence, by C. T. Taft, C. M. Murphy, and S. K. Creech

MILITARY TRAUMA AND INTIMATE PARTNER VIOLENCE

During military training and in the war zone, violent behavior is frequently reinforced and modeled, and it is often considered a necessary means for resolving disputes, in particular during armed conflict. These contingencies may lead to an increased propensity to use IPV in conflicts within intimate relationships, in particular, when the individual has PTSD (Taft, Watkins, Stafford, Street, & Monson, 2011). We are not aware of any published research that has examined specific links between military training and IPV behaviors, although some authors have written about how military training experiences may be related to aggression outside of the military context. For example, in his book *Trained to Kill: Soldiers at War*, Dr. Theodore Nadelson (2005) wrote about how military training may serve to disinhibit aggression: "Military training is meant to wrest the soldier out of the civilian and throw him into action. To do that, training must remove conscripts from the framework of the inhibiting force that civilization has raised against killing" (p. 43).

There is also reason to believe that military and civilian trauma do not operate in exactly the same manner when we think about IPV risk. Taft, Watkins, et al. (2011) recently published a meta-analysis (an empirical summary study of all available research studies) examining the statistical association between PTSD and IPV in both military and civilian samples and were able to conduct some comparisons across groups. They found a sizable overall relationship between PTSD and IPV. Interestingly, the association between PTSD and IPV was considerably stronger in military studies than civilian studies, although the association was still statistically meaningful in civilians. This finding was consistent with a prior meta-analysis that showed PTSD resulting from military trauma to be more strongly associated with anger and hostility than PTSD resulting from civilian trauma (Orth & Wieland, 2006).

A number of possible factors may help explain these differences between military and civilian samples. For example, prolonged trauma exposure involving severe life threat may have a particularly detrimental impact on social information processing such that veterans may come to view all others as potential threats to their safety and self-esteem upon their return home from military combat. Furthermore, military training experiences that serve to disinhibit aggressive behavior and reinforce violent responses to difficult situations may prime a veteran to respond with aggression when stressors or traumatic reminders are present. It may also be the case that military trauma, in contrast to some forms of civilian trauma, has a stronger interpersonal component. For example, the loss of close comrades may produce greater emotional avoidance or disengagement than that which might be associated with natural disasters or being a victim of crime.

In an earlier laboratory study of Vietnam combat veterans (Taft, Street, Marshall, Dowdall, & Riggs, 2007), when reminded of prior traumatic experiences, veterans exhibited a strong anger response and anger increased to a greater extent than other emotions, such as anxiety. Thus, military stressors and reminders seem to elicit a particularly strong anger response that may contribute to faulty social information processing and risk for IPV.

Studies that have examined the relationship between military war zone stressor exposure and IPV have focused primarily on measures of traditional combat exposure. Measures of combat exposure tap into events that are considered stereotypical, observable warfare experiences, such as receiving enemy fire, firing weapons, and going on special missions or patrols. In an early study that examined war zone stressors and IPV, Gimbel and Booth (1994) found a significant relationship between combat exposure and a composite variable they termed *marital adversity*, which included IPV, among a large, representative sample of Vietnam veterans. Orcutt, King, and King (2003) later found that combat exposure was associated with IPV in part because of its relationships with perceptions of threat in the war zone, and PTSD. *Perceptions of threat* refers to the veterans' assessments as to whether war zone experiences were harmful to their personal safety, with an emphasis on interpretations of and feelings about these experiences.

Only a limited amount of research has examined the link between exposure to war zone atrocities and IPV or other forms of aggression. Measures of war zone atrocities assess the degree to which one participated in, or witnessed, extreme acts of military abusive violence toward others. In an early study that examined this association, Beckham and her colleagues (Beckham, Feldman, & Kirby, 1998) focused on the link between atrocities exposure, as measured by the Vietnam Era Stress Inventory (Wilson & Krauss, 1983), and general interpersonal violence several years after deployment. The atrocities measure included six items assessing situations such as "the hurting, killing or mutilation (e.g., cutting off ears, putting heads on sticks, placing bodies in grotesque positions) of Vietnamese." The results indicated that exposure to atrocities was indeed related to severity of aggression, though this association was reduced when statistically adjusting for other factors.

In our laboratory, we and our colleagues (Taft et al., 2005) have examined links among combat exposure, perceived threat, and atrocities exposure and IPV in a subsample of the nationally representative sample of Vietnam veterans previously studied by Orcutt et al. (2003). In comparisons between violent and nonviolent veterans with PTSD, only exposure to war zone atrocities differed significantly. In other words, among veterans with PTSD, exposure to atrocities represented a unique risk factor for IPV, whereas the other two war zone stressor factors did not. These findings suggest the possibility that exposure to extreme and abusive violence in the war zone may disinhibit abusive violence upon return from the war zone. It is also possible that this form of war zone exposure leads to higher risk for IPV because it poses a greater risk for PTSD and disruptions in the core themes we discussed in Chapter 1, including problems with trust, self- and other-esteem, and power and control.

POSTTRAUMATIC STRESS DISORDER AND INTIMATE PARTNER VIOLENCE IN VETERANS

Of psychiatric problems linked with military trauma and IPV, PTSD by far has been the most heavily studied and discussed. As we have noted, veterans diagnosed with PTSD have consistently been shown to be more likely to engage in physical and psychological IPV than veterans without PTSD, and PTSD severity is associated with IPV severity (Taft, Watkins, et al., 2011). For example, in the nationally representative National Vietnam Veterans Readjustment Study (Kulka et al., 1990), approximately one third of male veterans with PTSD were identified as having been violent toward their partner during the previous year, a rate 2 to 3 times higher than that for men without PTSD (Jordan et al., 1992). These research findings are consistent with another meta-analysis that reported that a PTSD diagnosis was significantly associated with more anger difficulties than any other anxiety disorder diagnosis, although the authors did not conduct subanalyses comparing veterans and nonveterans (Olatunji, Ciesielski, & Tolin, 2010).

The relationship between trauma and IPV in veterans has also been shown to be largely explained by the presence of PTSD symptomatology. PTSD predicts IPV even when one statistically adjusts for a range of other factors, such as early life stressors and personality disorder features (O'Donnell, Cook, Thompson, Riley, & Neria, 2006; Orcutt, King, & King, 2003). In other words, it does not appear that trauma by itself increases risk for IPV; instead, the determining factor is whether that trauma exposure leads to symptoms of PTSD. If one is exposed to military trauma and does not develop significant PTSD symptoms, that individual's IPV risk looks very much like the IPV risk for civilians. As an example, a large nationally representative study of Vietnam veterans found that the annual prevalence rate of IPV among those with PTSD was 33%, whereas the rate of IPV among those without PTSD was 15% (Jordan et al., 1992; Kulka et al., 1990).

To better understand aggressive behavior it is not sufficient to simply look at correlations between variables. Etiological models of aggression and IPV have increasingly moved toward consideration of how various factors work together to increase risk. In other words, to gain a better understanding, it is helpful to know who might be at risk, under what circumstances, and how multiple risk factors operate together.

A particularly interesting model, the I^3 theory, was developed by Finkel and colleagues (Finkel, 2007; Slotter & Finkel, 2011) to explain aggressive behavior. The theory is based on an interaction among *instigating factors* (external circumstances or situations that trigger an individual to behave aggressively), *impelling factors* (those that make the individual more likely to respond aggressively to the instigating factors; these can be evolutionary and cultural, personal, dyadic, or situational), and *inhibiting factors* (those that counteract the instigating and impelling factors to prevent acting on the urge to behave in an aggressive manner). According to the I^3 model, an individual will engage in aggression only when the strength of instigating and impelling forces exceeds the strength of the forces for the inhibition of aggression, and thus it is critical to understand the relevant forces at play in a particular population and how they interact with each other. As Finkel (2007) argued, an individual may experience aggressive impulses, though he or she may or may not engage in actual aggression if no instigating factors are present and/or due to the presence of inhibitory or disinhibitory factors.

Finkel's (2007) I^3 model is consistent with previously described social information processing models of aggression and IPV (Chemtob, Novaco, Hamada, Gross, & Smith, 1997; Taft, Walling, et al., 2011) that highlight the role of PTSD symptoms. One can think of PTSD as an impelling factor in the I^3 model—a characteristic that increases the likelihood of responding to instigating events in an aggressive fashion. In addition, a number of disinhibiting factors, such as a substance use problems and traumatic brain injury (TBI), often co-occur with PTSD. An instigating factor for a military service member or veteran may be a relationship disagreement or conflict a situation that reminds him or her of a prior trauma, or a benign relationship event that activates hostile thoughts and negative interpretations of the partner.

Relatively few studies have looked at combinations of risk factors in the prediction of IPV in military populations. Among the potential disinhibiting risk factors for IPV, substance use problems have received the most attention. For men, alcohol abuse or dependence is the most highly comorbid psychiatric problem with PTSD in representative veteran samples (Kulka et al., 1990). The *self-medication hypothesis*, whereby alcohol is used to reduce the distress and anxiety that accompany PTSD symptoms, and drinking is maintained by the negative reinforcement from symptom relief, is often used to explain this relationship (Haller & Chassin, 2014). Savarese, Suvak, King, and King (2001) examined the interrelationships among PTSD hyperarousal symptoms, indexes of alcohol consumption, and IPV in a representative sample of male Vietnam veterans. In addition to main effects of drinking quantity and hyperarousal symptoms on physical and psychological IPV, interactive effects were also obtained such that the effects of PTSD hyperarousal on physical IPV were exacerbated by increased alcohol consumption.

TBI may also be an important disinhibiting factor in the context of PTSD given that they co-occur at high rates (Hoge et al., 2008; L. A. Nelson, Yoash-Gantz, Pickett, & Campbell, 2009). TBI has been associated with use of IPV in civilian and veteran samples, presumably at least in part because of its association with social information processing deficits (see Pinto et al., 2010). However, one published study did not find PTSD and TBI to have this interactive effect on IPV risk; instead, the data suggested that among those who may possess underlying antisocial features, having a history of head injury may lead to increased IPV (Kachadourian, Taft, O'Farrell, Doron-Lamarca, & Murphy, 2012). Another study, however, found that TBI and PTSD, when co-occurring, greatly increased general aggression risk in a clinical sample of veterans (Elbogen, Beckham, Butterfield, Swartz, & Swanson, 2008).

A question that is often asked is whether women veterans are similarly affected by trauma and PTSD when it comes to interpersonal functioning and IPV in particular. It is interesting that results from the previously mentioned meta-analysis showed that PTSD was more likely to be associated with use of IPV in men than in women (Taft, Watkins, et al., 2011), although the researchers did not have a large enough sample to directly compare women veterans and women civilians on the associations of interest. Taken together with some other prior civilian research (M. W. Miller & Resick, 2007), available data suggest that men are more likely to exhibit aggression outwardly when they experience trauma and PTSD, whereas women are more likely to develop internalizing problems, such as depression. However, an overall lack of research on women's violence, in particular, violence on the part of women veterans, makes gender comparisons tentative and inconclusive. It is our hope that future studies will be expanded to more fully study women veterans' experiences of trauma and potential for violence, especially given that women represent an increasing proportion of service members and are increasingly exposed to combat and other forms of military trauma (Vogt et al., 2011).

SUMMARY

Military trauma has been linked to the use of IPV, and PTSD symptoms resulting from trauma largely account for this relationship. Different forms of military trauma, including traditional combat exposure, perceptions of threat in the war zone, and exposure to atrocities, have all been related to heightened IPV risk. PTSD resulting from military trauma has been more strongly related to IPV risk than PTSD resulting from civilian trauma. This may be due to the prolonged life threat that is involved with military trauma, the role of military training, or perhaps a strong interpersonal component for military trauma. Trauma-related IPV, like all IPV, is a complex phenomenon with multiple risk factors. Therefore, it may be helpful to examine how different risk factors interact to increase risk. The limited available data suggest that PTSD is more strongly associated with use of IPV in men than in women, although much remains to be known about the etiology of violence for women veterans and service members.

3

TRAUMA AND INTIMATE PARTNER VIOLENCE IN CIVILIAN POPULATIONS

An abundance of research has documented the connection between childhood trauma and the use of intimate partner violence (IPV), much of it focusing on the intergenerational transmission of violence and correlations between experiencing and/or observing physical punishment, violence, and/or abuse in childhood and subsequent use of IPV as an adult (Jankowski, Leitenberg, Henning, & Coffey, 1999; Rosenbaum & Leisring, 2003; Wareham, Boots, & Chavez, 2009; Whitfield, Anda, Dube, & Felitti, 2003; Widom, 1989; Wood & Sommers, 2011). If one compares and contrasts the military and civilian literatures on trauma and IPV, one will note that the military literature places more focus on adult trauma and trauma-related psychopathology, such as posttraumatic stress disorder (PTSD), and the civilian literature focuses more on childhood trauma, with very little emphasis on PTSD symptoms. These differences in focus are somewhat understandable considering the aforementioned stronger link between PTSD and IPV use in military samples (Taft, Watkins,

http://dx.doi.org/10.1037/14918-004
Trauma-Informed Treatment and Prevention of Intimate Partner Violence, C. T. Taft, C. M. Murphy, and S. K. Creech

et al., 2011) and given that military trauma seems to be a stronger correlate of IPV than childhood trauma in samples of veterans (Taft et al., 2005). However, the available evidence indicates that trauma is linked with IPV use in civilians as well as service members and veterans and that, as we discuss in this chapter, similar processes explain these associations.

As we discussed in Chapter 1, the social information processing model of IPV was initially developed in civilian samples, and there is considerable research evidence in the civilian literature to support this model (e.g., Taft, Schumm, Marshall, Panuzio, & Holtzworth-Munroe, 2008). Instead of resummarizing the literature on social information processing in civilians who use IPV, in this chapter we review research on the intergenerational transmission of violence as well as studies that have examined links among civilian trauma exposure, PTSD, and IPV. We also discuss civilian women's use of IPV given that heretofore we have primarily focused on studies of men, and there is some available research on both genders in civilian samples.

INTERGENERATIONAL TRANSMISSION OF VIOLENCE

The notion that violence in childhood is related to violence in adulthood is nothing new. Decades of research supports the "intergenerational transmission of violence" as a key explanation for IPV (Kalmuss, 1984; Stith et al., 2000; Straus, Gelles, & Steinmetz, 1980; Widom, 1989). We know that approximately 45% of individuals who engage in IPV have witnessed IPV in their family of origin, and approximately 60% have been the victims of childhood physical abuse when growing up (see Rosenbaum & Leisring, 2003). Heyman and Slep (2002) reported that each act of interparental (father to mother) violence exposure in childhood was associated with an 8% increase in IPV use, and each act of direct childhood physical abuse experienced was associated with a 15% increase in IPV. Such findings are usually explained by social learning models (e.g., Bandura, 1977), according to which children exposed to violence learn to become violent themselves by directly observing violent parents. Social cognitive theories further indicate that violence-exposed children may develop positive expectations about the interpersonal effectiveness of violence and schemas (beliefs about one's self and others), or interpersonal scripts, that support the use of violence. Some research findings support social learning mechanisms by demonstrating that childhood trauma exposure is related to the development of negative beliefs about gender and interpersonal violence, which in turn are related to IPV risk (Reitzel-Jaffe & Wolfe, 2001). Such social learning models and research findings are also entirely consistent with social information processing models in that schemas developed in childhood provide the stored knowledge base of social information that influences the manner in which we interpret and respond to social situations at each step in social information processing.

Stith et al. (2000) conducted a meta-analysis that summarized the available research on the intergenerational transmission of IPV. Not surprisingly, this analysis demonstrated that both experiencing and witnessing abuse in childhood were linked to use of IPV in adulthood. It is interesting, and consistent with the aforementioned gender differences found in the relationship between PTSD and IPV use, that Stith et al. (2000) also found that the relationship between childhood trauma and adult IPV use was weaker for women than for men. This may occur because of previously discussed differences between men and women in internalizing versus externalizing problems following trauma exposure.

TRAUMA EXPOSURE, POSTTRAUMATIC STRESS DISORDER, AND USE OF INTIMATE PARTNER VIOLENCE

Trauma, PTSD, and social information processing deficits have rarely been discussed in intergenerational transmission models of IPV. One way to begin to understand the degree to which trauma and PTSD may play a role in civilian IPV use is to examine persons who have been referred to intervention for IPV in the community.

We are aware of three studies that have looked at trauma and PTSD in samples of men who use IPV. Dutton (1995), who examined a sample of 132 men who used IPV and 44 demographically matched controls, found elevated levels of trauma symptoms in the IPV group and psychological profiles consistent with PTSD on a commonly used personality measure. He also found that reports of parental rejection and lack of warmth, and parental verbal and physical abusiveness, were linked with trauma symptoms.

Rosenbaum and Leisring (2003) discussed the potential role of powerlessness in those who use IPV in the context of early trauma exposure. These clinical researchers questioned why trauma was not more widely considered in IPV intervention:

> Curiously, exposed males merit sympathy, consideration, and understanding only so long as they are children. Once they become abusive adults, they join the ranks of batterers and any attempt to view them as victims of a violent history is somehow seen as diminishing their responsibility for their aggressive behavior. Domestic violence, according to the prevailing zeitgeist, is about power and control, or more specifically, about the batterer's need to exert power and control over his female

partner. The question of why some men have the need to exert power and control over their intimate partners is rarely, if ever, addressed. (Rosenbaum & Leisring, 2003, p. 7)

Thus, as we discussed in Chapter 1, where we introduced the social information processing model, some people who have experienced childhood abuse and neglect may feel a profound sense of powerlessness that influences their beliefs about power and control and contributes to abusive behavior. Rosenbaum and Leisring (2003) went further and suggested that the poor efficacy of previous interventions for those who engage in IPV may be because trauma and related psychological difficulties were not addressed in these programs. The researchers reported results from a study of 118 men referred to an IPV intervention program and a comparison group of 149 men. The findings indicated that approximately 13% of the violent subsample likely had PTSD, nearly double the estimated base rate in the general population. Furthermore, among the men in the IPV group, those with PTSD engaged in more frequent and severe IPV than those without PTSD. In addition to reporting more physical and emotional abuse as children than the nonviolent group, members of the IPV group reported that their parents were less involved in their lives, more punitive, and less affectionate, and they lacked stability, nurturance, security, and love.

In the third study of which we are aware that has examined trauma and PTSD in samples of men who use IPV, we and our colleagues recently studied traumatic events experienced by 217 men who were court-mandated to enroll in a 41-week group IPV program to develop a better sense of the various forms of trauma these men may have been exposed to (Maguire et al., 2015). We found extremely high rates of trauma exposure, with 94% of participants reported experiencing at least one trauma in their lifetime. The death/illness/injury of a loved one was the most frequently reported type of trauma (76%). More than half (56.6%) of the sample reported experiencing adult physical assault, and more than one third (39.6%) had witnessed another person being physically assaulted during their lifetime. Approximately 60% reported experiencing some type of child abuse, including childhood physical assault (18.9%), childhood sexual assault (8.2%), and witnessing family violence growing up (32.7%). The greater the number of traumas experienced, the greater the individual was at risk for using both physical and psychological IPV. Furthermore, consistent with research findings we have previously described for military samples (Orcutt, King, & King, 2003), PTSD symptoms were related to both forms of IPV use (i.e., physical and psychological) and helped to statistically explain relationship between experiencing trauma and psychological IPV behaviors. In other words, trauma was related to PTSD symptoms, which in turn were related to severity of psychological IPV use.

THE ROLE OF TRAUMA IN INTIMATE PARTNER VIOLENCE FOR WOMEN

As we discussed in Chapter 2, PTSD seems to be a stronger predictor of IPV use in men than in women; however, the link is still evident in women. Almost all of the research evidence about these relationships has come from studies that were conducted with men who have used IPV, although there is some available research that has examined women's use of IPV. The use of violence by trauma-exposed women is an important topic because women are increasingly being court-mandated to IPV intervention, and women are at risk for various forms of trauma.

Swan, Gambone, Fields, Sullivan, and Snow (2005) examined the interrelationships among a host of IPV risk factors in a sample consisting primarily of African American women receiving clinical and/or legal services. They focused on the role of childhood abuse in women's IPV given some earlier findings suggesting that childhood abuse increases women's risk for IPV use (Leisring, Dowd, & Rosenbaum, 1999; Magdol, Moffitt, Caspi, & Silva, 1998). Almost all of the women in this sample who used IPV also experienced IPV, suggesting that they were experiencing ongoing trauma in their relationships. Regarding childhood trauma, 36% reported childhood physical abuse, 39% experienced emotional abuse, and 35% had experienced sexual abuse as children. These experiences of adult and child abuse, as well as PTSD symptoms, were related to a higher risk for engaging in IPV, which is generally consistent with the literature on men's use of IPV.

In a court-mandated sample of women, Hughes, Stuart, Gordon, and Moore (2007) similarly examined the roles of childhood trauma and PTSD symptoms and women's use of IPV. Consistent with Swan et al.'s (2005) study, these researchers found that experiencing childhood violence and IPV in adulthood were related to engaging in IPV for these women. Interestingly, however, PTSD symptoms were not related to engaging in IPV for this sample of women.

Our research team examined the role of PTSD in use of IPV in a sample of women who had been exposed to a flood (Taft, Monson, Schumm, Watkins, Panuzio, & Resick, 2009). As with the prior studies, IPV victimization was strong a predictor of IPV use, and PTSD symptoms also were related to higher use of physical and psychological IPV. The pattern of results indicated that PTSD symptoms contributed to general problems in the relationship, and this in turn related to problems with IPV. Our findings suggested that forms of trauma such as natural disaster exposure may place women at risk for abusive relationships.

More recently, Kendra, Bell, and Guimond (2012) examined links among child abuse, PTSD, and anger arousal in dating violence in a large sample of female college students. Their findings indicated that child abuse victimization was associated with physical and psychological dating violence, and the data further suggested that PTSD and anger arousal help explain this relationship. In other words, child abuse was related to anger arousal and PTSD, which in turn were associated with engaging in both forms of dating violence.

SUMMARY

Research has long demonstrated a link between childhood trauma exposure and violence in adulthood, including IPV. Explanations for this intergenerational transmission of violence have typically relied on a social learning perspective, which is consistent with social information processing models in that both emphasize how trauma affects schemas and cognition. Studies of men court-mandated to IPV intervention have demonstrated high rates of prior trauma exposure and PTSD. Research findings regarding trauma, PTSD, and IPV suggest that trauma-informed interventions may be useful for preventing and treating women's IPV in addition to men's IPV; however, this relationship is weaker in women than in men, and by far the greatest predictor of women's use of IPV is her partner's use of IPV.

4
ASSESSMENT

Effective therapeutic work with trauma-exposed individuals who are engaging intimate partner violence (IPV) begins with the intake interview and assessment. We advocate a trauma-informed and multimethod approach that combines therapeutic interview, motivational interviewing (MI) approaches, and completion of brief questionnaires. In this chapter, we describe assessment procedures and approaches that are useful before therapeutic activities are initiated. We focus on assessment of trauma exposure, traumatic stress symptoms, depressive symptoms, and other common trauma-related difficulties and disorders that may be linked to IPV. We emphasize the inclusion of brief, formal psychological assessment of these constructs to provide objective measurement for both the client and the clinician, to formulate an understanding of the scope of the client's problems compared with normative data, and to generate appropriate treatment referrals as needed. In settings where a psychologist is not available to conduct the intake assessment,

http://dx.doi.org/10.1037/14918-005
Trauma-Informed Treatment and Prevention of Intimate Partner Violence, by C. T. Taft, C. M. Murphy, and S. K. Creech

treatment programs can consider partnering with psychologists to conduct the assessments and make treatment recommendations to be carried out by nonpsychologist treatment staff members. The assessment and intake session as we describe it will last approximately 60 to 90 minutes.

The goal of the intake session may not necessarily be a comprehensive diagnostic assessment but rather to elicit an understanding of the client's presenting problems, history of exposure to trauma, mental and behavioral health symptoms, anger and use of aggression, and motivation for change. By approaching the intake session as a therapeutic assessment, the clinician sets the stage for positive change and helps to counter hostile misappraisals and inaccurate perceptions regarding the assessment, treatment, and therapist that may be prevalent in this population.

Therapeutic assessment is a brief and structured approach to individual assessment that emphasizes three primary tasks: forming a collaborative relationship, building empathy, and collective inquiry into the nature of the client's problems. Although true therapeutic assessment involves multiple sessions that are structured according to a specific format (for more information, see Finn & Tonsager, 1997), we believe that the general principles and approach to assessment as a therapeutic intervention are useful here. As such, the goal of therapeutic assessment is not simply gathering information to formulate a diagnosis and treatment plan but instead to gather information and share it with the client in a way that helps him or her to make changes (Finn & Tonsager, 1997). Clients are shown their test results, and these are discussed in a meaningful way. Results from a recent meta-analysis of 17 research studies that used psychological assessment as a therapeutic intervention indicated that this approach has a positive and meaningful impact on treatment—especially treatment process (Poston & Hanson, 2010). Thus, in undertaking clinical work with those who have engaged in IPV, use of therapeutic assessment approaches may initiate a positive therapeutic process and therapeutic alliance. A positive therapeutic alliance is especially important in this work, as is discussed in Chapter 6, this volume.

MI strategies have been shown to be useful in initiating work with those who engage in IPV (Murphy & Maiuro, 2009). MI was developed as a therapeutic strategy in recognition that clients present to treatment at different levels of readiness for change (Rollnick & Miller, 1995). Although developed for use with alcohol- and drug-dependent clients who often present to treatment with high levels of resistance, its principles are relevant and useful in work with trauma-exposed individuals who engage in IPV. Consistent with our recommendation that clinicians attend to therapeutic alliance carefully, MI emphasizes the use of high levels of empathic listening, creating a nonjudgmental and nonadversarial environment, and a focus on autonomy and choice. For example, goals include increasing awareness of causes and consequences of negative behaviors and the benefits of change. Readers may find a more thorough review of MI principles and strategies in several excellent books written about MI more generally (W. R. Miller & Rollnick, 2012) and about using this approach with those who engage in IPV (Murphy & Maiuro, 2009).

JUSTICE SYSTEM INVOLVEMENT

Justice system involvement is likely to be common in this population. In our experience, some clients are mandated by the justice system to receive treatment, whereas others may be seeking treatment in advance of a pending mandate or to improve the dispensation of their case. In this case, clients will likely need the clinician to report certain information back to the justice system on their behalf. In most cases, this is limited to reporting on treatment enrollment, attendance, and progress. Other clients may be justice involved and seeking treatment out of an intrinsic desire to get help; in this case, no reporting will be needed, although the client may ask for documentation at a later date. The relationship between the assessing and treating clinicians and the justice system will be determined by the specific circumstances of the treatment setting, applicable state regulations, and conditions set forth by the justice system. We recommend that clinicians adopt clear standards for the type and amount of information that will be shared and the mode of information sharing (e.g., phone, letters) and that they are ready to communicate these standards to both the client and the justice system. It can also be helpful to set forth clear guidelines to clients with regard to timing of requests for letters or phone calls to avoid last-minute requests.

REFERRAL CONTEXT

At the outset, it is useful for clinicians to consider the context in which clients are referred and their previous exposure to mental health treatment and the justice system if applicable. Given that many clients present to treatment after an IPV incident that could have involved jail time and mandated treatment, they may present with extensive anger toward the clinician, who is viewed as part of the punitive justice system. We thus advocate beginning with an overview of confidentiality, including legally mandated limits to confidentiality and any required or recommended communication with legal referral sources (if applicable). This information can help the client understand how and whether the clinician is connected to other systems. An overview of the procedures for the day and goals of the assessment will also help clients gain a greater sense of understanding, especially when they are new to treatment.

It is also helpful to consider how social information processing deficits can influence the ways in which a client may present for care and his or her attitude toward receiving care. For example, as we discussed in Chapter 1, trauma-related problems in social information processing can lead to misappraisal of events, an overly hostile attribution bias, emotional avoidance and avoidant coping strategies, and reduced ability to generate and enact socially competent responses to normal challenges that emerge in relationships and other social interactions. Within the context of an intake assessment, these deficits can lead to anger and mistrust of the therapist, a perception that the treatment will be punitive in nature, and to hostility, defensiveness, and nonadherence to the assessment. Thus, it can be helpful to review how the client was referred and the purpose of the assessment. For some clients, it can also be helpful for the therapist to normalize these reactions, noting that such thoughts and feelings are common among individuals presenting for IPV treatment services.

It is also useful to consider the role of empathy and therapeutic stance toward the client. In addition to such anger toward "the system," clients can often present with entrenched denial of any and all problems, instead blaming their partner or the justice system. On the opposite side of the spectrum, clients can present with extensive guilt and shame about an IPV incident or charge and may evidence intense depressive symptomatology. Not only can these negative emotions and cognitions impede forming rapport and a positive start to treatment, but perceptions of provider bias or judgment can reinforce the client's beliefs. It is thus helpful for the clinician to examine and eliminate any provider bias toward clients who are accused of or who endorse having engaged in IPV. Adopting a nonjudgmental, open, and empathic yet firm stance is essential at the outset of treatment. Although it could be tempting to err on the side of sympathy, skirting direct discussion of the IPV, we strongly caution therapists against this. Balancing compassion with clear and direct language about the client's IPV helps facilitate understanding and paves a pathway toward change (Finn, 2005).

Equally important is consideration of the role of posttraumatic stress disorder (PTSD) symptoms because these may manifest in anxiety about the assessment process. Hyperarousal and reexperiencing symptoms may interfere with concentration and with developing a positive therapeutic alliance. Similarly, avoidance symptoms may drive responses to assessment questions that seem vague or that minimize responsibility for aggressive behavior. Alternatively, shame and guilt related to traumatic experiences such as sexual abuse can manifest in suspiciousness of the therapist and a reluctance to engage in the therapeutic process altogether. Clients with severe PTSD symptoms may experience an extreme affective response in session and in rare cases may experience a dissociative episode. Core themes related to traumatic experiences can also affect the therapeutic process. For example, hostility and suspiciousness toward the therapist may in fact be driven by client experiences of traumatic events over which they had no control. Core themes and cognitions about trust and control may be at the heart of such hostility and suspiciousness. Accordingly, behavioral responses to a new situation like an intake assessment may include attempts to control or disrupt the session to assuage strong emotions.

In their work on trauma-informed assessment and screening, Fallot and Harris (2001) suggested that underreporting of traumatic experiences and providers' underrecognition of these experiences are common in professional settings. Specifically, traumatic experiences may not be reported by clients because of current safety concerns; past stigmatizing system responses that have blamed, pathologized, or conveyed disbelief and client feelings of shame and guilt can all contribute to client underreporting of trauma (Fallot & Harris, 2001). On the clinician side, lack of training in trauma, uncertainty about how to respond to client experiences of trauma or abuse, and fears about upsetting clients can contribute to a reluctance to screen or assess for traumatic experiences (Fallot & Harris, 2001). In addition, clinicians may fear screening if there are no available referrals and a problem is identified.

Several strategies may help to mitigate the impact of these issues on the intake process. First and foremost, the clinician must appreciate the need for flexibility in his or her approach and recognize that not every client may be ready to discuss experiences of traumatic events or symptoms of PTSD. In such cases, we might break the intake into two sessions because this will facilitate rapport and trust, and we are always willing to slow down a session or change course if the client experiences strong reactions to the assessment. However, it is important that clinicians take care not to support and reinforce client avoidance symptoms. Taking a moment to acknowledge that the client may be having negative emotions or might feel reticent to respond to questions and whether he or she is willing to continue can often go a long way toward improving rapport and trust; doing so often helps the client to overcome the impulse to avoid the assessment questions as well. Allowing the client to have some control over the order of topics discussed can also help. To that end, clinicians can present clients with a range of topics that must be covered, and the client can be encouraged to select the order of the discussion.

Second, clinicians should be familiar with strategies for helping clients manage extreme emotional responses, such as grounding techniques and breathing exercises, and clinicians must take care to manage their own affect, tone of voice, and response to the client. Clinicians must communicate empathy for traumatic experiences and how symptoms may be affecting a client's ability to respond to the assessment, but they must do so in a manner that does not convey judgment or a sense that the clinician is unable to manage or regulate his or her own affect. Appropriate clinician responses are firm when needed but always empathic, nonjudgmental, and flexible.

To combat the impact of hyperarousal symptoms on concentration, clinicians might consider including written handouts documenting confidentiality procedures and expectations discussed (e.g., treatment referral). Clinicians should also examine the physical location of their space, attending to and eliminating environmental and emotional variables that can make individuals who have experienced trauma uncomfortable. Among others, these include loud and unpredictable noises that can occur in a hospital or urban setting, privacy of space in which the interview is to occur, and letting the client know his or her rights as well as the expected session length, topics, and goals. Many of the principles of creating a trauma-informed service system are relevant in this context, especially for clinicians who are new to screening for trauma. We refer the reader to the resources available through the National Center on Trauma Informed Care website: http://www.samhsa.gov/nctic. In addition, we encourage clinicians to actively research and seek out low-cost community referral resources that may be available to clients who need additional mental health treatment.

BEGINNING THE INTERVIEW

To build rapport, we advocate beginning the interview with questions about the circumstances that brought clients to treatment and allowing some time initially for them to "tell their story." Clinicians may find they are the first person to inquire into and hear clients' side of the story. In addition to building rapport, this discussion also provides insight into motivation for change and an understanding of justice system involvement and any pending legal charges. As part of this discussion, clinicians are encouraged to inquire into clients' goals for treatment and, if possible, whether they have any goals for the assessment itself—for example, "finding out if I have an anger problem." MI principles are used here, with an emphasis on empathic listening and understanding clients' perspective on their problems and interest in change. The case study at the end of this chapter provides examples of this approach to assessment. Exhibit 4.1 includes tips and key domains to consider when conducting the intake assessment.

EXHIBIT 4.1
Intake Assessments

Tips for the Intake Assessment
Discuss confidentiality at the outset.
Use a nonjudgmental, open, and empathic stance.
Conduct the interview in a private space.
Use a multimethod assessment of mental health and substance abuse symptoms.
Employ a therapeutic assessment approach.
Use motivational interviewing techniques.
Be aware of referral options and hotline numbers.
Give feedback and set goals.
Key Domains of the Assessment
Referral context and justice involvement
Exposure to trauma and posttraumatic stress disorder symptoms
Childhood exposures and family environment
Drug and alcohol use
Depression
Traumatic brain injury/head injury
Relationship functioning and past, present intimate partner violence experiences and engagement
Partner interview
Safety
General anger problems
Readiness for change

CLIENT BACKGROUND AND ASSESSMENT OF TRAUMA EXPOSURE AND SYMPTOMS OF PTSD

As we discussed in the previous chapters, exposure to potentially traumatic events and symptoms of PTSD can have an impact on emotional and interpersonal processes that may increase risk for IPV. PTSD is classified in the *Diagnostic and Statistical Manual of Mental Disorders* (fifth edition; *DSM–5*; American Psychiatric Association, 2013) as a trauma- or stress-related disorder that includes four symptom clusters in response to direct or indirect exposure to death, threatened death, actual or threatened serious injury, or actual or threatened sexual violence (Criterion A). Symptoms of intrusion (Criterion B) are best defined as involuntary reexperiencing symptoms, and this category includes symptoms such as intrusive, involuntary, and recurrent memories of the trauma; distressing nightmares; and dissociative reactions (flashbacks), in addition to distress and physiological reactivity after exposure to trauma-related cues. Symptoms of avoidance (Criterion C) refer to the client's effortful attempts to avoid trauma-related reminders or stimuli such as thoughts and feelings, or actual stimuli such as people, places, or objects. The symptom cluster of negative alterations in cognitions and mood (Criterion D) includes seven possible symptoms that are persistent in nature: inability to recall important features of the trauma; negative beliefs about the self or the world; distorted blame of self or others for the trauma or consequences of the trauma; negative emotions such as guilt, anger, fear, or shame; markedly diminished interest in significant activities; feeling alienated from others; and the inability to experience positive emotions. Alterations in arousal and reactivity (Criterion E) includes the symptoms of anger and irritability; self-destructive/reckless behavior; problems with concentration; hypervigilance; exaggerated startle; and sleep disturbance. Symptoms must last at least 1 month and cause clinically significant distress or impairment.

In the *International Classification of Diseases* (10th revision; *ICD–10*; World Health Organization, 1992), PTSD is also classified as a stress-related disorder resulting from exposure to a stressful event or situation that is catastrophic or exceptionally threatening in nature (Criterion A) and likely to cause pervasive distress in almost anyone. Criterion B of the *ICD–10* includes persistent and distressing reexperiencing symptoms more specifically described as remembering or reliving the stressor through intrusive flashbacks, recurring dreams, vivid memories, or distress when exposed to reminders that may be associated with the stressor. Actual or preferred avoidance of circumstances associated with the stressor is Criterion C of *ICD–10* for PTSD. In Criterion D, there must be either (a) inability to recall important aspects of the stressor or (b) persistent hyperarousal symptoms, such as difficulty falling and staying asleep, irritability or anger, hypervigilance, concentration problems, and exaggerated startle. In contrast to the *DSM–5*, *ICD–10* requires that Criteria B, C, and D are all met within 6 months of exposure to the stressor. There is also no minimum duration of symptoms required as in *DSM–5*, and *ICD–10* does not explicitly mention distress or impairment.

As discussed earlier, the association between symptoms of PTSD and aggression has been demonstrated across populations (Taft, Watkins, et al., 2011), and the arousal and reactivity cluster of PTSD symptoms is most frequently associated with aggression (Savarese, Suvak, King, & King, 2001; Taft, Schumm, Marshall, Panuzio, & Holtzworth-Munroe, 2008; Taft, Vogt, Marshall, Panuzio, & Niles, 2007). The avoidance and numbing symptoms of PTSD seem to most affect relationship satisfaction (Evans, McHugh, Hopwood, & Watt, 2003; Solomon, Dekel, & Mikulincer, 2008). Therefore, assessment can provide important feedback for clients with regard to how symptoms of PTSD may be influencing their intimate relationships and to determine whether clients may benefit from referral to PTSD treatment.

Assessment for PTSD typically begins with asking clients about exposure to traumatizing events. This can be done either by administering a list verbally or asking clients to examine a list and check off any events that have occurred to them. One commonly used measure of trauma exposure is the Life

Events Checklist—5 (LEC–5; Weathers, Blake, et al., 2013b). This checklist screens for exposure to 16 potentially traumatizing events (e.g., natural disaster) through the client's lifetime and has been modified to be consistent with *DSM–5*. For each item, the client checks off one of the following answer choices: *Happened to me*, *Witnessed it*, *Learned about it*, *Part of my job*, *Not sure*, *Doesn't apply*. One criticism of the LEC measure is that it does not assess for frequency of exposure; therefore, another commonly used measure is the Traumatic Life Events Questionnaire (TLEQ; Kubany et al., 2000). The TLEQ assesses exposure to 22 types of traumatic life events, including the number of times each occurred and whether fear, helplessness, or horror was present, although these criteria have been removed from *DSM–5*. At the time of this writing, a TLEQ for *DSM–5* has not been released.

Although a variety of structured interviews for a diagnosis of PTSD exist, the gold standard interview is the Clinicians Assessment for PTSD Symptoms for *DSM–5* (CAPS–5; Weathers, Blake, et al., 2013a). This structured interview is administered verbally by the clinician and can take anywhere from 45 to 60 minutes to complete. The CAPS–5 assesses for the presence of the 20 *DSM–5* symptoms of PTSD using standardized questions to make a current or lifetime diagnosis of PTSD related to a single index trauma. The presence of each symptom is determined (yes–no) in addition to a rating of the frequency and intensity of the symptoms, which are then combined into a single severity score. We refer the reader to excellent assessment resources and web-based trainings available at http://www.ptsd.va.gov/professional/index.asp for more detailed information on PTSD diagnosis and use of the CAPS–5.

In clinical settings in which comprehensive diagnosis is not the goal of the intake, clinicians can use a PTSD symptom screening measure such as the PTSD Symptom Checklist for *DSM–5* to assess for symptoms (PCL–5; Weathers, Litz, et al., 2013; the scale is available by request at http://www.ptsd.va.gov/professional/assessment/adult-sr/ptsd-checklist.asp). The PCL–5 is a 20-item self-report checklist that assesses the presence of 20 *DSM–5* symptoms of PTSD in the past month on a 0- to 4-point scale (0 = *not at all*, 4 = *extremely*). Cut-points that may suggest a PTSD diagnosis are still being validated; however, it is currently suggested that a cut-point score of 38 may be suggestive of possible PTSD (Weathers, Litz, et al., 2013).

In addition to inquiring about traumatic experiences and symptoms of PTSD, it can be helpful to assess experiences of family violence in childhood. In previous chapters, we discussed how adverse childhood experiences such as maltreatment or exposure to interparental violence can negatively affect the development of interpersonal and emotional functioning. These types of experiences may be missed in the PTSD assessment process, yet they can influence beliefs about relationships, intimacy, and trust, while shaping how an individual learns to express emotions such as anger. In addition to items on the trauma checklists mentioned earlier, to assess exposures to maltreatment in childhood, clinicians can inquire verbally into family history, including whether there was domestic violence in the home; family practices of discipline; how family members generally expressed anger; and whether the client experienced physical violence at home. Gathering this information can be a powerful moment when clients are able to make connections between such childhood experiences and adult relationship problems.

ASSESSMENT OF OTHER MENTAL AND BEHAVIORAL HEALTH PROBLEMS

Substance abuse is a known risk factor for IPV. Problem drinking has been associated with IPV use in two meta-analytic reviews that examined results across numerous studies (e.g., Foran & O'Leary, 2008; Stith, Smith, Penn, Ward, & Tritt, 2004), and higher levels of drug use and drug-related problems have similarly been associated with IPV across numerous studies (Moore et al., 2008). In addition, substance abuse may increase IPV among those already at risk (Parrott, Drobes, Saladin, Coffey, & Dansky, 2003; Savarese et al., 2001).

To assess for current substance use problems clinicians can conduct a verbal interview or administer a brief self-report measure. One quick and well-validated measure of drug abuse is the Drug Abuse Screening Test (DAST; Skinner, 1982). The DAST is a 28-, 20-, or 10-item, yes–no measure that screens for potential problematic involvement with drugs, with higher scores representing greater potential for drug use problems. Suggested cutoffs indicating a referral to treatment may be needed are 3 and above for the 10-item measure and 6 and above for the 20-item measure, but clinicians should also inquire into the amount used and length of use in making determinations.

Similar to the DAST is the Alcohol Use Disorders Identification Test (AUDIT; J. B. Saunders, Aasland, Babor, de la Fuente, & Grant, 1993). The AUDIT is a well-validated and frequently used 10-item questionnaire that assesses problematic drinking behavior. Items record the amount and frequency of drinking, symptoms of alcohol dependence, and problems caused by alcohol. Scores are easily summed, and a cutoff of 8 is suggested as indicating risk for problems with alcohol use and the potential need for a referral to treatment. Both the AUDIT and the DAST are available for clinical use and can be found at http://www.integration.samhsa.gov/clinical-practice/screening-tools.

As mentioned earlier, the screening for substance use disorders should also include screening for IPV and anger in the context of these disorders when indicated. Sample questions might be the following: "How is your anger when you are using ___?" or "In the last incident we talked about, had you been using any alcohol or drugs?" During the feedback portion of the intake, clinicians can directly share with clients where their score falls compared with established norms, whether a referral is being made, and the possibility that greater use of drugs and alcohol can lead to greater problems with anger and aggression.

TRAUMATIC BRAIN INJURY

Traumatic brain injury (TBI) has been theorized as an important health condition that may disinhibit IPV in individuals who are at increased risk (Finkel, 2007; Taft, Walling, Howard, & Monson, 2011). TBI often co-occurs with PTSD, particularly in military veteran samples (e.g., Hoge et al., 2008) and has been associated with IPV use in civilian samples (for a review, see Pinto et al., 2010). TBI is a leading cause of injury, disability, and death in the United States, with estimates indicating it affects up to 1.7 million Americans annually (Coronado, Thurman, Greenspan, & Weissman, 2009; Faul, Xu, Wald, & Coronado, 2010). Most instances of TBI observed in IPV treatment samples reflect closed head injuries caused by accidents, military combat exposures, assaults, or other blows to the head, and such injuries range from mild to severe (Faul et al., 2010). For example, on the mild side, this type of injury is most often referred to as a concussion and is linked to short-term symptoms such as headache or difficulty concentrating. On the severe side, a traumatic brain injury can cause lasting problems including changes in cognitive and motor function, sensation, and emotional problems such as increased depression, aggression, and problems with impulse control. TBI is often associated with deficits in executive cognitive functioning. Cognitive deficits in these areas have been shown to impede social information processing by enhancing distorted thinking in response to relationship challenges (Persampiere, Poole, & Murphy, 2014).

The H.E.L.P.S. TBI Brain Injury Screening Tool is an easily administered measure designed for use by professionals who are not experts in traumatic brain injury (Picard, Scarisbrick, & Paluck, 1991; available at http://www.doj.state.or.us/victims/pdf/traumatic_brain_injury_and_domestic_violence.pdf). One of the defining characteristics of determining whether a traumatic brain injury is mild to severe is the length of time a person was unconscious or had amnesia after the initial injury. The H.E.L.P.S. refers to five key assessment domains that may indicate a referral for further evaluation is necessary: (H) hit head or having been hit on the head; (E) being seen in the emergency room, hospital, or the doctor because of an injury to the head; (L) loss of consciousness or a period of being dazed and confused because of an injury to the head; (P) problems in daily life that were not present before the injury such as headaches, dizziness, or anxiety; and (S) sickness such as brain tumor, meningitis, and other medical issues that can cause a TBI. A positive screen for possible TBI is indicated when there is an affirmative answer to H, E, or S and an affirmative answer to L or E together with the presence of two or more problems that were not present before the injury. Additional resources on assessment of traumatic brain injury can be obtained at http://www.brainlinemilitary.org.

DEPRESSION

Although most frequently considered a consequence of IPV victimization, some studies have linked depression to increased risk for IPV (Lipsky, Caetano, Field, & Bazargan, 2005). Further research is needed, but this link may be associated with social information processing deficits secondary to the negative thought patterns that are commonly associated with depression. For example, Beck's (1979) cognitive theory of the development and maintenance of depression posits that the cognitive triad—negative schemas, dysfunctional attitudes, and cognitive distortions—are central to depression. Activation of the cognitive triad is posited to lead to negative automatic thoughts that work to influence emotions, actions, and symptoms of depression (Beck, 1979). As we discussed in our review of social information processing deficits and IPV, such negative automatic thought patterns may lead to misinterpretation of social cues and events, hostility and negative attributions, and a decreased ability to respond appropriately respond to relationship challenges.

A wealth of brief assessment instruments for depression exists. As with other domains, clinicians may choose to conduct a more structured interview or to use a brief screen for depression. The well-validated Patient Health Questionnaire—9 (PHQ–9; Kroenke & Spitzer, 2002) is a nine-item self-report measure that maps on to the nine *DSM–IV* symptoms of depression as well as an overall rating of symptoms severity. Clients respond with a rating of how frequently they experienced each symptom in the past 2 weeks on a 4-point scale (0 = *not at all* to 3 = *nearly every day*) with higher scores reflecting increased symptomatology. Suggested cutoffs of 5, 10, 15, and 20 are considered indicative of possible mild, moderate, moderately severe, and severe depression (Kroenke, Spitzer, & Williams, 2001). The PHQ is free and available at http://www.phqscreeners.com.

ASSESSMENT OF RELATIONSHIP DIFFICULTIES AND IPV

At the core of the initial assessment is gathering information on the frequency and severity of IPV and problems with anger. The gold standard assessment for IPV is the Revised Conflict Tactics Scales (CTS2; Straus,

Hamby, Boney-McCoy, & Sugarman, 1996). The CTS2 contains 39 questions that assess for physical, psychological, and sexual IPV experiences and engagement in the context of an intimate relationship. Clients respond to each item with the frequency that each has occurred in the past year on five scales: Psychological Aggression, Negotiation, Injury, Sexual Coercion, and Physical Assault. Scores can be summed according to whether any IPV has occurred in the past year, referred to as the *prevalence score*. Scores can also be summed to account for the number of times IPV behaviors have occurred in the past year, referred to as *frequency scores*. There are also methods of scoring the measure according to minor and severe types of violence. See http://pubpages.unh.edu/%7Emas2/ctsb.htm for detailed information. The CTS2 is not freely available, however, and it must be purchased from Western Psychological Services (http://www.wpspublish.com). For additional information on other measures of IPV, the Centers for Disease Control and Prevention published an excellent compendium reviewing available assessments (M. P. Thompson, Basile, Hertz, Sitterle, & Centers for Disease Control and Prevention, 2006).

In addition to administering a self-report measure of IPV, specific clinical interview approaches are useful for providers seeking to assess for IPV. In addition to reluctance to disclose, many clients who have engaged in violence or are victims of violence experience significant guilt, shame, and distress when discussing past actions or intimate relationship problems. To inquire verbally into IPV, we advocate using a general-to-specific approach in which clinicians start with general questions about the length and quality of the intimate relationship, followed by more specific questions about physical and psychological IPV such as, "What happens when you have an argument or fight with your partner?" "Do you and your partner call each other names when you are arguing?" "Has it ever gotten physical between the two of you during a fight?" and "How long has this been going on?"

It may also be useful to assess for overall relationship functioning if the client remains in an intact couple. Such assessment provides important information on other domains of the relationship that can be useful in therapy and in goal setting. Brief measures such as the Couples Satisfaction Index (Funk & Rogge, 2007), a 32-item self-report measure of a variety of domains of relationship satisfaction might be considered. Alternatively, the clinician can briefly interview the client regarding important domains such as communication, time together, parenting, intimacy, and general happiness in the relationship. Often such discussion can generate additional goals for treatment, for example, "I'm concerned about the impact of our fighting on the kids."

ASSESSMENT OF ANGER

Understanding the extent of anger management problems is another important aspect of the assessment. The State–Trait Anger Expression Inventory—2 (STAXI–2; Spielberger, 1989) comprises 57 items that measure both the experience and expression of anger, and studies of the measure have supported adequate discriminant and convergent validity (Deffenbacher, Oetting, Lynch, & Morris, 1996). The psychometric properties of the measure have also been supported in military samples (*State–Trait Anger Expression Inventory Professional Manual*; Spielberger, 1989), and partner-violent men score higher than nonviolent men on this measure (Barbour, Eckhardt, Davison, & Kassinove, 1998). In addition, partner-violent men who display pathological anger profiles on the STAXI have been found to have higher violence recidivism after group cognitive behavioral therapy than partner-violent men who report less extreme problems with anger (Murphy, Taft, & Eckhardt, 2007).

The STAXI–2 comprises six scales: five subscales and the Anger Expression Index (AX; Spielberger, 1989). The State Anger Scale measures the individual's present experience of anger (i.e., "How I feel right now"). The Trait Anger Scale measures anger over time (i.e., "How I generally feel"), and the Anger Expression scales specifically measure reactions and behaviors when angry. The AX index provides a measure of anger expression, anger suppression, and control over the anger response. Although the STAXI–2 offers clinicians a great deal of information about a patient's anger and behavioral responses to anger, the STAXI–2 does not specifically measure aggression or incidents of aggression. However, the STAXI–2 does have norms that can be used to examine each client's anger compared with other samples that can be useful in providing feedback to clients about their anger.

ASSESSING MOTIVATION FOR CHANGE

There are two readiness-to-change measures that were developed specifically for use in IPV treatment settings (see also Chapter 6, this volume, where we discuss the utility of considering stages of change in IPV treatment). Although it is important to note that both have been criticized for poor construct validity (Eckhardt & Utschig, 2007), they may still be of some utility in a clinical setting for gathering information on clients' readiness for change. The Safe at Home Instrument for Assessing Readiness to Change Intimate Partner Violence (SAH; Begun et al., 2003) comprises 35 items measuring readiness to change using transtheoretical model of behavior change constructs (TTM; Prochaska & DiClemente, 1982). Content was developed using IPV treatment experts as informants. The items do not explicitly mention violence, focusing instead on relationship conflict, readiness to change, general attitudes, and the current situation. Three subscales can be derived from responses can also be calculated: Precontemplation, Contemplation and Preparation/Action, and a Readiness to Change Index. The SAH has been revised to include items that map on to the maintenance stage of change and to include gender-neutral language (Begun et al., 2008), with acceptable findings for indices of measurement validity.

A second measure that may be of some utility is the University of Rhode Island Change Assessment—Domestic Violence measure (URICA–DV; Levesque, Gelles, & Velicer, 2000). The URICA–DV also maps onto TTM stages of change, and items were adapted from a previous measure that is not specific to domestic violence, the URICA (Levesque et al., 2000). The URICA–DV comprises 20 items designed to assess readiness to change physical violence toward a partner and four subscales (Precontemplation, Contemplation, Action, Maintenance) as well as a global Readiness to Change Index score can be calculated from responses. Preliminary analyses suggested evidence of construct validity for the measure (Levesque et al., 2000). Data from studies of the URICA–DV have suggested that men who fell into the clusters of Precontemplation and Contemplation were more likely to be in the early stages of treatment, whereas men who were in the Action stage were more likely to have used violence cessation strategies and more behavior change processes (although this was unrelated to treatment length; Eckhardt, Babcock, & Homack, 2004; Levesque et al., 2000). Such information may prove useful to clinicians seeking to understand where new clients fall on the continuum of readiness to change.

PROVIDING CLIENT FEEDBACK, ASSESSING READINESS FOR CHANGE, AND GOAL SETTING

As we discussed previously, one goal of therapeutic assessment is to gather information and share it with clients in a way that helps them to make changes (Finn & Tonsager, 1997). As such, clients should be given feedback on their scores on each of the assessment measures completed. It can be useful to compare scores with population norms, as well as to note directly when clients have exceeded cutoffs. In addition, when feedback is shared, this can initiate a larger discussion about the extent to which PTSD symptoms, drug and alcohol use, or depression may be affecting relationship anger and aggression. Clients can be asked whether each problem is something they would like to work on as a goal, and therapists can engage the client in creating a plan of action. In MI, another relevant therapist activity is to help raise the client's awareness of discrepancies between clients' values and goals and their problematic behaviors. For example, continued problems with anger management and alcohol use may be discrepant with the client's value of being a caring partner and the goal of having a healthy and loving relationship. An example of providing some of this feedback is given at the end of this chapter.

INCLUDING PARTNER ASSESSMENT OF IPV

We strongly recommend including the partner in the assessment process by privately and confidentially interviewing her or him. Many state domestic violence standards require "victim contact" for the purposes of notification, risk assessment, and resource provision (Maiuro & Eberle, 2008). To facilitate such assessment, clinicians can ask clients for their permission to contact their partner, and partners can be contacted by phone. One purpose of such assessment is to detect possible under- or overreporting of IPV by the client and to obtain the partner's perspective on the relationship. Previous studies of concordance rates in large justice-involved samples have suggested that obtaining both partners' reports can minimize underreporting, especially with regard to determining violence severity, and that agreement about violence levels was higher at intake than at follow-up (Heckert & Gondolf, 2000a, 2000b).

Our laboratory recently completed two studies examining concordance rates and correlates of male veteran and female partner IPV that highlight the importance of obtaining partner report of IPV. In both studies, there were low rates of agreement between veterans and partners on incidents of physical and psychological IPV (LaMotte, Taft, Reardon, & Miller, 2014; LaMotte, Taft, Weatherill, Scott, & Eckhardt, 2014). Findings from both studies also indicated that greater relationship satisfaction was related to reporting less IPV than one's partner reported. In addition, partner PTSD symptoms were associated with overreporting of both their own and the veterans' IPV, whereas veteran PTSD symptoms were associated with underreporting their own IPV (LaMotte, Taft, Weatherill, et al., 2014). In the second study, results indicated that for both veterans and partners, making more positive and less negative relationship attributions was associated with reporting less IPV than one's partner reported (LaMotte, Taft, Reardon, & Miller, 2014). Thus, PTSD symptoms and relationship satisfaction may affect the amount of IPV reported, and obtaining reports from both members of a dyad may be important for accurate assessment.

Another purpose of including partners in the assessment process is to make sure they have received information about resources that are available to them and to assess for their safety. The first line of inquiry in a partner assessment must be to determine whether the partner is alone and able to speak confidentially. When we conduct such calls, we are ready to provide hotline and referral numbers over the phone and to lead partners through safety planning (see Chapter 5, this volume, for further detail). We start the call by going over the purpose of it clearly, emphasizing that we will not be sharing information back and forth between partners, although we make them aware that their partner is in an IPV treatment program. There are four important safety concerns that must be addressed on such calls:

1. Does the partner feel safe in his or her current situation?
2. Does the partner feel that she or he or any children are in current danger?
3. Does the client have access to any weapons?
4. Does the partner have a safety plan?

Partners often have a positive response to these calls and are willing to give their input regarding abuse in their relationship and to engage in safety planning. However, the clinician must also respect that partners may not wish to participate in the interview. Reporting laws vary by state as to whether there is mandated reporting for IPV; therefore, clinicians should be aware of the provisions in their specific state or province and setting. In all such contacts, partners must be informed at the outset about confidentiality and mandated reporting.

After safety and confidentiality are discussed and there is an understanding between the assessor and the partner, assessment of IPV and relationship factors can begin. We have typically administered questionnaires such as the CTS2 and other relationship satisfaction measures over the phone to examine the partner's report of recent relationship aggression. We also inquire into partners' understanding of any legal issues, such as a no-contact order and pending legal charges, and we ask partners open-ended questions about whether they have anything to add about their relationships that would be important to know. This information is then integrated into the assessor's case formulation, but it is not shared with clients.

CASE STUDY

Frank is a 32-year-old Caucasian male who was referred through the justice system for an evaluation and treatment. He is employed at an electronics store, and he and his girlfriend, Jenny, have been living together for about 2 years. Jenny is a teacher. Frank has been exposed to several car and machine accidents during earlier work as a truck driver, and his father was extremely physically abusive toward him when he was a child, once breaking his arm. Frank was also stabbed several years earlier when he and his friends got into a fight at a bar. Frank is currently being charged with a domestic violence offense, and there is a no-contact order in place prohibiting him from staying at home. He is currently residing with a friend. Despite the no-contact order, he and Jenny have been exchanging text messages, and he hopes they can reconcile. Frank is also on methadone maintenance treatment due to a heroin addiction, and although he is sober from alcohol as well, this is a struggle for him during times of stress.

Frank completed the CTS2, STAXI–1, PCL, and AUDIT as part of his assessment, in addition to a measure of general intimate relationship adjustment and exposure to head injury. His scores revealed that although psychological IPV is particularly high, he also reported using minor violence against Jenny in the past 6 months, with a history of more severe violence in the past. Frank's PTSD symptoms were also extremely elevated, and alcohol use was a problem. Frank described a persistent problem with anger and irritation toward others that he does not manage well.

Transcript of Session

Therapist: Thanks for coming in today, Frank. I know you had to take the bus to get here, and I appreciate that you were able to make it on time. How are you doing today?

Client: I'm here, aren't I?

Therapist: Yes, you are, and I am glad. If it's OK with you, I'd first like to give you an overview of what we're going to be doing today and the purpose of this appointment.

Client: Fine.

Therapist: OK, here is a handout that goes over what I am going to tell you so you can follow along. As I mentioned on the phone, this is an intake appointment for our treatment program here. In this program, our goal is to help people who have problems with anger and aggression learn how to have better relationships with others, control their anger, and end violence. [clear and direct; includes paper handout in addition to verbal information]

Client: Well, I don't really see why I have to come to this when it was my girlfriend Jenny that started this whole thing. I mean, it's really stupid, the cops didn't even ask her any questions; they just came and took me away.

Therapist: It feels like you are being singled out. [reflection statement; nonconfrontational]

Client: Yeah, how can I fix a situation where my girlfriend is always yelling and screaming at me for no reason? I think this whole thing is blown out of proportion, and I don't see why I have to do this program.

Therapist: I understand, it's frustrating that you are the one that isn't able to live at home anymore and you are being ordered to get treatment when there were two people involved. Given that neither one of us has control over the requirement to do this program, maybe we can come back to talking more about that later. First, I want to finish going over this form so you know what to expect today and what my role is. Would you like to do that? [doesn't get thrown off track by comment; empathic statement about situation; emphasis on personal responsibility]

Client: Uh-huh, sorry.

Therapist: Alright.

[Therapist continues to go over issues of confidentiality and session structure, then begins assessment.]

Therapist: OK, I know that was a lot of information. Do you have questions right now?

Client: No.

Therapist: Great. I mentioned a while back that I wanted to hear more about what happened a few weeks ago that led up to this no-contact order and referral. So what happened? [asking the client to tell his story]

Client: Yeah, well, I came home from work a little late. My girl just started screaming at me that I was out with this other girl from work and why couldn't I ever be on time.

Therapist: So your girlfriend, Jenny, thought you were late because you were out cheating on her.

Client: Yeah, she always thinks that—it's a constant argument. Anyway, sometimes I just get so mad that I don't even want to be there. So I just took off on my bike and went to my friend's house. She kept texting me all night. I went home really late and I had been drinking, and when I walked in the door she started screaming at me again. I slammed my cell phone against the wall, and I started screaming back, and I guess I pushed her and she sort of fell into the door to the kitchen and then she ran into the bedroom and locked the door and wouldn't talk to me. Next thing I know, the cops were there and I was getting arrested. But, I mean, she was pushing me too. She was going crazy—but they arrest me and don't ask her any questions. It's really messed up. Now I can't even go back home, and I have to deal with all this stuff. I had to ask off work to get here, and they don't like that.

Therapist: OK, thanks for sharing that with me. Is that the first time you guys have had a fight like that? [nonjudgmental stance]

Client: No, it's been bad for a while. I really love her, but she's got problems, you know. She really pushes my buttons. I think she does it on purpose.

Therapist: I see. What about you, do you see a problem with your own anger? [beginning to bring client into assessment process]

Client: I don't know. People just are the way they are, right? I know I have problems, but it's really not that bad.

Therapist: So you don't really see this as a problem. That is something we can look at if you are interested. Have you ever wondered how your anger compares with other men's?

Client: Not really. I mean, I guess we all get angry. I know sometimes I can be pretty nasty—name-calling and stuff like that. But that's normal.

Therapist: OK, so you see this as normal for you. Sometimes the way we handle things when we are angry becomes a pattern, and it's hard to see if there is maybe a way to do things differently. Would you be interested in getting some feedback today about your anger?

Client: Yeah, I guess. My friends do say I get pretty scary sometimes. Like last week I punched this guy in the face because he was looking at me the wrong way at a bar.

Therapist: Your friends have told you that maybe your anger is scary. If we could help you understand and control your anger a little better, is that something you'd be interested in? [asking client to join in assessment process]

Client: Well, there's nothing to understand, really. I just get so angry I black out.

Therapist: Would there be any benefits to you if you could change that? [pros and cons of change]

Client: Change what?

Therapist: To change your anger, maybe to slow down the process so you have less of those blackouts.

Client: Yeah, I guess, maybe I'd get in less trouble. Sometimes it doesn't go so well for me at work either.

Therapist: I'm hearing two benefits there, one is that you might get in less trouble, and another is that maybe things would be better at work. Can you see any downside to working on your anger?

Client: Well, I guess I'd have to come to these appointments every week. It's not cheap, you know.

Therapist: Right, there is definitely a financial cost and a cost to your time. That's true. What about in your relationship? Would there be a downside there if you could control your anger better?

Client: I mean if we could stop fighting all the time, maybe we would get married.

Therapist: So another benefit might be that you guys would finally get married. Your relationship with Jenny is really important to you.

Client: Yeah.

Therapist: What if things stay the way they are? [generating change talk]

Client: Then I don't think we can be together. . . . And I don't know if I'll be able to stay sober. I can't keep living with my friend.

Therapist: So there's a risk to your sobriety, that's really important, and you don't think you and Jenny will be able to stay together if you don't work on your anger. [pause] Well, what are you going to do? [emphasize personal responsibility change]

Client: I'm here. I guess I'll try this group or whatever you talked about on the phone. I mean I have to do it anyway or they are going to send me to jail.

Therapist: Right, so even though this is all sort of forced and you don't want to be here, it sounds like you are willing to put your best foot forward.

Client: Yeah. But how can you really help me—I mean she's involved too.

Therapist: Well, that is something we should talk about, and we will talk about more. As you know, you can only change yourself and your behavior. We can't force anyone else to change. In this program, you will hear us repeatedly emphasize that you are responsible for your own behavior. That is our philosophy. But sometimes in our work we find that when clients make changes, they find that their partner also makes changes in response. The first thing, and the most important thing, is to help you learn to better manage your anger without getting aggressive. [balancing empathy with direct statement that IPV must stop]

[Frank nods]

Therapist: OK, so we will talk more, but first it can be helpful to see how you are doing with a lot of different types of anger, so I will have you complete some forms that will tell us some more about that, and we can see how you are doing in general. Are you OK with that?

Client: Yep.

Therapist: Great. I'll get you set up with a clipboard. At the end of the session today, I can score these and give you a little feedback.

[Client fills out forms.]

Therapist: Thanks for filling out that paperwork, Frank. I really appreciate it. We will take a look at it toward the end of our visit today, and I'll give you a little more information about those forms. I'd like to ask you a few more questions.

[Clinician continues intake interview.]

Therapist: OK, Frank, I've taken a look at those questionnaires you completed and I scored them. Let's take a look at them together.

Client: OK.

Therapist: So here is the first one [reviewing CTS2]. It looks like with you and Jenny—you are describing that it is really common for both of you to insult or swear at each other and do things like name-calling and shouting when you are in a disagreement. It was less common for you to push, shove, or grab, but that did happen in the past 6 months, and once it looks like you are saying it got really bad, and Jenny had to go to the doctor because of a fight with you. Does that seem accurate? [giving feedback]

Client: Yeah, I mean there are some times when we've pushed and shoved each other and thrown stuff, but usually it's the verbal stuff that we get into most. When we get into an argument, we go right into the name-calling.

Therapist: So it sounds hard for you to resolve even minor disagreements without things getting out of hand with verbal abuse toward one another. [paraphrase]

Client: Yeah, we don't talk to each other very well.

Therapist: Would you like to include that as a treatment goal? Improving your communication skills when you are in a disagreement?

Client: That would go a long way. I don't want to be calling her names like that, and I don't want to be called names myself, but I don't know if I can.

Therapist: Let's give that a shot. I definitely think you can, and we will really focus on that in our treatment program. One thing I want to make sure we talk about, though, is the physical violence that has happened. Is it OK if we talk about that for a bit? [communicating confidence that client can change; direct statement about physical violence; asking permission before directly giving advice]

Client: I wouldn't call it violence. There is the one time when it got really bad, but I haven't done anything like that in a long time.

Therapist: It seems like things are going better because it has just been pushing and shoving, maybe grabbing in an argument—but no one got injured. Calling it physical violence seems like an exaggeration to you. [rolling with resistance]

Client: Right.

Therapist: It sounds like this has gotten you into trouble, though. You mentioned before that your anger gets out of hand, right—that you black out sometimes and your friends said you could be scary? [backward focus]

Client: Yes.

Therapist: So then it sounds like that is very risky for you, because any time you are getting angry, when pushing and shoving happens, it could get worse right? I mean, is that what happened that one time you were describing, when it got really bad?

Client: Yeah it is, I pushed her onto the ground and she broke her arm, so that's why I just take off now.

Therapist: The taking off has been working because you can get out before you "black out," but there is still some physical violence going on as well as the verbal abuse. What do you want to do about that?

Client: Like I said, I don't want to be doing that stuff, it just happens. I don't know.

Therapist: It sounds like you want to get a handle on this, but you don't know how.

[Client nods.]

Therapist: One thing that might work for you is if we can help you to manage your anger better without you having to take off and without you using any abuse toward Jenny. Would that be something you would like to work on?

Client: Yeah, if I could do that, maybe we would resolve some things.

Therapist: OK, how about we include that as a goal?

[Client nods.]

Therapist: But I also need your commitment that you are not going to use any violence during the course of treatment. Any use of violence—even the pushing or shoving—is a problem that we are very concerned about. This is one of the things I want to give you feedback on. Most people do not use violence in their relationships, and any violence is too much—because it hurts Jenny physically and psychologically, and it hurts you, too. You have been pretty emotional when talking about this. [directly but empathically addressing consequences of violence]

[Client nods]

Therapist: Right—I can see that this is all hard on you, and it got you into these legal troubles as well, right? I am also hearing that it is important to you to learn some new ways of handling things and you are willing to do so without resorting to violence. [highlighting Frank's values, asking for commitment]

Client: Yes, definitely.

Therapist: So at this point, you are willing to work on improving your communication and learning some new ways to manage your anger without using violence toward others and you are willing to attend our program here. [summarize so far]

[Therapist continues to discuss feedback with Frank.]

SUMMARY

In this chapter, we described a number of therapist activities and assessment approaches that are useful in initiating effective therapeutic work with individuals who are engaging in IPV. Specifically, we emphasized using the principles of therapeutic assessment and MI, as well as adopting an empathic and flexible stance that directly addresses the client's use of IPV. In addition to assessing for the extent of IPV and its consequences, we described a trauma-informed and multimethod approach to the assessment of trauma exposure, traumatic stress symptoms, depressive symptoms, and other common trauma-related difficulties and disorders that may be linked to IPV. This assessment approach also includes inquiry into problems with substance abuse, anger, and motivation for change. Finally, we highlighted the importance of confidential partner assessment, which provides an important external source of information about the client's IPV and allows the clinician to offer mental health and safety resources to the partner.

5

SAFETY CONSIDERATIONS

For both women and men, experiences of physical and psychological intimate partner violence (IPV) are associated with risk of physical health problems and injury, as well as mental health problems such as posttraumatic stress disorder (PTSD) and depression (Coker et al., 2002; Rhodes et al., 2009). Psychological IPV in particular has been shown to have detrimental effects on health that are as strong, or stronger, than effects observed for physical IPV (Coker et al., 2002; Pico-Alfonso et al., 2006) and stronger and more unique associations with PTSD symptoms (Street & Arias, 2001; Norwood & Murphy, 2012). At the extreme end of the spectrum, IPV also carries a risk of suicidal thoughts and actual or attempted suicide and/or homicide (Campbell, Glass, Sharps, Laughon, & Bloom, 2007; Ellsberg et al., 2008; Rhodes et al., 2009). In addition to risk for partners, there is also risk of negative health outcomes in children exposed to IPV (e.g., Carlson, 2000; Edleson, 1999), including an association between IPV and child abuse (Campbell & Lewandowski,

http://dx.doi.org/10.1037/14918-006
Trauma-Informed Treatment and Prevention of Intimate Partner Violence, by C. T. Taft, C. M. Murphy, and S. K. Creech

1997; Herrenkohl, Sousa, Tajima, Herrenkohl, & Moylan, 2008). Finally, though rarely discussed, violence or harm to pets and animals may also be associated with IPV (Ascione et al., 2007). It is clear that providers working in the field of IPV have to include safety planning in their programs.

The duty to protect potential victims from harm by clients is a general legal and ethical requirement of mental health practice. In the treatment of those who engage in IPV, this duty is complicated by the fact that there is ongoing risk to a potential victim who likely has some awareness of this risk from previous IPV experiences. Also, the distinction between a general risk of violence over time and an imminent threat of violence at a specific point in time can be difficult to distinguish in these situations. Routine partner outreach and assessment are crucial to clarify risk and promote safety. In fact, we believe that significant effort to establish partner contact is an essential element of ethical practice in the treatment of IPV.

FORMAL RISK ASSESSMENT

A number of instruments have been developed to assess for IPV risk, including the Danger Assessment (DA; Campbell, Webster, & Glass, 2009), the Domestic Violence Screening Instrument (DVSI; Williams & Grant, 2006; Williams & Houghton 2004), the Ontario Domestic Assault Risk Assessment (Hilton et al., 2004), and the Spousal Assault Risk Assessment Guide (SARA; Kropp & Gibas, 2010; Kropp & Hart, 2000). These measures vary as to whether they are completed by the partner (DA); by a clinician using a criminal record review (DVSI); or through using a variety of methods including interviews with the client and partner, record reviews, police reports, and measures of IPV and drug and alcohol use (SARA). Some provide a list of overall risk factors endorsed, whereas others, such as the SARA, are intended to help structure clinician judgment about risk. In an excellent review of these instruments, Kropp (2008; see also Bowen, 2011) suggested that each contains similar content and possesses some reliability and validity; however, he also cautioned that each predicts recidivism only moderately well. Therefore, if clinicians decide to include a risk measure as part of their assessment battery, this should be done in combination with other assessment approaches and in consideration of each client's situation and idiosyncratic risk factors that may increase the likelihood of future and continuing violence.

Multiple studies have found that the combination of including women's perceptions of risk with either a risk prediction instrument such as the DA or a list of risk factors significantly improves prediction accuracy (Heckert & Gondolf, 2004). Using data from a sample of 177 women whose partners were involved in court-ordered batterer's intervention treatment, Weisz, Tolman, and Saunders (2000) examined whether the women were better at predicting future severe IPV than a statistical approach that used a number of empirically defined risk factors. Results indicated that women's estimates of the likelihood that their partner would be violent during a dispute with them over the next year significantly predicted severe IPV as measured at a follow-up assessment. In addition, several Time 1 risk factors, including past restraining orders and injuries; IPV between a focal incident and court date; threats to drop charges; forced sex; choking or strangling; controlling behavior; accusations of an affair; and kicking, biting, or hitting, all predicted severe violence at the second interview. Results suggested that the combination of victim prediction and the consideration of risk factors may improve the accuracy of prediction. In a similar study, Cattaneo and Goodman (2003) found that partner violent clients' abuse of alcohol and general levels of violence, severity of IPV, and partner assessments of dangerousness were significant predictors of repeated IPV. Thus, the literature has indicated that an extremely important aspect of risk assessment is the inclusion of partner report, as is assessed by Campbell's DA measure (Campbell et al., 2009).

PARTNER SAFETY PLANNING

In addition to providing important information on IPV frequency and severity, contacting partners for assessment also provides an avenue for the provision resources that promote safety. Across several studies McFarlane and colleagues examined whether safety-promoting interventions with women who have experienced IPV is effective (McFarlane, Groff, O'Brien, & Watson, 2006; McFarlane et al., 2004). In one study, 75 women receiving services at a family violence unit received six safety intervention calls in which they were provided with information about safety-promoting behaviors such as hiding money or documents in case of need to exit, removing weapons from the home, and establishing a code word with friends or family that signified the need for help (McFarlane et al., 2004). Results indicated that safety-promoting behaviors were improved compared with a control group who did not receive the intervention, and additional safety behaviors acquired following intake were practiced for up to 18 months. Another study tested the efficacy of either receiving a wallet-sized referral card containing a safety plan and local information on IPV services or receiving the wallet referral card plus nurse case management about IPV and resources. Results indicated that both treatment groups adopted increased safety behaviors and reported reductions in IPV (McFarlane et al., 2006). Exhibit 5.1 is an example script of a partner interview based on those used in our programs.

EXHIBIT 5.1
Sample Partner Assessment Script

I am calling from the _____. We are interviewing partners of individuals who are participating in our program to stop relationship conflict and aggression. Your partner gave us your name to contact you to see whether you would take part in a phone interview. We'd like to ask you some questions about your perspective on how things have gone in your relationship with [name of partner]. We can also give you some information on local resources that may be available to you. If this is a convenient time, I can give you some details about the interview and our program. This will only take a few minutes. Is this a convenient time?

YES NO NOT INTERESTED

Better time to call back? Day: _____ Time: _____ Better #: _________

IF YES, CONTINUE

During the interview today, you may refuse to answer any question you do not feel comfortable answering. You may stop your participation at any time, for any reason. Your refusal will not affect your partner's eligibility for treatment, and he will not be given any information about your responses. If during our telephone conversation, you feel you no longer have enough privacy where you are, you may end the interview by saying "I'm too busy to talk right now, can I call you back?"

Information collected for the purposes of this interview will be kept confidential. You will not be told anything about what your partner has said to us, and your partner will not be told anything about your responses. Your partner will not be informed of whether or not you agree to participate, and he will be able to be in our treatment program (and receive care) even if you do not agree to participate.

Is it OK if I ask you some questions now?

IF NO: "Thank you anyway."

IF YES: "Would you like to do it now or at a later time?"

Preferred date/time: ___________________

Safety

TO BEGIN THE INTERVIEW, SAY, "To begin the interview today, I'm going to give you our number in case you need to interrupt the interview. It is __________. Are you in a quiet, private space?"

1. "I'd like to find out whether you feel safe in your current situation with [partner's name]."
2. "Are you still in a romantic relationship with [partner's name]?" ___Yes ___No
3. "If applicable, are you planning to leave or end your relationship with [partner's name]?" ___Yes ___No
4. "Do you feel that you or your children are in current danger of physical harm?" ___Yes ___No
5. "What about any family pets—do you feel they are in current danger of physical harm?" ___Yes ___No
6. "Does [partner's name] have access to any weapons?" ___Yes ___No
7. "Do you have a safety plan to use if you feel in danger?" ___Yes ___No

   IF YES, obtain details of safety plan ("What would you do? Where would you go?")

   IF NO, discuss general details of safety planning and connect to a helpline and/or local resources.

   "It is important to think through ways to keep yourself and your children safe. Although you may feel that the violence was a single incident, or will not be frequent, it is still important to think about creating a safety plan."

EXHIBIT 5.1
Sample Partner Assessment Script *(Continued)*

8. "Where is a place you can go if you need to leave your home? What about inside your home?"
   - "Visualize your house and identify safe places (rooms that have two exits, rooms without knives or weapons or hard surfaces, rooms with phones) where you can go."
9. "What would you need to take with you if you had to leave in a hurry?"
   - "You might think about putting some money and copies of important documents aside. These could include copies of your passport, bank statements, birth certificates, and so forth."
   - "Create a 'necessity bag' of items you (and your children) will need if you need to leave the home quickly. You can keep this at work or at a close friend's house."
10. "If you have children or pets, how could you get them to safety as well? What would they need if you had to leave with them in a hurry?"
    - Share community resources for options for pets if available.
11. "Is there someone in your life you can talk to about what is going on?"
    - Discuss benefits of letting others in life know about situation, if applicable, and assist in troubleshooting
12. "Have you considered your legal options?"
    - This might include going to the police or district courthouse to get a restraining order in place. Share information on how to access the justice system.
13. "Do you feel need help accessing physical or mental health care?"
    - Offer a list of community resources and phone numbers. Provide direct contact if possible.
14. Always offer a hotline: "If you would like it, I have a 24-hour toll-free number that you can call from anywhere in the country for help for domestic violence. [If person is interested:] That number is 1-XXX-XXX-XXXX."
    - "If you feel you cannot keep this number safely, some women in the past have copied it and placed it in their shoe."
15. Introduce other assessment measures such as CTS2 [Conflict Tactics Scales] and risk assessment measures.
    - "Now I'd like to ask some detailed questions about things that may have happened when you were in an argument with [partner's name]."

Campbell (2001) suggested that there are five important aspects of safety planning that should be addressed: (a) lethality or dangerousness, (b) whether the partner intends to stay in the relationship, (c) the partner's emotional well-being, (d) available resources (community, family, job), and (e) involvement of children. Increased emphasis has recently included pets as an important area to consider because concern for the welfare of an animal may make it difficult for women to access an emergency shelter (Ascione et al., 2007).

With regard to lethality assessment, Campbell (2001) recommended assessing for threats of lethality, including with weapons; the presence of weapons in the home; and obsessive jealousy, and then informing the partner that these are risk factors for homicide so that she is able to make an informed decision about what to do. This can be done in combination with administration of the DA risk instrument (Campbell, 2001; Campbell et al., 2009) and should include asking whether the partner perceives that she or he is in danger or is not safe. If responses suggest risk of lethality is present, the clinician must make referrals to local shelter services, recommend that weapons be removed from the home, and in situations where danger seems imminent, the clinician may be required to contact law enforcement in conjunction with state and facility requirements for duty to warn.

If a partner discloses that she or he intends to end the relationship and leave the home, the clinician should help the partner with safety planning for this potentially dangerous event. This is extremely important because some data have suggested that the risk of homicide is high during such a period (Campbell et al., 2003). If the partner plans to stay in the relationship, he or she might be assisted in safety planning for how to access support resources, including those available through the justice system, if needed. If the clinician detects that a partner is need of referrals for psychological treatment, these should be provided.

RISK MANAGEMENT PLANNING FOR THOSE WHO ENGAGE IN INTIMATE PARTNER VIOLENCE

Compared with those who experience IPV, less information is available with regard to recommendations for safety and risk planning in the context of treatment for those who engage in IPV. Kropp (2008) described four features of a risk management plan: (a) monitoring, (b) treatment, (c) supervision, and (d) partner safety planning. *Monitoring* includes repeat assessments with the client, partner, and other providers involved in the case and may include behaviors such as examining missed appointments, field visits, and drug tests. *Treatment* includes treatments for IPV as well as mental health problems. *Supervision* refers to any justice system imposed limitations such as no-contact orders, probation, or jail time. Finally, the goal of *safety planning* is to bolster the resources of the partner in case of future or ongoing violence despite all other efforts. Throughout this chapter, we have discussed specific domains that contribute to risk of IPV and that should be part of ongoing safety and risk assessment. We also refer the reader to additional safety and stabilization strategies for those who engage in IPV, addressed in Chapter 12.

CLINICIAN PREPARATION FOR SAFETY PLANNING

Perhaps the most important aspect of safety planning is resource building and planning on the part of the clinician. Clinicians working with this population should form alliances with local domestic violence shelters and become aware of legal, mental health, and economic resources available to both those who experience and engage in IPV. Vetere and Cooper (2001) referred to community relationship building as forming a "stable third" who helps share and manage the risks of treatment for domestic violence. Regular contact between agencies helps strengthen such alliances. In addition, funding for local shelter and mental health services is highly variable from year to year, and such alliances will keep clinicians aware of important changes to available resources. Specific to the justice system, we recommend providing education to probation officers and others involved with regard to specific limits of confidentiality that may be different between settings.

We have found it is also extremely helpful to understand how to enact rarely used provisions for safety and risk planning, as well as to understand fully the legal obligations of all involved. For example, what are the circumstances under which a clinician must involve the justice system or child protective services, and what is the most clinically appropriate way to do so? Clinicians may commonly find that they are aware that a no-contact order is being broken, but under what circumstances must this be reported, and how will the clinician do so? The answers to these questions will be determined by each clinician's state and institutional practice guidelines. Another example involves the procedures enacted when weapons are present. Prior to advising that weapons be removed from the home, clinicians should contact local law enforcement to determine the process by which a client can turn weapons in, as well as other options for weapons removal that do not involve law enforcement. Sometimes the legal situation of the client may require that they have no weapons, and this is also important to know. It is important to prescreen all hotline and other shelter service phone numbers that may be offered, both to make sure that numbers are correct and to gather information to be used when clients invariably ask what will happen when they call.

SUMMARY

IPV has myriad and potentially lethal consequences for partners, with risks extending to children and pets. There are several validated measures that exist to assist in evaluating risk assessment that were reviewed in this chapter, and available evidence suggests that each predicts IPV recidivism moderately well (Kropp, 2008). In this chapter, we argued that including partner interviews in the assessment process is crucial for accurately assessing IPV risk as well as for providing resources and that successful safety and risk intervention will depend on forming relationships with the larger community of providers. We concluded by offering a sample partner assessment telephone script that is similar to those we have used in the past.

6
PROCESS CONSIDERATIONS

Discussion of any intervention designed to end and prevent a problem behavior necessitates a consideration of process factors. *Process factors* refer to the process of therapy or the nonspecific factors that may influence treatment outcomes beyond the use of specific therapy techniques. The most commonly discussed process factors are the therapeutic alliance and motivational readiness for change. We argue that it is likely that the less-than-impressive research findings in evaluation studies of intimate partner violence (IPV) programs are due in large part to a failure to consider these process factors that have been shown to represent the most important ingredients for change across a range of populations and problems. Many community IPV interventions are not even considered therapy at all, which ultimately may undermine our collective knowledge about what brings about behavior change. Some have long argued that many in the IPV field downplay the importance of a collaborative therapeutic relationship, empathic listening, group cohesion,

http://dx.doi.org/10.1037/14918-007
Trauma-Informed Treatment and Prevention of Intimate Partner Violence, by C. T. Taft, C. M. Murphy, and S. K. Creech

and related processes shown to promote success in other areas of psychotherapy and directed behavior change (Daniels & Murphy, 1997; Jennings, 1987; Murphy & Baxter, 1997).

Not only have such process factors been neglected clinically but also in research studies as well. Researchers in the IPV field have focused considerable attention on attempting to document the overall effectiveness of interventions (Babcock, Green, & Robie, 2004) and identifying different subgroups of those who engage in IPV (Bender & Roberts, 2007), although little work has examined process-related factors that may contribute to more positive outcomes and ultimately lead to improvements in IPV programs. In the general psychotherapy literature, process factors are often more influential in determining successful outcome than type of intervention (Krupnick et al., 1996), and thus warrant our careful attention.

Trauma histories can have a major impact on the process of therapy. If a client presents to IPV intervention with a history of childhood abuse and other violence victimization in adulthood, for example, it may require greater effort to facilitate a positive therapeutic environment. Previously discussed themes that may be affected by trauma, such as difficulties trusting others, often play out in therapeutic relationships. Therefore, our efforts to facilitate a positive therapeutic alliance take on even greater importance when working with a trauma-exposed population.

In this chapter, we review the research and clinical literature on process factors and how to enhance good therapy process in our work with this population. First, we address the use of confrontational tactics in IPV interventions. We then discuss the literature on the therapeutic alliance and motivational readiness for change as they apply to IPV intervention. Finally, we address issues of guilt, shame, power and control, trust, and self-esteem that often accompany trauma and IPV, and that may bring important process considerations.

USE OF CONFRONTATIONAL TACTICS

Some clinicians and researchers have argued that standard group treatment approaches for IPV that focus on gender reeducation and socialization may foster a confrontational rather than a therapeutic atmosphere (Mankowski, Haaken, & Silvergleid, 2002; Murphy & Baxter, 1997; Taft & Murphy, 2007). Critics have argued that widely adopted intervention approaches for this population recommend that providers use confrontational tactics to counter victim blaming, denial, minimization, or rationalization of IPV by the client and that they should do this by challenging the client directly or by encouraging group members to confront one another. Group leaders may be encouraged to impose other negative sanctions, such as group dismissal or lengthening the course of intervention for clients who are seen as difficult or resistant. Discussions of trauma histories and related problems such as posttraumatic stress disorder (PTSD) that are associated with IPV are often discouraged or vigorously challenged in these interventions and are not met with empathy. These factors are viewed as rationalizations or justifications for abusive behavior, and the therapist may be considered to be colluding with the client's rationalizations by empathizing.

A number of other factors may increase the likelihood that confrontational tactics will be used in IPV intervention. First, many programs treating court-mandated clients do not draw clear boundaries between treatment and punishment and may see themselves as an extension of the criminal justice system (Murphy & Baxter, 1997). Second, those who engage in IPV are sometimes thought of by providers as "primitive" men who are incapable of insight or positive behavior change, leading some providers to resort to punitive tactics when confronted with client resistance (Jennings, 1987). Third, the severity and impact of IPV may create a sense of alarm in providers, who may react by attempting to bring all IPV and rationalizations to an immediate halt, and thus confrontational tactics are used (knowingly or unknowingly) as a sort of crisis intervention (Jennings, 1987). Fourth, some providers may unconsciously react aggressively to the defensiveness or hostility of the abusive client (Taft & Murphy, 2007). Some providers may have difficulties showing therapeutic empathy and concern for the welfare of abusive clients, who are often hostile toward providers, controlling and manipulative in their interpersonal relationships, and self-centered or clinically narcissistic. Last, most IPV program providers simply have not been trained in the importance of process factors and how to facilitate a positive therapeutic process.

THE THERAPEUTIC ALLIANCE

The most studied and written about process factor is the *therapeutic alliance*, a measure of the strength of the therapeutic relationship between the client and therapist. One influential model indicates that the therapeutic alliance consists of agreement on the goals and tasks related to therapy, as well as the bond formed between client and therapist (Bordin, 1979). A positive therapeutic alliance has been found to be an important factor in therapeutic change for a wide variety of treatment populations and treatment modalities (Friedlander, Escudero, Heatherington, & Diamond, 2011; Marsh, Angell, Andrews, & Curry, 2012; Martin, Garske, & Davis, 2000). Many consider it to be the most promising integrative common factor in psychotherapy.

Though it is admittedly often difficult to form a positive therapeutic alliance with abusive clients, a strong alliance is crucial in motivating these individuals for treatment and bringing about successful behavior change. It logically follows that if abusive clients do not believe the therapist is there to help them and do not agree with the goals and tasks of treatment, they will not work toward developing new coping strategies and better ways to handle their anger. Sonkin and Dutton (2003), in their application of attachment theory to interventions with men who engage in IPV, discussed how a positive therapeutic relationship was necessary for exploring prior unresolved trauma and abuse perpetrated by childhood attachment figures that may underlie abusive behavior.

A small research base has indicated that the facilitation of a more positive therapeutic alliance is associated with greater IPV intervention compliance. In a qualitative analysis of a sample of treatment-seeking maritally discordant couples reporting husband to wife physical IPV, Brown, O'Leary, and Feldbau (1997) found that the most frequently provided reason for dropout was a mismatch of the goals for therapy with the provider, a key component of the alliance. Cadsky, Hanson, Crawford, and Lalonde (1996) similarly reported lower dropout among clients whose self-identified problems matched the focus of the treatment program. Rondeau, Brodeur, Brochu, and Lemire (2001) found that greater therapeutic alliance ratings were associated with treatment retention in men in IPV intervention in Canada, and the alliance was the strongest predictor of treatment compliance.

The therapeutic alliance has also been associated with reductions in abusive behavior in IPV programs in research studies. Brown and O'Leary (2000), in a treatment study of self-referred married couples reporting serious husband-to-wife physical IPV, found that higher observer alliance ratings obtained during the first session were associated with reductions in both physical and psychological IPV following intervention. Taft, Murphy, King, Musser, and DeDeyn (2003), in a primarily court-mandated sample of men participating in a 16-session cognitive behavioral treatment program for IPV, found significant correlations between both early and late therapist alliance ratings and measures of IPV at 6-month follow-up such that higher alliance was associated with reductions in IPV. In addition, significant associations were found between therapist alliance ratings and treatment adherence, assessed through compliance with homework assignments. In a qualitative study, Rosenberg (2003) conducted in-depth interviews with completers of an IPV program. Approximately 86% indicated that connection with the group leader was helpful. More recently, Boira, del Castillo, Carbajosa, and Marcuello (2013) reported relationships between the therapeutic alliance and the usefulness of the program and its content in a small sample of men in an IPV intervention.

Murphy and Baxter (1997) speculated that confrontational tactics, particularly in the early stages of therapy with men who engage in IPV, have detrimental effects on the alliance. Others have similarly argued that highly directive interventions lead to a lack of access to important client cognitive resources, hindering IPV intervention (Mooney & Padesky, 2000). The negative impact of confrontation on the therapeutic alliance is likely to be magnified in trauma-exposed populations. Given that many abusive clients were themselves victimized in childhood or at some other point in their lives (Dutton, 1998), issues of mistrust must often be overcome in developing a positive therapeutic alliance that will lead to true behavior change (Rondeau et al., 2001). When a provider responds to a traumatized client in a confrontational manner, this could elicit trauma-related feelings of mistrust, damage the therapist–client relationship, and hinder intervention efforts. Moreover, as Scalia (1994) argued, confrontation with those who engage in IPV may contribute to increases in clients' trauma-related reservoir of anger and risk of abusive behavior.

Confrontational approaches also reinforce negative themes, or *schemas*, around issues related to power and control (Murphy & Baxter, 1997; Safran & Muran, 1996). For example, when providers engage in confrontational behavior, they are reinforcing the idea that someone is always in control of the other in interpersonal relationships and/or is more powerful than the other. The client may also be angered in having felt belittled or attacked by the provider, which may serve to invoke or remind the client of prior traumas during which they experienced similar feelings. A likely outcome of these processes is that the client becomes less amenable to change and, in fact, angrier. Clients may display these reactions in outward hostility and defensiveness or in passive compliance designed to fulfill an externally imposed requirement for treatment without engaging in genuine self-exploration.

Conversely, psychotherapy scholars have long argued that supportive, alliance-building approaches counter negative interpersonal schemas. Research shows that a positive alliance leads to greater interpersonal functioning and an increase in one's ability to garner social support from others (Kivlighan & Shaughnessy, 1995; Mallinckrodt, 1996). In other words, if the provider and client are able to develop a positive alliance and work collaboratively toward behavior change, this can help overcome trauma-related challenges to therapy, improve the client's relationships, and reduce the risk of IPV.

MOTIVATIONAL READINESS FOR CHANGE

Prochaska and DiClemente's (1982, 1992) transtheoretical model has been used extensively in substance abuse and health behavior research to describe how individuals undergo intentional behavior change (Evers et al., 2012; Heather, Hönekopp, Smailes, & UKATT, 2009; Prochaska, Johnson,

& Lee, 2009). One key element of the model focuses on five stages of change (precontemplation, contemplation, preparation, action, maintenance) representing distinct cognitive markers individuals pass through to undergo successful behavior change. This model can be conceptualized as a wheel or a spiral of change because most individuals pass through the stages several times before they permanently change their behavior (DiClemente & Scott, 1997). According to this model, the therapist should match their approach with the stage of change the patient is in, because different processes of change operate within different stages. The individual's stage of change at any given time is thought to reflect their current motivational state. Thus, the stage of change on entry into treatment may be thought of as the individual's motivational readiness for engaging in a program of treatment. Research has demonstrated that the success of treatment tends to be a function of the individual's stage of change on entry into treatment (Prochaska & DiClemente, 1992).

In the *precontemplation* stage of change, individuals have not yet considered the possibility that they have a problem or have to change their behavior. Individuals in the precontemplation stage usually only present to therapy as a result of external pressure from a spouse, another family member, an employer, or the courts. When individuals enter the *contemplation* stage, they are considering change but have yet to make a commitment to taking action. Typically, individuals alternate between accepting that they have a problem and need to change and justifying their current behavior. When individuals decide to make a change, they have moved into the *preparation* stage. This is the stage at which the person first appears to be clearly motivated to change. If individuals then choose a change strategy or take active steps toward change, they have moved into the *action* stage. Next is the *maintenance* stage, in which individuals continue to change their behavior and attempt to maintain the gains made during the action stage. For example, if an alcoholic quits drinking and has not relapsed for a reasonable period (e.g., 6 months), he or she is considered to be in the maintenance stage.

The goal of therapies that use this model is the successful long-term maintenance of the gains made. If individuals are not able to maintain their gains and they begin engaging in the problem behavior again, they have relapsed. As mentioned previously, relapses are common, and it is usually the case that individuals must go through the stages of change numerous times before they are able to maintain their gains permanently. However, individuals usually learn from their relapses, may begin the subsequent change effort at a later state (contemplation or preparation), and may move more quickly through the early stages than they did in earlier change attempts.

The transtheoretical model may be particularly relevant with regard to those who engage in IPV, particularly in terms of the referral status and attitudinal and cognitive factors often ascribed to these individuals (Murphy

& Maiuro, 2009). The mode by which these individuals enter intervention programs differs from most other treatment populations in that they are often court referred. As a result of this, many enter against their will. O'Hare (1996) found that court-referred patients were over 10 times more likely to be precontemplators, as measured by the Stages of Change Scale, than were voluntary patients in his sample of outpatient mental health clients presenting to treatment for a variety of problems. Precontemplators may not respond to active directive interventions and are the most resistant clients. In addition, violent individuals in early stages of change are more likely to either not be engaged in treatment or drop out from treatment prematurely (Eckhardt, Holtzworth-Munroe, Norlander, Sibley, & Cahill, 2009; Scott, 2004). In contrast, individuals who voluntarily seek psychological help have likely moved past the precontemplation stage of change and are usually more motivated for therapist intervention.

DiGiuseppe, Tafrate, and Eckhardt (1994) addressed several common beliefs held by angry clients that reflect early stages of change. They argued that angry individuals often feel that their anger is justified and appropriate, blame others for their outbursts, and claim the recipient deserved the expression of anger. Likewise, those who engage in IPV have been found to deny or minimize the effects of their IPV and claim that their violence was either justified or caused by external factors (Pence & Paymar, 1993; Smith, 2007). These statements reflect early stages of change and are likely to have a negative impact on treatment. As DiGiuseppe et al. argued, angry individuals often do not agree on the goals and tasks of therapy because they see their expressions of anger as appropriate. In addition, they may perceive therapist attempts at changing their anger expression as a sign that they are not believed and that the therapist is not on their side, which could prevent a positive emotional bond from forming. This would likely be compounded by a confrontational approach to therapy. Individuals in earlier stages of change may require less intense interventions in an attempt to move the individual toward the action stage. In the substance abuse literature, W. R. Miller and his colleagues have shown that confrontational therapist tactics are associated with higher client resistance during treatment and greater substance abuse following treatment, whereas higher therapist expressions of support and empathy are predictive of less client resistance in therapy and better outcomes (W. R. Miller, Benefield, & Tonigan, 1993; W. R. Miller, Taylor, & West, 1980).

As noted, some work has shown that motivational techniques facilitate compliance and enhance outcomes in IPV intervention (Murphy & Maiuro, 2009). In a prior study, we used a quasi-experimental design to examine the effectiveness of supportive telephone calls and handwritten notes from therapist to client after missed sessions in a treatment program for partner violent men (Taft, Murphy, Elliott, & Morrel, 2001). The cohort who received this intervention attended a significantly larger number of intervention sessions and had significantly lower dropout rates when compared with a cohort that did not receive this intervention, even after controlling for the demographic and background factors that often predict attendance. Clinicians who participated in this project commented that clients had spontaneously thanked them for the personal note, indicating that this gesture may have been particularly important in facilitating return to treatment after a missed session.

In a more recent quasi-experimental study examining program compliance, Scott, King, McGinn, and Hosseini (2011) examined a motivational interviewing adjunctive therapy component and treatment adherence in a large sample of highly resistant men who engage in IPV. These researchers found that highly resistant clients who were administered the adjunctive intervention evidenced lower dropout than both resistant and nonresistant clients receiving the standard IPV intervention without the adjunctive intervention.

In a related study of IPV intervention, Alexander, Morris, Tracy, and Frye (2010) compared a group treatment program based on helping clients move through the stages of change with a cognitive behavioral gender reeducation approach in a large sample of predominantly court-referred men. Interestingly, results indicated that the stage-of-change intervention was more effective than the standard intervention for those clients who were initially lacking in motivation, whereas the cognitive behavioral intervention was more effective for those who evidenced higher levels of motivation before treatment. These data suggest the utility of tailoring IPV intervention to client readiness for change.

IMPACT OF CORE THEMES RELATED TO TRAUMA ON THERAPY PROCESS

We have previously discussed how certain themes related to trauma may underlie negative trauma reactions as well as abusive behavior. We discuss some such themes in this section, with a focus on how they may affect the therapeutic relationship and how the provider might effectively deal with negative client behaviors related to these themes. Specifically, we discuss core themes related to guilt and shame, power and control, trust, and self-esteem.

Guilt and Shame

To facilitate a positive therapeutic environment, it can be helpful for providers to consider possible reasons for clients' rationalizations for their abusive behavior and outright denial of their IPV. Often a discussion of guilt and shame can help a client to recognize that it is difficult to acknowledge one's abusive behavior. Despite their conceptual overlap, shame and guilt function differently. Whereas guilt tends to be more associated with empathy and acknowledging the impact of one's behavior (de Hooge, Zeelenberg, & Breugelmans, 2007), shame is associated with attempts to deny or escape from responsibility (Tangney & Dearing, 2002). Gilligan (1997, 2003) theorized that aggressive acts are maladaptive attempts to escape shame and associated feelings of weakness, inferiority, and worthlessness. Studies have similarly shown a link between shame and the use of both physical and psychological aggression in dating relationships (Dutton, van Ginkel, & Starzomski, 1995; Harper, Austin, Cercone, & Arias, 2005).

Shame may help account for the relationship between PTSD and IPV. Sippel and Marshall (2011), using a modified Stroop task, found that the relationship between PTSD and IPV behaviors was mediated by facilitated color naming of shame-related words. These results suggest that PTSD may be associated with shame-processing biases, which in turn lead to IPV. Relatedly, Hundt and Holohan (2012) found that shame, guilt, depression, and PTSD were all significantly associated with IPV, though shame was the strongest predictor and mediated the relationship between PTSD and IPV. Evidence has also indicated that attempts to escape from shame may be accompanied by aggression (Stuewig, Tangney, Heigel, Harty, & McCloskey, 2010; Thomaes, Bushman, Stegge, & Olthof, 2008; Thomaes, Stegge, Olthof, Bushman, & Nezlek, 2011), and many IPV episodes occur in the context of prototypically shame-inducing events (e.g., arguments regarding jealousy, infidelity, or betrayal; Fenton & Rathus, 2010).

Taken together, the available clinical and research findings on shame are not only helpful in better understanding the etiology of IPV but also provide clues with respect to clinical interventions that may be effective or ineffective for this population. Considering that shame-inducing events may serve as a functional antecedent to episodes of IPV, it stands to reason that more confrontational, shame-inducing interventions would be countertherapeutic with this population. Conversely, approaches that do not serve to label, stigmatize, or otherwise shame the client will likely facilitate a better therapeutic relationship and readiness for change.

The experience of shame may also prevent taking responsibility for abusive behavior. Abusive individuals may deny or minimize their abusive behavior because of feelings of shame. In other words, at some level, they recognize that they have engaged in abhorrent behavior, but powerful feelings of shame provoke a denial reaction, so they avoid coming face to face with the reality of their behavior and the damage it has caused. This can often come to light in frank discussions with abusive clients about what might get in the way of discussing their prior abusive behavior. When we talk openly to abusive clients about what makes it difficult to disclose their IPV and discuss its impact, clients will sometimes discuss how powerful feelings of shame get in the way. This is a positive line of discussion with abusive clients because it may help lower client resistance and remove cognitive barriers to discussions of abusive behavior.

Power and Control Conflicts

Conflicts related to power and control are common among those who have experienced trauma and also underlie abusive behavior. Such conflicts can be difficult to manage in the therapy context as well because it may be difficult to establish positive therapeutic relationships with controlling clients, and such clients may view mainstream providers as authority figures attempting to control them. The more the therapist attempts to show abusive clients "who is boss," the more the clients will react negatively to the provider and refuse to join him or her in attempting to change their behavior. The therapist wants to avoid reinforcing the client's view that one person is always controlling the other person in every relationship. Though therapists have to establish certain "ground rules" for therapy to be helpful, they should avoid attempting to force the client to change or to exert their own power over the client nontherapeutically. This can be a challenge to even seasoned clinicians because clients with conflicts related to power and control may display open hostility toward providers and otherwise attempt to thwart change efforts. The therapist is encouraged to "roll with the resistance" (W. R. Miller & Rollnick, 2002) and to maintain a calm, therapeutic stance while attempting to understand the client's perspective.

Trust Difficulties

It stands to reason that when clients have conflicts related to trust, they may have a more difficult time establishing a positive therapeutic relationship. The client may have been betrayed or let down by others and generalized mistrust to virtually everyone, relationship partners and treatment providers alike. It is important for the provider to have an understanding of potential trust issues at the outset and be mindful of the timing of more active interventions when the client is not ready or willing to work together with the provider in a collaborative manner. Establishing trust occurs when the provider conveys a genuine interest in understanding the client, as well as his or her reasons for having difficulties trusting others. Again, if the therapist engages in confrontational behavior that mirrors previous negative relationships in which trust has been betrayed, it may be exceedingly difficult to reestablish the trust that is so critical for positive treatment gains to take place. At the same time, it is important for the therapist to assist clients in recognizing their difficulties in trusting others and how these difficulties developed and to help clients understand how their trust difficulties affect the therapeutic relationship and their abusive behavior.

Low Self-esteem

Low self-esteem is common among abusive individuals who have been exposed to trauma. Perhaps clients have been abused themselves at some point in their lives or are currently experiencing abuse. Clients may have had a difficult time adjusting to life after a trauma and their self-esteem may be low as a result of their own abusive or otherwise problematic behavior. Some abusive clients with low self-esteem may have a tendency to attempt to lower others around them, including providers. Others may have difficulties mustering the energy to engage actively in behavior change efforts. The provider should be aware of these different dynamics and work with clients to help uncover cognitive distortions related to how they are viewing themselves, orient clients toward more reasonable perceptions of themselves and others, and help them develop an understanding of how their low self-esteem contributes to their abusive behavior and difficulties maintaining a positive therapeutic relationship.

Uncovering Themes Affecting the Process and Outcomes of Therapy

In this chapter, we have discussed how some themes underlying trauma reactions and abusive behavior may affect the therapeutic relationship. Although these issues may be challenging for the therapist, encountering them can also be incredibly therapeutic and game changing when it comes to ending abusive behavior. When the therapist can help abusive clients to understand how their prior trauma has affected their views of the world and how their views of the world affect their progress in therapy (and, more important, their abusive behavior), clients may achieve a much greater understanding of the causes of their problems. This uncovering work can be an early step in recognizing the need for change and understanding the best course forward to attempt to resolve trauma-related distortions and end abusive behavior.

In working with trauma-exposed individuals, although we want to avoid more confrontational tactics, this does not mean that we "collude" with them in victim blaming, denial, or minimization of IPV. Rather, we take a firm stance that the individual is responsible for his or her abusive behavior, but we do so in the context of a relationship in which there is genuine interest in understanding the client and recognizing how the client has learned these abusive patterns. We work to understand the prior traumas clients have experienced and how this affects their current relationships, and this will help clients see that we recognize that they are not abusive by nature. When we work to understand our clients and how their problems developed, we get away from stigmatizing or labeling them simply as "batterers," and we show that we are listening to their stories. Many clients have told us that we were the first to do so.

Spending the early therapy sessions on understanding clients' experiences, including their trauma histories, leads our clients to more openly discuss their abusive behavior and make genuine efforts to change. When we try to force change without first showing trauma-exposed clients that we are genuinely interested in hearing their stories and understanding how their abusive behavior developed, clients often shut down or otherwise tell us what they think we want to hear until they have completed the course of the intervention.

Validating clients' difficulties in their current or past situations is also therapeutic. Again, this does not mean that we validate their statements suggesting that they are the "victims" in their situation or their partner is to blame, but rather to validate whatever they are struggling with personally and to acknowledge the impact that trauma and related problems have had on them. The provider should be careful to maintain a stance of understanding and validation while not joining clients in rejecting their own role in their problems or failing to take responsibility for their IPV.

CASE EXAMPLE OF TRAUMA-RELATED THERAPY PROCESS CHALLENGES

A Vietnam veteran several years removed from his military service is court-ordered to receive therapy for IPV. He presents to therapy overtly angry, expressing hostility toward the intake worker conducting his initial assessment. During his first therapy session, he states to his therapist that he "has nothing to say"—he is there only because he has to be there and has no intention of actively engaging in therapeutic work. The therapist is tempted to terminate therapy immediately and tell the client that his probation officer will be told of his noncompliance. The therapist resists this impulse, however, in an attempt to roll with the client's resistance and better understand it.

After three difficult sessions, the client shows up unannounced to the therapist's office, asking to speak with him. The client, tearful and agitated, tells the provider about a traumatic event that occurred during boot camp. The client was drafted into the military despite a severe back injury he had previously sustained. His commanding officer was convinced that he was faking this injury and forced the client to do humiliating and excruciatingly painful drills through the night on multiple occasions. The veteran has had difficulties with authority figures ever since this and has difficulties trusting anyone else, including his relationship partner, which has contributed to his controlling and abusive behavior. The client explains to his therapist that he has never disclosed these events to anyone because they bring about great feelings of anger, humiliation, and shame. Following this discussion and further processing of this event, the client becomes actively involved in the therapy process and joins the therapist in working on ending all abusive behavior.

SUMMARY

For other treatment populations, process factors have been shown to be more important than the type of treatment provided, though in IPV interventions confrontational tactics that hinder a positive group process are all too often used. In this chapter, we reviewed how trauma-related issues involving guilt and shame, power and control, mistrust, and self-esteem difficulties can all negatively affect the process of therapy and hinder treatment progress. The therapeutic alliance and motivational readiness for change are critical process factors to consider in any trauma-informed IPV intervention, and available research has indicated that the facilitation of both of these is associated with greater intervention compliance and reductions in post-intervention IPV. Finally, we provided some strategies for facilitating a positive treatment process, such as allowing clients to tell their stories and helping them to identify how trauma has affected their relationships.

II

TRAUMA-INFORMED INTIMATE PARTNER VIOLENCE INTERVENTIONS AND EXAMPLES

7

GROUP INTERVENTIONS

Group intervention is the standard format for intimate partner violence (IPV) programs delivered in the community. This chapter discusses group-based interventions and considerations when addressing trauma and IPV. Information presented in this section should provide group leaders with strategies for facilitating a positive group process that is conducive to therapeutic change, as well as help them to navigate typical treatment issues and manage difficult situations that sometimes arise in group interventions with this population.

GROUP COHESION

Group cohesion refers to the "connectedness of the group, demonstrated by working together toward a common therapeutic goal, constructive engagement around common themes, and an open, trusting attitude which allows

http://dx.doi.org/10.1037/14918-008
Trauma-Informed Treatment and Prevention of Intimate Partner Violence, by C. T. Taft, C. M. Murphy, and S. K. Creech

members to share personal material" (Budman, Soldz, Demby, Feldstein, Springer, & Davis, 1989, p. 341). Group cohesion reflects the degree to which the members are able to work together constructively to further the therapeutic work. Not surprisingly, clinical research on group cohesion across a range of treatment populations has found higher levels of cohesion to be associated with positive therapeutic outcomes (Ellis, Peterson, Bufford, & Benson, 2014; Gallagher, Tasca, Ritchie, Balfour, & Bissada, 2014; Joyce, Piper, & Ogrodniczuk, 2007; Schnur & Montgomery, 2010).

Given that those who engage in IPV are typically thought of as a "treatment-resistant" population, a primary goal of the therapist is to foster motivation and develop a shared and collective sense that group members need to take positive and proactive steps to change their problematic behavior. Without this shared goal between client and therapist of recognizing and ending abusive behavior, treatment gains will likely not be achieved. In contrast, it is possible for group members to achieve a sense of cohesion with each other yet not work together toward reducing or ending their abusive behavior. In this regard, some early writings on working with those who engage in IPV suggested that group cohesion among these individuals could be detrimental at times, given their tendency to deny or minimize the effects of their IPV and claim that their violence was either justified or caused by external factors (Pence & Paymar, 1993; Ptacek, 1988). It is conceivable that clients could support such attitudes and beliefs held by other group members, thereby developing a sense of cohesion that is not conducive to therapeutic change. Negative peer influences may also escalate when one or two highly vocal and persuasive group members with antichange or antisocial attitudes become informal group leaders, further usurping the therapists' influence.

Fortunately, our direct observations of recorded group therapy sessions with those who engage in IPV reveal that this dynamic is rare. In addition, we believe that this occurs under specific conditions—namely, when therapists display inadequate levels of empathic reflection; use a punitive, shaming, or blaming tone; and use language that separates themselves from the group (e.g., regularly referring to *you* or *you all* vs. *us* and *we* in verbalizing general statements to the group). Thus, we view group cohesion as almost always conductive to a favorable group environment that promotes cessation of IPV, with rare exceptions that are largely preventable by proper therapist selection and training in group facilitation skills. We have never had to remove anyone from one of our trauma-informed IPV groups to preserve positive group cohesion, but we have, on a handful of occasions, discussed disruptive group behaviors with individual clients before or after the group session to process and address underlying thoughts and feelings that may be contributing to the problem.

When group members bond in therapy, this increased support and encouragement can be healing in and of itself, and we know that social support helps lessen the impact of trauma on a variety of problems such as posttraumatic stress disorder (PTSD; Ozer, Best, Lipsey, & Weiss, 2003; Wright, Kelsall, Sim, Clarke, & Creamer, 2013). Indeed, some clinical research findings indicate that higher or increasing group cohesion has been related to better treatment outcomes in the treatment of PTSD (Ellis et al., 2014). In our aforementioned study of a primarily court-mandated sample of men participating in a 16-session cognitive behavioral treatment program for IPV, greater cohesion among group members assessed both early and late in the course of treatment was found to be associated with reductions in physical IPV after intervention (Taft, Murphy, King, Musser, & DeDeyn, 2003).

Group members also often qualitatively describe the benefits of group cohesion and getting the perspective of others who have experienced similar issues. In Rosenberg's (2003) interview study that asked completers of an IPV program about its most helpful elements, support from other group members was the most highly endorsed item, affirmed by approximately 96% of participants. These findings suggest that perceived support from group members may play a particularly important role in abusive clients' intervention experiences and in their efforts to change abusive behavior patterns.

Detailed analysis of group behavior reveals some obvious and direct links, and some subtle and complex links, to changes in IPV. Clients who verbalize more protherapeutic attitudes during group sessions have lower rates of psychological and verbal IPV after treatment (Semiatin, Murphy, & Elliott, 2013). Specifically, protherapeutic group behaviors include expressing more positive and less negative views about treatment, taking more personal responsibility for one's own abusive behavior, and providing more positive responses to support other group members' change talk. Analysis of the effects that other group members have on the individual's change process reveals more complexity. Specifically, group responses to counter-therapeutic expressions (e.g., verbalizations that blame others for one's problems or that support the use of coercive or abusive behaviors) appear to have different effects early, versus late, in group therapy. In early treatment sessions, when other group members respond to counter-therapeutic statements in a supportive and nonconfrontational fashion, the individual tends to reduce his or her counter-therapeutic expressions over time. Later in the group treatment process, the opposite pattern appears, and greater challenge from fellow group members is associated with reduced counter-therapeutic talk (Meis, 2008).

Facilitation of a positive group environment is likely to be especially important when working with trauma-exposed groups. Trauma-exposed individuals may have a more difficult time trusting others, and establishing and maintaining relationships may be particularly challenging. Trauma and trauma-related problems such as PTSD have been shown to negatively affect social support networks just as social support has been shown to affect PTSD (King,

Taft, King, Hammond, & Stone, 2006). In other words, trauma and its effects can essentially drive away one's sources of support, and thus developing relationships in the group therapy context can be healing. The sharing of experiences in the group context among those who have difficulty with relationships may be especially powerful given that these group members may have no other sources for advice or support. Moreover, when individuals have experienced a similar trauma, they may develop an especially powerful bond that may be more difficult to establish between the client and a therapist who has not had similar experiences. For that reason, the therapist is likely to be more effective in conveying a message or clinical skill if she or he can assist the group members in appropriately teaching one another and processing the issue than if the group leader "teaches" the information in a more didactic format.

FACILITATING POSITIVE GROUP PROCESS

In his important book on the fundamental principles and practices for experiential group psychotherapy, Yalom (1995) discussed a number of therapeutic factors for successful group therapy. Here, we touch on the relevance of trauma for some of these critical elements, as well as therapist behaviors that are beneficial for positive group process.

Yalom discussed the importance of the "installation of hope" in group. This may be particularly important for those who have experienced trauma because they may feel hopeless about their interpersonal problems and how to improve their relationships. Many group members we have treated present to the assessment or first treatment session fully expecting that it is impossible for them to make positive changes. Individuals with chronic PTSD or who have unsuccessfully sought help for trauma-related problems in the past may feel even more resigned to believing that things simply cannot get better. Therefore, it is critical that the group leader(s) convey that it is in fact highly likely that they will see significant changes in how they manage anger and relationship conflict as a result of group. We often inform our group members that it is natural to have doubts about therapy but add that many others in the past have had similar doubts yet have experienced positive growth and change.

It is also important to highlight other obstacles that trauma-exposed group members have overcome simply to make it to group. Perhaps they have overcome substance abuse issues, for example, or maybe their trauma-related symptoms were previously more severe before they received help. The traumatized group member may have a difficult time being in a room full of other people because of symptoms of PTSD, especially if their trauma involved interpersonal victimization by other men. As a group leader, it is important to highlight to group members how they have overcome trauma in various ways, and learning to manage their anger and IPV is something that they also have the capability of doing.

Yalom (1995) noted how the "universality of experience" and "group identification" with one another are powerful forces for change. When trauma-exposed group members discover that there are others who can relate to their experience, they often describe a great sense of relief. Group members who share a particular background (e.g., military background, social background) can identify with one another and help guide the other to positive change. Sometimes differences among group members can similarly be a powerful force for change. For example, an older group member may help steer a younger group member in the right direction, guided by his past experiences with a particular problem that he successfully navigated.

The group can also serve an important function for conveying information. For example, group members can help educate others about symptoms of PTSD and resources for receiving help or can relay experiences of help seeking for trauma-related issues. Because trauma-exposed group members may be isolated from other sources of social support, they may be cut off from sources of information to which others have greater access. Group members can also be much more potent forces of change than group leaders at times. For example, a group member who helps identify and correct negative thought patterns in another group member may be considered more credible than a group leader who does not have the same shared experiences as the two clients.

Interpersonal learning refers to direct learning about emotions and interpersonal realities that occur in the group. When trauma-exposed individuals learn from each other and come to experience feeling accepted and valued, they will more openly and honestly discuss their struggles and their true thoughts and feelings. This is particularly important for trauma-exposed individuals because it is likely that they have difficulties trusting others and expressing themselves openly, and they may feel that nobody values them as a person. We have heard many group members state that they feel free to speak more openly in group than in any other context, that this is extremely helpful for them, and it also helps boost low self-esteem.

Much informal communication skills training may also occur through the supportive dialogue of group. Surprisingly, research comparing structured cognitive–behavioral to supportive therapy for IPV offenders revealed notable communication improvements in a supportive group therapy condition that contained no explicit communication skills training (Morrel, Elliott, Murphy, & Taft, 2003). Similarly, a review of group treatment session recordings reveals many instances in which group members respond to one another with patience, empathy, and concern, leading to the hypothesis that such group interactions may provide a natural (uncontrived) vehicle for communication skill development.

Yalom (1995) referred to *catharsis* as the expression of emotions that have not been formerly expressed, or perhaps not clearly labeled or experienced. Group members may be only partially aware, for example, of deep shame related to their trauma histories, yet the effects of this shame may be quite clear in their relationship problems. Expressing these feelings in group may provide the individual with some relief, especially when the group shows understanding and compassion. We have found that this expression of emotion in trauma-exposed groups is an element that group members often describe as most helpful by the end of group. Many trauma-exposed individuals report difficulties in understanding and expressing emotions, and emotional avoidance is a core PTSD symptom. Therefore, getting in better touch with feelings and ways of expressing them can serve a critical function for improving relationships and other areas of personal functioning.

Last, *altruism* and *existential factors* go hand-in-hand in groups of trauma-exposed clients. Altruism refers to group members providing each other with help and support, and existential factors refer to the sense of purpose and meaning in life. As discussed, when people experience a trauma, it typically affects the way they view the world in a number of respects, and for many, it leads to existential crises or a search for meaning in general. When group members assist each other with emotional and tangible forms of support, they feel like they are a part of something positive that helps provide meaning. A supportive and productive group can be extremely meaningful for its members. If they feel like they have made a difference in another individual's life, it gives their own life greater meaning.

LEADER TASKS AND TECHNIQUES

Group leaders engage in other important group facilitation techniques in working with trauma-exposed clients. For example, leaders should always strive to use empathy and supportive listening in the group context. This does not mean empathizing with victim blaming or rationalizations for IPV, but rather other critical elements of the individual's experience and struggles for making positive behavior change. The goal is for other group members to model these therapist communication behaviors and establish a supportive, listening environment that encourages self-disclosure both within and outside of the group. The group should feel like a safe place for the exploration of personal and interpersonal problems. This is especially important for trauma-exposed individuals, who may have difficulties trusting others or establishing and maintaining interpersonal relationships.

When working with trauma-exposed clients, it may be especially important to comment on group process and to identify important group dynamics and intragroup conflicts. For example, group members may be observed misinterpreting other group members' actions or intentions in negative ways similar to how they might misinterpret partner behaviors and intentions. The group leader should be attentive to group interactions at all times and make process comments to the group, asking them to describe what they themselves are experiencing and observing in other group members.

During group discussion and exercises, traumatized group members may be particularly likely to engage in avoidance behaviors when it comes to describing their feelings or personal experiences. This may involve focusing exclusively on other group members' difficulties without discussing their own or otherwise shifting the focus of group discussion to "lighter" topics. Group leaders should be attuned to client attempts at avoidance, gently reflect to the group member what they are noticing, and ask the client and group members if they are similarly noticing attempted avoidance. It is important to bear in mind that avoidance is a hallmark feature of PTSD, but it can also accompany trauma in the absence of a formal PTSD diagnosis. Moreover, avoidance may not simply involve trauma reminders but also the expression of feelings with others.

It is important that group leaders offer encouragement and positive reinforcement for healthy relationship behaviors and effective anger deescalation strategies used by group members. It is possible and perhaps likely that clients who have experienced significant trauma have not had much positive feedback directed toward them. They may have been taught that they were worthless or unworthy of positive regard from a young age, and they may have internalized these beliefs. Trauma-exposed group members respond extremely well to praise and positive reinforcement for things they handle well in group, and this is a major factor in enhancing and maintaining motivation for behavior change. It can at times be a challenge for group leaders to find elements in the client's story to praise and reinforce, but there is usually something about the client's response that represents positive intentions, the desire or motivation to change or an improvement over previous behavior.

Even seemingly small therapist behaviors in between sessions can go a long way in enhancing motivation and engagement in treatment. Sending a personalized, handwritten note to group member when he or she misses a group session expressing concern and summarizing the group can have a powerful impact on group attendance and uptake (Taft, Murphy, Elliott, & Morrel, 2001). We have observed several group members personally thank their group leaders for such gestures that may take on additional weight when the client has experienced a life filled primarily with abuse, violence, and little positive regard.

When conducting groups with trauma-exposed individuals, it is important to highlight positive changes rather than focusing on what the group member did wrong. Reinforcing positive coping behaviors will have a more powerful impact than focusing exclusively on the negative responses. Especially for clients with abuse histories or who have otherwise been given negative messages about themselves, commenting on positive changes they have made will go a long way toward encouraging the group member to continue to strive for behavior change. Asking questions such as, "How is this different from what you've done in the past?" can assist in highlighting changes group members have made that they may not have been actively thinking about. Trauma-exposed individuals have a tendency to focus on what they have done wrong instead of what they are doing right, so it is important that group therapists challenge these negative ways of thinking and assist clients in recognizing their own positive change efforts.

SUMMARY

Group intervention is the standard treatment format for court-mandated IPV programs in the community. Facilitating a positive group environment is critical for the success of trauma-informed group intervention, and the cohesiveness of the group has been shown to predict reductions in IPV following treatment. Facilitating a positive group environment is particularly challenging yet important for trauma-exposed individuals because trusting others may be difficult for them. We discussed several fundamental factors necessary for successful group intervention based on Yalom's (1995) work, incorporating trauma-relevant issues and themes into these features of successful group therapy and describing key leader tasks and techniques that promote a therapeutic group process for this population. Examples include using empathy and supportive listening, commenting on group process, countering client avoidance attempts, providing encouragement and positive reinforcement, and maintaining an optimistic focus on positive gains made.

8

EXAMPLE OF GROUP INTERVENTION

In this chapter, we describe the Strength at Home Men's Program to provide an example of a trauma-informed group intimate partner violence (IPV) intervention that is currently being implemented across multiple sites within the VA Healthcare System. The program has been shown to be an efficacious IPV intervention in multiple pilot studies (Love, Morland, Menez, Taft, MacDonald, & Mackintosh, 2015; Taft, Macdonald, Monson, Walling, Resick, & Murphy, 2013) as well as in a randomized controlled trial (RCT; Taft, Macdonald, Creech, Monson, & Murphy, 2015). In fact, it is the only IPV intervention shown to be efficacious in a military veteran population via RCT. The program has yet to be studied via RCTs in samples of civilians or women who engage in IPV, but given the previous discussed evidence of the applicability of the social information processing model across treatment populations, we expect that the intervention could be successfully implemented outside of the male veteran context.

http://dx.doi.org/10.1037/14918-009
Trauma-Informed Treatment and Prevention of Intimate Partner Violence, by C. T. Taft, C. M. Murphy, and S. K. Creech

In this chapter, we first provide an overview of the program. We then describe and discuss the session-by-session content, highlighting trauma-informed program elements and providing examples of handouts and material administered. Next, we offer notes related to program referral and group composition. Finally, we review the available research evidence for the program. The material presented in this chapter is intended to provide the reader with an example of a trauma-informed IPV intervention. We emphasize the trauma-informed components and strategies of the intervention in this chapter and give examples of some of the program materials. The manual is not publicly available at this time, although the reader is encouraged to contact the book authors for more information about the program and its implementation and how to gain access to a fuller set of program materials.

STRENGTH AT HOME MEN'S PROGRAM OVERVIEW

The Strength at Home Men's Program was designed to reduce and end IPV in light of the trauma histories and negative life events so commonly reported by those who engage in IPV. The program draws on existing cognitive behavioral interventions, specifically incorporating components of cognitive behavioral therapy for IPV (Murphy & Scott, 1996), anger management and assertiveness training (Grace, Niles, Quinn, & Taft, n.d.), relationship-focused treatment of posttraumatic stress disorder (PTSD; Monson & Fredman, 2012), and cognitive processing therapy (Resick & Schnicke, 1992). We developed the program through collaboration with clinical researchers who were instrumental in developing these approaches, including Candice Monson, Patricia Resick, and Christopher Murphy. The program is tailored to those who may or may not be new to psychotherapy. The intervention is intended to end IPV in current relationships and prevent IPV in future relationships by helping clients to identify and correct misappraisals across a range of potentially difficult situations and to develop effective communication and conflict resolution skills. The program is intended for those who have engaged in recent physical IPV or other coercive, controlling, or abusive relationship behaviors.

The Strength at Home Men's Program is a 12-week intervention (we have also developed longer versions) conducted by a cotherapist team with at least one doctoral-level clinician in a group therapy format, typically with six to eight clients per group. It is important to note that this group structure, although consistent with other interventions for problem behaviors such as substance use problems, as well as psychiatric conditions, head injury, and a host of other problems, is a departure from standard interventions delivered in the community. Community programs are generally considerably longer with larger group sizes and less highly trained group leaders. The differences between our program structure and those of programs in the community stem from the nature of the work done within the intervention and how it is conceptualized. Our program is considered intensive group therapy, in contrast with purely psychoeducational community programs. With highly trained clinicians, small group sizes, and the use of cognitive behavioral therapy techniques, each group participant is expected to be a highly active participant, and all clients discuss their problems with relationships, trauma, and IPV in depth throughout the course of group. Because the purpose of the group is to help uncover abusive patterns that have developed over time and to illuminate the ways in which previous traumatic and stressful events may contribute to the client's problems, the work we do is indeed "therapy" and not simply psychoeducation.

Strength at Home targets social information processing deficits that are associated with IPV. Several aforementioned common themes that may underlie relationship difficulties are also targeted. Although the program is not a direct treatment for PTSD, it was designed to be highly sensitive to the fact that many partner-violent individuals have histories of traumatic stress exposure that negatively affect their relationships. The group is conducted in a supportive, nonconfrontational atmosphere by two coleaders. It follows a closed-group format involving weekly 2-hour sessions. Each session contains brief instructional material; group activities to discuss, learn, and practice new behaviors; and flexible time to solve ongoing problems, explore change efforts, and build group cohesion.

The initial phase of Strength at Home provides psychoeducation on IPV and common reactions to trauma, and there is a focus on setting goals, enhancing motivational readiness for change, and building group cohesion and a positive therapist–client therapeutic alliance. The second phase focuses on conflict management skills to help clients understand the components of their anger and to deescalate situations before they become highly conflictual or abusive. During the third phase, specific coping strategies are covered, with a focus on identifying and correcting negative thought patterns contributing to anger and IPV, and coping with stress more effectively. The fourth phase focuses on enhancing communication skills, and the final session focuses on gains achieved over the course of the intervention and plans for continued change. Across all of the sessions, group members complete in-session practice exercises and are provided "practice assignments" to consolidate and apply information learned in group.

The program was written with several goals in mind. First, we wanted to provide enough structure and group tasks to guide leaders who have limited experience with IPV interventions. Second, we wanted to retain flexibility so that leaders have time and freedom to explore and expand on important material that arises during sessions. Programmatic flexibility also allows group leaders to build a healthy and constructive group process by dealing with conflicts within the group, engaging in problem solving around current life difficulties, and addressing the needs of group members at different stages of the change process. Leaders are often able to weave program material into group discussions even if group members bring up situations that are not directly relevant to the weekly topic. Leaders should never dismiss participants concerns by saying "We'll cover that in Week 5" or "That's not the focus for today," nor should they attempt to relate current concerns to the weekly session topic artificially. It is more helpful to clarify participants' concerns, promote empathy in the group, and engage in brief problem solving.

SESSION DESCRIPTION

Session 1. Introduction and Welcoming

This session introduces clients to the structure, expectations, and philosophy of the group. After initial introductions and discussion of group philosophy and goals, the leaders lead a discussion of the "pros" and "cons" of IPV, a motivational strategy. Leaders then give insight into the structure and expectations for the group, explain the importance of practice assignments, and answer questions about the group. The main clinical tasks are to begin establishing a therapeutic alliance with each group member, to validate and address group members' concerns and reservations about counseling, to model and encourage healthy group interactions and group cohesion, and to facilitate motivation for behavior change.

It is helpful for group leaders to be aware of potential client concerns as the first treatment session proceeds. If clients have experienced severe interpersonal trauma, they may have difficulty simply sitting in a room with several other men. For some clients, being in the group environment can be a significant trigger for their trauma reactions. For example, one recent client who had been the victim of a gang rape by several men while on deployment found himself unable to sit down for more than a minute or two during his first group session. Simply being around a group of other men in an enclosed space brought on so much anxiety for this client that he requested to take frequent breaks during this first session and displayed palpable physical signs of anxiety the entire session, creating discomfort not only for himself but for other group members as well. He subsequently missed two group sessions and then requested individual therapy because of his difficulties.

At the outset of the first session, when describing the nature of the group, members are informed that group leaders will not prompt them to go into detail about their traumatic events. However, discussions will sometimes center on trauma and how it affects relationship difficulties and problems with managing anger. This is important to clarify with group members because some clients, particularly those with PTSD, may be concerned that they will be pressured to reveal traumatic material either before they are ready to disclose it or in a group context that will be particularly anxiety provoking for them. The processing of traumatic material is often critical for successful treatment of PTSD but may be challenging in group IPV intervention. Letting group members know that they will not be pressured to discuss aspects of their trauma can be a relief for some of our clients. However, typically group members express no concerns or difficulties in describing traumatic events in the group.

When discussing the philosophy of the group via the "Group Philosophy" handout (Appendix A), we discuss how factors such as trauma and prior stressful experiences may contribute to conflict in relationships, but trauma can be addressed without resorting to violence and IPV. This is an important point to convey to both providers and clients. Acknowledging that trauma contributes to IPV risk does not mean that trauma "causes" IPV in a deterministic fashion. IPV is not an inevitable consequence of trauma exposure and related problems. Rather, trauma is a risk factor for IPV that should be understood and possibly addressed, but ultimately the client is responsible for his or her behavior. In other words, we can discuss how trauma negatively affects relationship conflict while making it clear that trauma exposure is not a justification for abusive behavior.

One critical element of the first session is the "pros and cons of IPV" exercise. This is a commonly used strategy in motivational interviewing to move clients along the stages of change and increase motivational readiness. Building on the last item from the "Group Philosophy" handout—"Violence and aggression in relationships is learned behavior, and it can be unlearned"—the exercise begins with the group leader asking the group members how people learn to be aggressive in relationships. Typical responses are that people learn to be aggressive by experiencing and witnessing abuse and aggression during childhood or through exposure to violent media depictions, violent neighborhoods, and environments growing up, for example. The therapist then makes the point that we also learn to be aggressive because we get something from it, and those "pros" of IPV help to keep the behavior going. After the group is only able to come up with a few temporary "pros" of IPV (e.g., temporary stress relief, win the argument, get point across), they are then asked to list the negative consequences of IPV. Group members typically create a long list of "cons" such as financial consequences, lost relationships, stigma of being labeled a batterer, legal consequences, negative effects on children, and occupational problems. The group leader then points out the disparity between the number of (temporary) pros and the long list of cons and begins to discuss how the group material helps meet the same aims of the pros without any of the cons.

This exercise assists clients in recognizing that their abusive behavior is reinforced by contingencies in their environment and helps demonstrate to clients that their behavior is not working for them. Perhaps equally or even more important, the exercise demonstrates to clients that their group therapists want to hear their open and honest perspectives about their own abusive behavior. Trauma-exposed clients may be reluctant to disclose personal details or acknowledge their IPV, but this exercise allows them to talk about their IPV in an open and interactive way, inviting them to disclose IPV while not feeling shamed in doing so. Moreover, this exercise sets the stage for open discussions about trauma and IPV throughout the course of group sessions and facilitates a positive group process.

Session 2. Trauma and Relationships

Group members explore their beliefs about healthy and unhealthy relationships and their goals for group. The session then shifts to discussing psychoeducational material that focuses on understanding forms of IPV and the impact of trauma on group members' relationships. The main clinical tasks of the session are to enhance motivation, to educate group members regarding IPV, and for group members to gain insight into the effects of trauma and difficult events they have experienced in their own relationships.

The discussion using the "Common Reactions to Trauma" handout (Appendix B) is typically the most difficult and emotional exercise over the course of the entire group. Group members often recount experiences of severe child abuse, military trauma and exposure to atrocities, and interpersonal trauma victimization, such as the experience of sexual abuse. The goal of this exercise is to discuss how these traumas have contributed to their relationship difficulties and abusive behavior, to increase understanding about how their abusive patterns may have begun and developed. Problems resulting from trauma, such as PTSD symptoms, depression, controlling behaviors, and self-esteem problems are also discussed. Often these group discussions will lead to treatment referrals for comorbid problems.

After the trauma discussion, group members sometimes express sadness regarding how their trauma has affected their lives and how they have destroyed their relationships and hurt others. This awareness work can be challenging because during this early phase in group, we are not yet providing active skills. For this reason, it is important that the group leaders convey to the group members that this intervention is trauma-informed and that we will be teaching them strategies that have been shown to work among others who have experienced trauma and many of the same problems they are experiencing. It is also helpful for group leaders to comfort clients and ensure them that it is a normal reaction for them to be upset by the group discussion.

The trauma discussion is often a time for group members to note shared and similar experiences with other group members and to continue to build positive group cohesion.

Session 3. Conflict Management I: Understanding Anger

This session begins with a discussion of the "Trauma Impact Questions" practice assignment (Appendix C) focusing on understanding how trauma has affected clients' relationships to continue the conversation on the impacts of trauma from the previous session and to facilitate clients' contemplation of this connection in between group sessions. The group discussion then shifts to a focus on understanding the anger response and expressing anger assertively. This material is designed to assist group members in recognizing and understanding the components of their anger and the importance of striving toward assertive expressions of anger. The practice assignment focuses on self-monitoring of the different components of group members' anger and further practicing assertive responses to anger.

The Trauma Impact Questions practice assignment asks group members how trauma has affected their relationships and what the most difficult consequences of trauma have been. In addition, the questions prompt group members to write about whether trauma has contributed to their abusive behavior and how it has affected the underlying common themes discussed throughout this book, including trust in one's partner, intimacy and closeness, and power and control issues. As the group progresses, these themes will arise in other exercises and assignments, such as in the self-monitoring assignments introduced later in this session. When these themes arise, group leaders should gently point this out to group members. Leaders should connect these themes to group members' past stressful and traumatic experiences and ways in which they respond to relationship situations. This is a critical task for group leaders to connect past traumas to current "themes" that may underlie abusiveness because it is these "stuck points" that contribute to IPV and that are most difficult to treat without the client recognizing them and making efforts to work through them.

Session 4. Conflict Management II: Time-Outs

This session is devoted to strategies to defuse difficult relationship situations in which IPV may result. After reviewing group members' self-monitoring practice and assertiveness assignments (Anger Analysis Form; Appendix D), Time-Outs are discussed. Group members learn to take a "break from the action" to cool down during difficult relationship situations. The rationale behind Time-Outs is discussed, and each group member begins developing a plan to use during potentially conflictual situations. The development of these plans is an important crisis management tool that helps ensure safety and provides a skill that helps to lay the groundwork for future work on communication.

Review of the self-monitoring Anger Analysis Form practice assignment is an early step in helping group members recognize their social information–processing deficits by monitoring their thoughts during anger-provoking situations and taking steps to reappraise potentially negative ways of thinking. When discussing self-monitoring assignments, group leaders should always be alert to negative interpretations of situations that may or may not be accurate. When such thoughts are evident, group leaders should attempt to facilitate the challenging of these negative interpretations, first by asking other group members if they had any thoughts about the manner in which the client interpreted the situation, and if that is not effective, by more directly challenging the client's faulty thoughts and soliciting more positive interpretations from group members. Because recognizing and correcting overly hostile and otherwise negative interpretations of situations is a process, it is important for group leaders to assist clients in working on this as early in the group as possible.

Recognizing and correcting social information processing deficits is also a key component to the Time-Out discussions, as illustrated in the "What to Do During Time-Out" handout (Appendix E). For example, material focuses on helping clients to be aware of their negative thoughts and replace them with more positive thoughts during Time-Out. Clients are also taught to think about what they would like to communicate with their partner when the Time-Out has ended and to be aware of feelings other than anger that can have an impact on one's cognitions and interpretation of the situation.

Trauma is also highly relevant during Time-Out discussions. Often clients will state that it is not possible for them to take a Time-Out. They describe their anger as an instantaneous reaction to a provocation or stressful situation that is beyond their control. Perhaps they learned to react to stressful situations with a strong immediate anger response as part of their military training or as a way to respond to stay alive in a war zone. There is no doubt that taking a Time-Out can be challenging for some. However, group members virtually always indicate that they are able to take a Time-Out by the end of group or at least recognize that they are getting angry before their explosion. In other words, despite the level of trauma a client experiences, our clients can always work on recognizing their anger warning signs (physiological reactions, feelings, and thoughts) before erupting into an aggressive outburst. It is simply not true that our clients explode without some kind of anger-escalation process that occurs beforehand; the key is to make that process as conscious to the client as possible.

Session 5. Coping Strategies I: Anger-Related Thinking

This session is devoted to exploring and identifying automatic thoughts associated with anger reactions that may characterize trauma-exposed abusive clients. Group discussions focus on developing reasonable appraisals of threat and of other people's intentions, and the group generates active coping thoughts to counter anger-enhancing thoughts. Session material focused directly on social information processing issues in trauma and IPV.

One of the exercises in this session is a discussion of the "survival mode" of functioning described by Chemtob and his colleagues (Chemtob, Novaco, Hamada, & Gross, 1997; Chemtob, Novaco, Hamada, Gross, & Smith, 1997; Novaco & Chemtob, 1998) via the "'Survival Mode' and Alternative Thoughts" handout (Appendix F). As discussed in Chapter 2, this model focuses on how trauma-exposed individuals develop a faulty sense of threat and are more likely to interpret other's intentions as hostile or threatening, even in ambiguous situations. The discussion initially focuses on the military context and how one may develop an overly negative and hostile perception of others. It then shifts to intimate relationships. Because they function in survival mode, clients may assume that their partner is being hostile when this may not necessarily be the case. We discuss how thoughts such as "She's just trying to manipulate me," "She's just trying to push my buttons," "She's trying to make me jealous," or "She's trying to control me" are common among those who have experienced trauma and negatively interpret partner intentions.

The main clinical goal of this session is simply to help group members understand that their thoughts and beliefs about their partners are not the final "truth" but are only one of many possible ways to view a partner's behavior and intentions. This can help some group members considerably as they begin considering alternative ways to view their partner's behavior. Group members are encouraged to continue to monitor their thoughts during difficult situations, not to assume that they know what others are thinking, to ask instead of guess, and to work toward trying to assume the best in others.

Session 6. Coping Strategies II: Dealing With Stress

This session focuses on stress and stress management because stress and anxiety may place men at risk for relationship adjustment problems and IPV. Practice assignments focus on identifying sources of stress and coping strategies for handling stress. The main clinical tasks of this session are (a) to help clients understand how external stress and problematic coping strategies contribute to negative interactions in their intimate relationships, (b) to deepen clients' awareness of the interpretations and thoughts that lead to high levels of emotional distress in stressful situations, (c) to help clients distinguish between problem-focused and emotion-focused coping strategies and to see the importance of matching coping strategies to the nature of the stressor, and (d) to help clients identify underused and overused coping strategies to enhance their motivation to develop and use additional coping strategies.

Group material describes how coping responses are relatively more or less effective depending on whether they are well matched to the nature of the stress. In particular, truly unavoidable or uncontrollable stressors require emotion-focused coping strategies to deal with the resulting distress. Attempts to alter the stressful circumstance itself will often create more distress in the long run if the circumstances are not within the individual's control. This concept can be readily illustrated by the pain and stress that is often generated by trying to change or control a relationship partner's behavior. On the other hand, the exclusive use of emotion-focused coping with stress that can be controlled is often ineffective. Many examples are available of stressful situations that are being avoided or improperly addressed when a more active, problem-focused approach would be more effective.

We find that our group members appreciate this session on stress and coping because trauma is associated with considerable stress, particularly if the client is suffering from PTSD, and group members often report a limited number of stress management strategize they use. Men often report that they rely exclusively on problem-focused strategies to "fix" problems. Emotion-focused strategies may not be an important part of men's coping repertoire, and therefore group leaders should encourage clients to increase their strategies for managing stressful situations for which they have no control over.

The session ends with a guided imagery relaxation exercise. Such relaxation strategies can be particularly important for trauma-exposed clients because they may be more likely to experience an overactive fight-or-flight response that ultimately can have a negative impact on social information processing abilities. The relaxation exercise can also be used to show the connection between our thoughts and our stress and anger. We have our clients first visualize and keep in their minds a recent anger-invoking situation, then rate their current level of anger on an "Anger Meter" (a 10-point scale; Appendix G); next, they participate in a 5-minute guided imagery relaxation exercise, and then we have them fill out the Anger Meter again. Typically, group members will report that their levels of anger were lowered by the relaxation exercise and that they are experiencing fewer anger-producing thoughts and physical signs of stress and anger.

Session 7. Communication Skills I: Roots of Your Communication Style

After discussing anger self-monitoring exercises and stress management strategies, group members participate in an exercise in which they write about and discuss how they learned their style of communicating anger and other emotions. Following the handout "Roots of Your Communication Style" (Appendix H), they discuss lessons learned as a child, growing up, and in the military. The primary clinical task of this material is to illustrate how men typically are socialized to be passive or aggressive, not assertive. This exercise is followed by a relaxation exercise to demonstrate the anger-reduction effects of these techniques.

This represents the first session focusing specifically on communication. It is important for group members to develop an understanding of how they learned to communicate the way that they currently do as a first step in unlearning dysfunctional communication patterns and strategies. A significant amount of trauma is often revealed in this session, and group discussions often can be animated, emotional, and poignant, which often facilitates group cohesion among members who can relate to each other's traumatic experiences.

Childhood trauma is invariably discussed during this session. We have yet to conduct a group session in which at least some group members do not reveal the experience of child abuse and neglect or witnessing interparental violence. The vast majority of group members report exposure to abuse, neglect, or other highly adverse childhood experiences, such as unstable caregiving arrangements, parental abandonment, or parental problems involving drug use, poor mental health, violence, or imprisonment. Group members often describe that these abusive experiences taught them to keep their thoughts and feelings to themselves, or else they would face more violence. They also discuss how witnessing and experiencing these events taught them to be aggressive, learning that one always has power over the other in relationships and that conflict is normative in relationships. Some group members also describe a moment in which they decided to turn the tables on the abuser and lashed out, seeking retribution or safety for their other parent who was being victimized.

In addition to the experience of abuse and neglect, group members discuss how they were generally not ever taught to express their feelings. To be "real men" in our society, boys are taught to keep their feelings in or to express their feelings outwardly in the form of anger and aggression. Few group members describe being taught to openly express their anger and the feelings that may underlie their anger, and most describe childhood environments in which it was deemed unacceptable to express feelings other than anger and toughness.

During the military portion of this discussion, group members discuss how they were trained to follow orders in the military and do what they were told. They also discuss how they were trained to channel all of their emotions into anger or to completing their mission. Group members typically indicate that a war zone or dangerous area was not a place for openly expressing feelings but rather for channeling any and all feelings into accomplishing their mission.

Typically, at the end of the group discussion focusing on the roots of the group members' communication style it becomes evident that members of the group learned to hold in all of their feelings during childhood and also in their military experience, to express their feelings outwardly in the form of aggression, or both. It is a rare group member who describes growing up in an environment in which he was encouraged to express his anger and underlying feelings in a more healthy and assertive manner. This discussion can assist group members in drawing links between their potentially traumatic backgrounds and negative relationship behaviors and begins to provide a road map to unlearning negative communication strategies. Group leaders may reflect to group members that it is not surprising that they experience profound difficulties in communicating with relationship partners because they never learned to appropriately and effectively communicate in an open, honest, and assertive manner. Group members often describe feeling validated after this discussion because they can begin to see that their difficulties may represent long-standing patterns that have been learned but that can be unlearned.

Session 8. Communication Skills II: Active Listening

After reviewing communication self-monitoring forms, group members discuss aspects of healthy and unhealthy communication, and then the group focuses specifically on active listening skills. Active listening skills are emphasized in this session because they are the foundation of good communication and are critical for deescalating conflict and enhancing intimacy. Listening skills are particularly important when significant trauma symptoms are present in one or both members of the couple because social information–processing abilities are often compromised by emotional arousal.

In addition to identifying and correcting cognitive misappraisals, improving listening skills is a key foundational component to successful IPV intervention among those exposed to trauma. Moreover, these two sets of skills operate together. Enhancing listening abilities is a critical component of accurately interpreting and responding to an ambiguous situation. If group members learn to truly listen to their partners rather than making assumptions and jumping to negative conclusions, this may lessen the likelihood that they will misinterpret the situation in an overly negative manner.

Group members are encouraged to attempt to develop an active listening mind-set in which understanding the other person's feelings takes priority. This might be difficult for trauma-exposed clients, who may have difficulty trusting others and who may have power and control issues. To listen to the other person means to give up that control and move from a focus on "winning" the discussion to really hearing the other person out without imposing one's own feelings or opinions. Group members are told that once their partner feels heard, they will have a better chance of having an opportunity to then express their own views.

Paraphrasing, clarifying through questions, and validating are the three main elements of active listening. To *paraphrase* means to put something into one's own words. Good listeners often paraphrase what the other person has said to find out whether they understand. This is a skill to help clients understand what their partner is saying or feeling. Almost nobody says things exactly the way they want to on the first try. Therefore, other people will often *clarify* themselves after what they have said is paraphrased. If clients lose the listening mind-set, they will be tempted to twist their partner's words to get their own point across.

Once the client adopts an active listening mind-set, they may realize that there are many things they do not understand about their partner's thoughts and feelings. They are told that the simplest approach is to ask, without judging or accusing, what their partner feels. Group members are also told that how they ask the questions can make a big difference. They should be careful not to interrogate their partner to prove their own point or to try to confirm their negative suspicions.

The highest level of active listening is when people understand what their partner feels and why he or she has these feelings. This is called *validation*—being able to understand why other people think, feel, or act the way they do. Validation occurs when the client can honestly say, "I see why you feel that way." This is a skill that is often difficult for trauma-exposed clients to master because they often find it difficult to get out of the negative mind-set that there is always a winner and loser in any conversation or disagreement, reflective of a power and control conflict. Validation occurs when clients and partners actively work to try to increase understanding and show the other that they value their feelings.

Session 9. Communication Skills III: Assertive Messages

After reviewing group members' communication self-monitoring forms, group discussion focuses on how to give an assertive message. Next, group members are introduced to a scripted role-play depicting both assertive messages and active listening, and then they practice these skills in session. The continued focus on enhanced communication skills is intended to reduce the negative association between trauma and communication skills deficits and to further improve relationship problem-solving and conflict resolution skills.

Group members are taught that the goal of assertive communication is to solve problems and enhance closeness through direct communication. By this point, a considerable amount of group material has focused on assertiveness, and this session provides some concrete strategies in delivering an assertive message—specifically, by (a) providing a clear and concise description of the behavior or issue at hand, (b) stating one's feelings about the issue and its effects, and (c) making a suggestion or request for the other partner on how the problem might be resolved.

As noted, boys and men are often socialized to keep their emotions in or to express them aggressively (Werrbach, Grotevant, & Cooper, 1990; Zeman & Shipman, 1996). Many men are not taught how to express their feelings and requests in an assertive fashion, and as a result, they resort to alternative modes of expression involving passive or aggressive behavior. It is common for our clients to "stuff" their anger for fear that they will respond aggressively or do or say something that they will regret. This may lead to pent-up anger, which results in aggressive outbursts. Aggressive outbursts undermine the effort to address legitimate grievances or problems. With every act of aggression, it becomes more difficult to discuss problems and less likely that the problems will be resolved.

Studies have shown that problems with assertiveness are higher among men who use IPV than nonviolent men (Maiuro, Cahn, & Vitaliano, 1986; Rosenbaum & O'Leary, 1981). Limited ability to express feelings and requests in an assertive fashion, and associated deficits in problem solving, are major elements of poor social competence observed in research on partner-violent men (Anglin & Holtzworth-Munroe, 1997; Taft, Schumm, Marshall, Panuzio, & Holtzworth-Munroe, 2008). Thus, assertiveness training is particularly important for this population.

Passive and aggressive communication behaviors may also represent forms of avoidance of trauma-related issues, other feared stimuli, and difficult emotions. Such avoidance may serve to maintain trauma-related problems such as PTSD because it prevents habituation and the processing and resolution of difficulties that the client is experiencing.

It may be helpful to highlight that assertiveness does not mean giving in to one's partner or others. It involves expressing one's emotions in a way that is not abusive but still gets one's needs met. Assertiveness involves mutual respect for both one's own rights and feelings and those of one's partner. Aggressive responses violate the other person's right to be treated with respect and convey a serious lack of concern for the other person's feelings.

Passive responses, in contrast, fail to respect one's own rights and feelings. The challenge for group members is to find the "middle-way" responses that are respectful of both one's own and the partner's feelings and rights.

A common cycle is as follows: (a) in individual responds passively to relationship issues by avoiding or failing to deal with problems that arise ("stuffing" angry or hurt feelings), (b) resentments and a list of grievances build up, and (c) the individual "blows up" with an aggressive response (cold or angry outburst) that expresses the built-up resentments and bad feelings.

We have found it helpful to make the point that openly discussing problems and issues in relationships can lead to a greater understanding and intimacy, and it might also lead to improvements in trauma-related problems such as PTSD because it counters avoidance. In general, assertively coping with trauma-related material and other unpleasant circumstances and feelings is extremely important to clinical recovery from trauma.

Some trauma-exposed group members may feel vulnerable communicating in an assertive manner. It will be important to gently challenge group members by asking them how well their current style of anger expression works for them and suggest that the long-term benefits of assertive communication are likely to outweigh the short-term discomfort. Other group members may contend that it "doesn't work" to use assertive responses because they cannot control others' responses. Remind group members that there are few situations (e.g., prison) where it is more effective to use aggressive or passive responses to conflict. There are often short-term benefits but long-term problems associated with aggressive or passive responses to conflict.

Session 10. Communication Skills IV: Expressing Feelings

Group members review their communication self-monitoring forms and the assertive messages and active listening practice assignment. Group material then focuses on how trauma-related avoidance can lead to difficulties expressing emotions in relationships. Strategies for expressing feelings are provided. Emotional expression skills are important for enhancing intimacy and understanding in relationships.

Often trauma-exposed clients find it easier to express anger than other feelings, even if other feelings underlie their anger. The first step in learning to better express underlying feelings is to become more aware of the feelings one is experiencing. Learning to identify feelings is often a difficult task for those who have experienced trauma. Often clients will describe not being aware of any feelings that they have other than sadness and anger. They may describe not experiencing any feelings at all, consistent with the emotional numbing symptoms or PTSD, or they may describe experiencing a lot of confusing feelings but not really knowing what feelings are beneath the anger.

As a first step in identifying feelings, we provide group members with a color-coded "Identifying Feelings" chart of several different emotions one may experience (rendered black and white in Appendix I). This includes the basic emotions of mad, sad, scared, disgusted, and glad as well as a range of intensities for these feelings and more complex emotions that may consist of more than one basic emotion. We ask our group members to describe which emotions they feel most frequently and which emotions they may have difficulty talking about. Often group members will note having difficulty expressing the "softer" emotions, such as feeling sad, anxious, or scared. We discuss how men have been socialized to avoid expressing those feelings and how the expression of such feelings is critical for healthy relationships.

Feelings are the glue that holds relationships together. Expressing one's feelings builds intimacy and trust. Couples who stay together and report the most satisfaction tell us that they share feelings—both positive and negative—with one another. Trauma-exposed individuals and their loved ones often avoid expressing their feelings or become emotionally numb. Both members of the couple may come to fear feeling judged, vulnerable, or out of control if they express feelings in their relationship.

When our clients avoid expressing their feelings, they feel more disconnected from their partner, and problems such as PTSD may not improve. We discuss with clients how they are better able to make sense of their feelings when they express them. They are also more likely to see that they can handle them without avoiding them. In other words, they become comfortable in emotional situations. Group leaders then ask group members how each of them avoids expressing feelings and why and whether they can remember a time when they felt closer to their partner after expressing their feelings about an issue.

Material on emotional expression ends with some tips for sharing feelings and listening to other's expressions of feelings. Specifically, group members are encouraged to practice identifying the feelings beneath their anger because anger often hides embarrassment, fear, hurt, or other emotions. It takes practice to get at the root of how one feels. Another tip for the expression of feelings is to use "I" statements rather than "you" statements so that partners do not feel they have been attacked or put on the defensive.

Group members are encouraged to be nonjudgmental and remember that there are no right or wrong feelings. Clients are also prompted to always remember to listen and not simply go into "fix-it" mode whenever their partner expresses feelings. Some trauma-exposed clients may be more likely to try to fix the situation rather than allowing their partners simply to vent about a difficult or stressful situation.

Session 11. Communication Skills V: Common Communication Traps

After discussing communication and completing self-monitoring assignments for expressing feelings, group material focuses on four important communication traps that undermine assertive communication. These traps include generalizing, mindreading, not staying focused on the issue at hand, and dwelling on the negative. Strategies to avoid these common communication traps and to cope productively when they arise are introduced and discussed in this session.

Perhaps the most important element of Session 11 is review of the clients' practice assignment, "Daily Feelings Expression—Individual," focused on the expression of feelings (Appendix J). For this and the next week, group members are asked to express a feeling to someone each day and chart this on a daily monitoring form. Participants are asked in session about how they felt when they expressed their feelings and whether it enhanced their sense of closeness with their partner or others. Group leaders assist in troubleshooting difficulties with emotional expression and discuss possible barriers to such expression.

It is important for group therapists to be mindful that those with significant trauma or PTSD may attempt to avoid this practice assignment. Such avoidance should be pointed out and openly discussed. The expression of feelings can be uncomfortable for those who have difficulty trusting others, who have difficulty relinquishing power and control in relationships, or who may have self-esteem problems and difficulty making themselves vulnerable. However, for these individuals, this assignment takes on even greater importance because enhanced communication and feelings expression may represent an important mechanism for navigating these relationship stuck points.

Session 12. Reviewing Treatment Gains and Planning for the Future

After discussing the emotional expression practice assignment, group members explore gains made in the group. They identify goals and strategies for future change, along with barriers to change and strategies to overcome these barriers. Much of the session is spent discussing thoughts and feelings about the group ending, exploring plans for future change, and saying goodbye. The primary clinical tasks are to help group members develop a realistic appraisal of changes made, identify areas needing continued attention, and generate strategies for continuing this work after the group ends.

We have yet to encounter a client who has not made positive changes from the beginning to the end of the group. We feel that it is critical to "build clients up" at the last group session, particularly trauma-exposed clients who have not had much positive reinforcement or support from others in their lives. We help group members point out positive changes the other members have made over the course of the group, and we add our own observations. This is important because often trauma-exposed clients have a tendency to focus on the negative with respect to their functioning. Typically, however, by Session 12, group members possess a less negative outlook and have no difficulty describing and discussing their accomplishments in a favorable manner.

During the last session, some group members express an interest in getting help for trauma-related problems beyond their abusiveness and relationship issues. Some get help for psychiatric issues such as PTSD and depression. It can be helpful for group members to share resources and to describe their own treatment experiences. A number of our clients entered our program with a fear of any form of treatment, but upon seeing that therapy can be helpful, they became more open to receiving care for other difficulties.

Group members are also encouraged to continue to provide each other with support and to take a realistic view of barriers to continue making positive changes. Trauma-exposed clients cannot be complacent in monitoring themselves and maintaining the proper mind-set for viewing the world and communicating effectively with others.

Evidence for Strength at Home Men's Program

We have conducted multiple pilot studies of the Strength at Home Men's Program, all of which have shown it to be effective in preventing and reducing IPV behaviors (Love et al., 2015; Taft et al., 2013). We also recently conducted an RCT of the Strength at Home intervention, comparing physical and psychological IPV outcomes between those receiving the Strength at Home Men's Program and those in an enhanced treatment-as-usual condition (Taft, Macdonald, et al., 2015).

In a pilot study conducted at the VA Pacific Island Health Care System, we had three primary aims: (a) to survey VA and community providers about their views on the need for, and availability of, military-specific IPA treatment services in the ethnically and culturally diverse community of Oahu, Hawaii; (b) to contribute to the emerging literature on Strength at Home and evaluate the feasibility of implementing the program in the diverse local community by conducting a pilot study using a sample of veterans and their partners; and (c) to obtain participant feedback on the acceptability of the program. A survey of 20 mental health professionals was conducted, and both quantitative and focus group data were gathered from six veterans. All of the mental health professionals surveyed expressed the belief that there was a need for an IPV program that is specific to military populations, and all reported they would be very likely to refer to such a program. Furthermore, approximately 70% felt IPV was an important or very important clinical issue for veterans they served, and

62% reported that existing services for this population in the community were poor.

Results from analysis of quantitative data from veterans indicated a significant reduction of psychological IPV use by veterans from baseline to 6-month follow-up (after treatment) as assessed by the Multidimensional Measure of Emotional Abuse (Murphy, Hoover, & Taft, 1999). Qualitative (focus group) data also indicated a positive participant response to Strength at Home. Veterans identified the specific focus on intimate relationships (rather than general anger management) and a smaller group size as things they liked most about treatment. All participants agreed that Strength at Home was well suited to the needs of veterans in the diverse local community.

We implemented a pilot study of the Strength at Home Men's Program, funded by the Department of Veterans Affairs and Department of Defense, before the conduct of the RCT to pilot test the intervention and make modifications (Taft et al., 2013). This study involved six participants, five veterans and one active duty service member, who all completed the first assessment and the 6-month follow-up assessment. Results indicated that overall, participants engaged in significantly lower physical IPV from pretreatment to 6-month follow-up (see Figure 8.1a). Differences for total, mild, and severe physical IPV were statistically significant, and effect sizes (*d*) were all greater than 1.0, indicating a large effect. Total and severe psychological IPV frequency, as measured by the Revised Conflict Tactics Scales (Straus, Hamby, Boney-McCoy, & Sugarman, 1996), also significantly declined from pretreatment to 6-month follow-up. Effect sizes for all measures of psychological IPV were large (>1.0; see Figure 8.1b).

The second phase of this research program funded by the Department of Veterans Affairs and Department of Defense was particularly important. This was the RCT phase, which is necessary for demonstrating the efficacy of a treatment. If we want to have confidence that a specific intervention is effective, it is imperative that we compare those who are assigned to that intervention and a comparison group that does not receive the treatment. Otherwise, we cannot state with confidence that participants would have reduced their IPV without the aid of intervention. Results for this study have recently been published in the *Journal of Clinical Psychiatry* (Taft, Macdonald, et al., 2015).

For this study, we compared those assigned to the Strength at Home Men's Program relative to those in an enhanced treatment-as-usual condition. In the latter condition, participants were provided safety planning information and information about resources and services related to IPV and trauma. Participants in this condition were free to receive any other care or abuser intervention within or outside of the treatment setting (VA hospital). Furthermore, they were specifically provided treatment referrals by the study

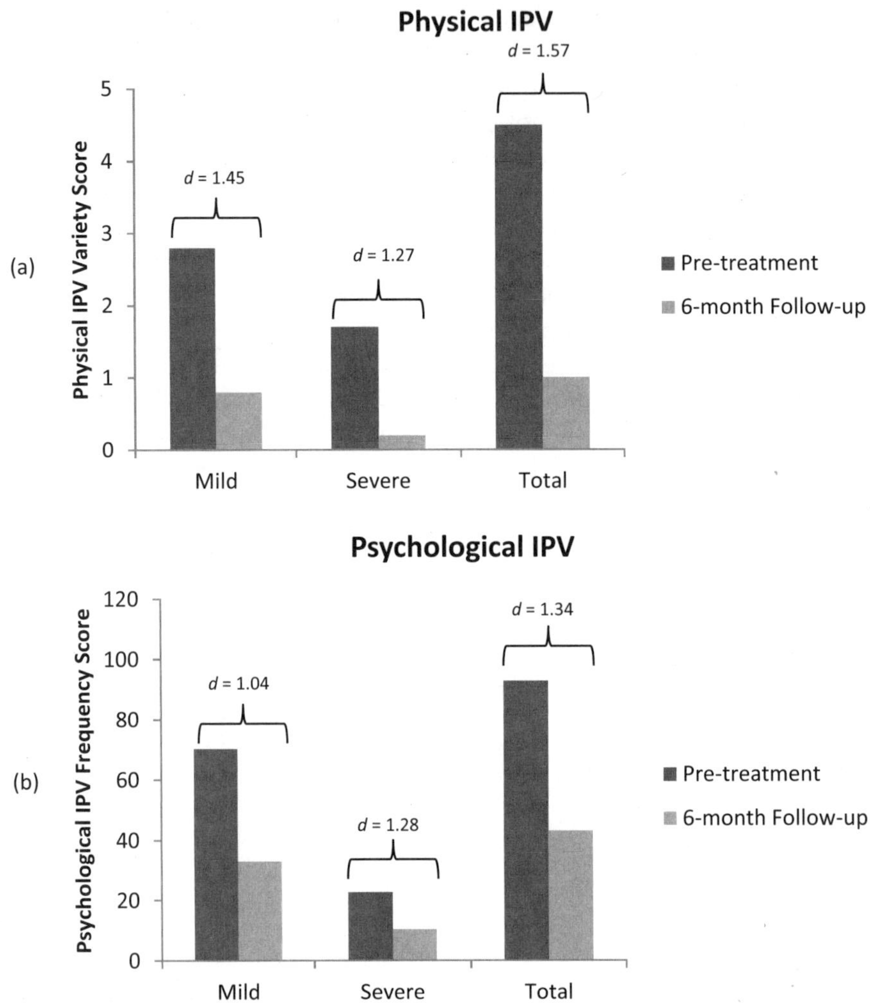

Figure 8.1. Pilot study results: (a) physical interpersonal violence (IPV) and (b) psychological IPV.

staff if indicated. Thus, these comparison group individuals received greater than the standard of care within the VA at that time.

In total, 135 male veteran participants were enrolled in the study across two study sites and were included in intent-to-treat analyses, the strongest design meaning that the data were examined regardless of whether participants completed the intervention. One hundred and eight female partners agreed to provide collateral information. Partners were not only asked about the abusive behavior of the veteran but were also provided information on services for IPV, clinical referrals, and safety planning information. Hierarchical linear modeling (Raudenbush, Bryk, Cheong, & Congdon, 2004; Singer & Willett, 2003) was used to investigate the effect of treatment on changes in use of IPV over time. Consistent with the hypotheses, there were significant time-by-condition effects such that participants in the Strength at Home Men's Program condition compared with the participants in the enhanced treatment-as-usual condition evidenced greater reductions in physical and psychological IPV use as measured by the Revised Conflict Tactics Scales (Straus et al., 1996).

In analyses examining different components of psychological IPV using the Multidimensional Measure of Emotional Abuse (Murphy & Hoover, 1999), a significant time-by-condition effect was also found such that Strength at Home Men's Program participants evidenced greater reductions in coercive, controlling behaviors over time than participants in the enhanced treatment-as-usual condition. Overall, the results suggest that the Strength at Home Men's Program was effective in reducing use of IPV over time.

When we looked at whether veterans engaged in physical IPV recidivism at each time point, we found that recidivism was significantly higher in the enhanced treatment-as-usual condition (43.3%) than the Strength at Home Men's condition (23.3%) at posttreatment. Differences were smaller at 3-month follow-up; 26.7% of enhanced treatment-as-usual participants recidivated compared with 18.5% of Strength at Home Men's group participants (see Figure 8.2).

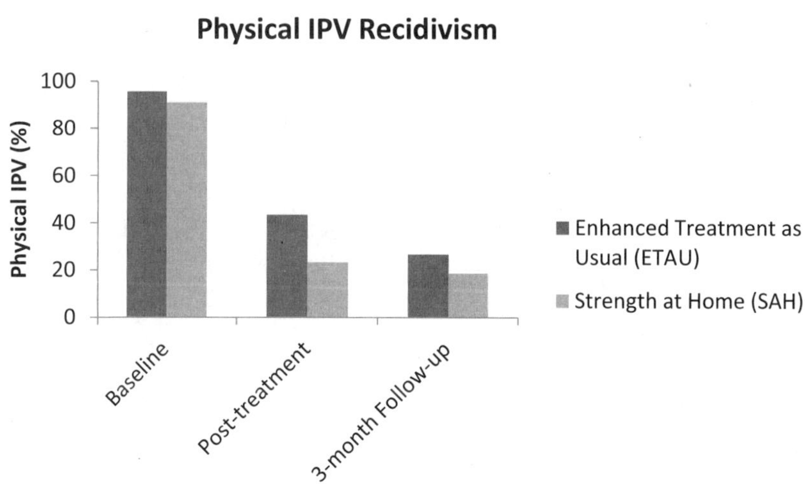

Figure 8.2. Randomized controlled trial results showing relatively lower physical intimate partner violence recidivism rates in the Strength at Home condition.

CASE EXAMPLE: TRANSCRIPT OF GROUP DISCUSSION

Therapist: Kevin, why don't you walk us through your anger analysis form for the week [see Figure 8.3]?

Client: OK. My situation was that we were driving over to my mom's house because she asked us to come over for dinner. Right before we were getting on the highway, I hit a pothole, and we got a flat tire. So I got out of the car to start changing the tire, and I couldn't find the jack. I could tell my partner was mad right away. Then my partner said it was all my fault because I was driving too fast. I said something sarcastic back, and then just waited on the side of the road for my friend to come help us. We didn't end up going to my mom's because I was too mad at that point and I wanted to be alone. So that's what happened.

Therapist: Wow, that sounds like a really challenging situation, Kevin. Would you mind telling us a little more about what you were thinking and feeling at the time and how you handled things?

Client: Physical reactions were muscles tight, teeth clenched, heart racing, rapid breathing, sweating.

Therapist: And when did the physical reactions start, Kevin?

Client: Oh, right away, and pretty much any time I drive.

Therapist: OK, go on, what were your feelings?

Client: So I circled, mad, disgusted—because the jack wasn't in the car—irritable and frustrated. My thoughts were "If I don't stuff my anger, I'll blow up" and "She is not on my side."

Therapist: And now let's flip the worksheet over. Can you tell us how you responded to the situation?

Client: Well, I didn't check many things under *Assertive*. I did use an "I" statement. Under *Aggressive*, I used inflammatory language and sarcasm, and I threw something.

Therapist: What did you throw?

Client: I had a soda bottle in my hand when I was looking for the jack and I threw it on the ground when I couldn't find the jack.

Therapist: What else did you check off?

Client: Under *Passive*, did not communicate thoughts and feelings, withdrew or walked away, dwelled on feelings of anger, used sarcasm.

Briefly describe a recent anger situation.

My partner and I were driving to my mom's house when we got a flat tire. My partner said something sarcastic about my driving. The jack was not in the car, which made everything worse. We didn't end up going to my mom's after all.

What were your physical reactions during this anger episode? (Please circle or add your own).

muscles tight	**teeth clenched**	**blood rushing**	**rapid breathing**	**sweating**
heart racing	**adrenaline rush**	**headache**	**stomach pain**	**trembling**

Add your own ______________________________

____

____

What were your feelings during this anger episode? (Please circle or add your own).

mad	**disgusted**	**rageful**	**jealous**	**ashamed**	**hurt**
sad	**glad**	**depressed**	**embarrassed**	**lonely**	**frustrated**
scared	**irritable**	**anxious**	**humiliated**	**guilty**	**horrified**

Add your own ______________________________

____

____

What were your thoughts during this anger episode? (Please circle or add your own).

"If I don't stuff my anger, I'll blow up."

"S/he is trying to push my buttons."

"I'll show her/him who they are dealing with."

"S/he is not listening to me, and I need to make him/her understand my side."

"S/he is not on my side."

"I'm going to get my way no matter what."

Add your own ______________________________

How did you respond to this situation? Check off your behaviors.

Figure 8.3. Anger analysis forms.

(*continues*)

ASSERTIVE:

____ Asked clarifying questions instead of making accusations

____ Communicated your needs without demeaning or being sarcastic to the other person

____ Expressed your feelings about the issue

____ Took a Time-Out

_X_ Used "I" statements (e.g., "I am upset" instead of "You make me upset")

____ Used polite language (e.g., no swearing or insults)

____ Approached problem with a constructive attitude and tone

____ Set limits (e.g., explain that you will not tolerate certain behaviors)

____ Suggested a compromise to a disagreement

____ Controlled your display of anger despite the other person's reaction

Add your own ______________________________

AGGRESSIVE:

____ Made verbal threats

_X_ Used inflammatory language (e.g., swearing and/or insults)

_X_ Raised voice or used a sarcastic/demeaning tone

____ Glared at or "stared down" the other person

_X_ Broke or threw something

____ Became physically aggressive

Add your own ______________________________

PASSIVE:

_X_ Did not communicate your thoughts and feelings

_X_ Withdrew or walked away in an attempt to avoid addressing the problem

_X_ Dwelled on feelings of anger and defeat without attempting to solve the problem

____ Used a form of negative distraction (e.g., drinking or other substance, risky behaviors)

_X_ Used sarcasm

Add your own ______________________________

Figure 8.3. Anger analysis forms. *(Continued)*

COOLING DOWN BEHAVIORS:

____Worked off your anger through physical activity or exercise

____Spoke to a friend or professional

____Used positive distraction (e.g., favorite hobby or activity)

____Created a soothing environment (e.g., put on music, took a warm bath)

____Treated yourself to something special (e.g., a nice lunch, a massage)

____Wrote down your feelings

____Did a deep breathing or relaxation exercise

Add your own ____

Figure 8.3. Anger analysis forms. *(Continued)*

Therapist: OK, and did you used any cooling down behaviors?

Client: No.

Therapist: Thanks, Kevin. Can we just go back quickly to the "I" statement that you said you used? Can you tell me more about that?

Client: Well, I said that I knew it was frustrating and I wanted to get going too, but sometimes these things happen.

Client: That's when she said that these things happen because I drive too fast.

Therapist: I see. And that's when you said something sarcastic back?

Client: Yeah, I said I can't control when there's a pothole on the road or something like that anyway.

Therapist: And you didn't end up going to your mother's after all?

Client: No, I was too angry. So after the tire got changed, I just drove home, and I sat in the backyard all night smoking. I didn't say anything else about it.

Therapist: [turns to group] OK, so how do you guys think Kevin handled this situation?

Client 2: That's rough, but I think he did OK. I mean driving around here is stressful, especially after Iraq, and I know he just got back about 2 years ago. So that really changes things for you forever basically. And then not to find the jack in the car, that would make me mad too. So I think he did OK.

Therapist: What do others think?

Client 3: Well, I think maybe they could have talked about it more.

Therapist: Hmm. That's interesting. Can you tell us more?

Client 3: I don't know, but maybe he could have said if he was feeling especially frustrated driving that, you know, it was a tough situation for him, or maybe he could have talked to her afterward about that, to maybe tell her that it was really stressful and he was under pressure and that it is hard to change a tire in a situation like that, you know. [The other group members nod in agreement.]

Therapist: Kevin, what do you think about what the guys are saying?

Client: I did tell her something like that, I said it was frustrating for everyone and these things happen.

Therapist: Right, and that's a good start. I think the group is also saying it may be useful to talk to your partner about what happened. Is that what people are saying?

Client 3: Yes, I think they still need to talk about it because they didn't resolve the problem.

Client: Use the assertive communication and all that.

Therapist: Yes, what could you say that would be assertive?

Client: I could say that I understand that everyone was frustrated, but that for me driving can be especially stressful and that I am sorry it went down the way it did. I was angry because she said that it was my fault for speeding, but I didn't say anything about how I was feeling. I just went in the backyard.

Therapist: What does everyone think about that? [The group members nod.] Is that something you could do Kevin?

Client: Yeah, I can try.

Therapist: I am also hearing you say that due to some of your experiences during your deployment, you are really keyed up when you drive. I am wondering if that may be a time when you are going into survival mode, and so you might misread some of the things people say and do as more hostile than they really are. Is that a possibility?

Client: Oh, yeah, for sure. She probably wasn't even sarcastic.

Therapist: So how can you handle that differently?

Client: I guess I can try to calm myself with the breathing. Try to give things some space before I react or I can ask if she's mad and not assume.

Therapist: I think that would go a long way. What does everyone think?

[Group continues.]

SUMMARY

In this chapter, we reviewed the Strength at Home Men's Program, a 12-session cognitive behavioral group intervention based on a social information processing model of IPV. Groups consist of individuals, not couples, and are therapy focused. Program phases include psychoeducation, conflict management, coping skills, and communication skills, with motivational interviewing strategies and group process–building interventions used throughout. We discussed the intervention session by session with a particular emphasis on trauma-relevant elements. A growing research base, including a recent dual-site RCT, indicates that the Strength at Home Men's Program is effective in reducing and ending physical and psychological IPV in relationships.

9

COUPLES INTERVENTIONS

At some point, clinicians working in the field of intimate partner violence (IPV) will need to decide whether it is appropriate to treat couples in which one or both partners has used aggression. This is a key controversy in the field, with the prevailing view for some time being that IPV should never be treated in a couples format. A closer look at research findings and theoretical perspectives from the past 20 years, however, reveals that couples treatment may be appropriate and effective for some couples.

IS COUPLES THERAPY APPROPRIATE FOR DYADS EXPERIENCING IPV?

Safety of the partner is the primary concern among those who argue against couples-based IPV intervention (Bograd & Mederos, 1999). Specifically, the concern is that partners who have experienced IPV might be intimidated

http://dx.doi.org/10.1037/14918-010
Trauma-Informed Treatment and Prevention of Intimate Partner Violence, by C. T. Taft, C. M. Murphy, and S. K. Creech

in therapy and that the issues discussed in treatment could compromise their safety if the abuser punishes her or him for what is said in the treatment context (see O'Leary, Heyman, & Neidig, 1999). In addition, because couples treatment emphasizes dyadic interaction and often focuses on behavioral skills acquisition, an important concern is that such treatment may not hold individuals accountable for their IPV and may place blame for IPV on the recipient (Gauthier & Levendosky, 1996). In addition, it has been argued that couples therapists, in seeking to take a neutral stance toward both members of the couple, might be overly neutral toward the use of violence and fail to acknowledge a context or pattern of power and control (Goldner, 1999).

However, it has also been argued that many IPV couples wish to remain in their relationships and want couples therapy and that treatment that fails to address the underlying troubled aspects of intimate relationship functioning will do little to prevent violence in the future (Stith & McCollum, 2011). Supporting this argument are studies indicating that standard batterer's intervention programs have little effect on recidivism (e.g., Babcock, Green, & Robie, 2004) and that intimate relationship distress is significantly associated with IPV across numerous studies, and thus treatment of the distress may help prevent or reduce IPV (Stith, Green, Smith, & Ward, 2008). Furthermore, psychological IPV has been shown to precede and predict physical IPV (Murphy & O'Leary, 1989; Schumacher & Leonard, 2005). The implication is that psychological IPV may represent an early risk factor for more severe types of IPV and that dyadic intervention may be required to intervene effectively.

To examine whether couples who had engaged in mild physical IPV could be treated safely using couple therapy, Simpson, Atkins, Gattis, and Christensen (2008) compared the efficacy of nonaggression-focused behavioral couples therapy in a sample of 134 couples with and without a history of mild physical IPV. Couples with moderate to severe relationship distress received up to 26 weeks of behavioral couples therapy and completed assessments before, during, and after treatment, including four times during a 2-year longitudinal follow-up. Results revealed that therapy did not increase rates of psychological or physical IPV. In addition, although couples with a history of mild IPV started treatment more distressed compared with the no-IPV group, treatment outcomes did not significantly differ between groups. Importantly, results also showed that risk for psychological IPV decreased when relationship satisfaction and individual functioning improved. Thus, results from this study indicate that couples therapy with those who have experienced mild aggression may be safe and beneficial; however, the authors warned that therapists must use the utmost caution in determining aggression severity and frequency. Furthermore, the authors suggested that although treatment does not appear to create risk for such couples, it may place them at risk to be denied treatment because of IPV; gender-specific treatment may feel unhelpful or irrelevant because it may not address underlying dyadic issues (Simpson et al., 2008). Along similar lines, a study comparing gender-specific to conjoint group treatments for heterosexual couples experiencing male-to-female IPV found no evidence that conjoint treatment led to greater fear or self-blame for abuse in women participants (O'Leary et al., 1999).

PREVALENCE OF IPV WITHIN RELATIONSHIPS

Of crucial importance to this topic is the research evidence on who engages in IPV in relationships. One view, influenced by the larger number of men who are arrested for domestic violence offenses and data collected from women seeking services in shelters, is that IPV is primarily committed by men against women (Carney, Buttell, & Dutton, 2007). For example, national studies that report rates of victimization have indicated that women experience higher rates of lifetime and recent victimization compared with men and that women are more likely than men to be injured in domestic altercations (Breiding, Black, & Ryan, 2008; Tjaden & Thoennes, 2000).

A contrasting perspective is one arguing that most IPV is bidirectional in nature. Results from large-scale community samples and meta-analyses have supported the view that there are many kinds of violence, including a large amount of bidirectional or reciprocal violence (Archer, 2000; Whitaker, Haileyesus, Swahn, & Saltzman, 2007). For example, Straus (2008) examined this issue in a sample of more than 13,000 university students from 32 nations and found that nearly one third of both female and male students reported physical aggression toward a relationship partner in the past year and that the most common pattern of aggression was bidirectional, with the least common pattern being male only. An examination of the couples treatment literature reveals that low-level relationship aggression is in fact a relatively common occurrence among those seeking treatment and that such aggression is often bidirectional in nature (for a review, see Simpson, Doss, Wheeler, & Christensen, 2007). Of particular concern is that many couples seeking relationship treatment do not identify IPV as a problem (Doss, Simpson, & Christensen, 2004).

It has been suggested that one explanation for the differing rates of IPV observed is that not all IPV in intimate relationships is the same (Johnson, 2011). For example, Holtzworth-Munroe (2005) and others have argued that one important variable to consider is severity level. Specifically, she argued that when community samples are used, there is not enough variation in severe violence, and therefore results are more likely to indicate that IPV is bidirectional, with women slightly more likely to use IPV than men. In contrast, when justice-involved, clinical, hospital, or shelter samples are used, results often support the hypothesis that IPV is largely committed by men against women (Holtzworth-Munroe,

2005). A recent review of the literature in clinical samples generally agreed with this hypothesis, finding that women appear to be more victimized, injured, and fearful than men (Larsen & Hamberger, 2015). In addition, this review concluded that men and women appear to engage in different types of psychological IPV, that men appear to be the predominant perpetrators of sexual IPV, and that women appear to be more likely to use physical aggression in response to aggression used against them (Larsen & Hamberger, 2015).

Johnson (2011) proposed a typology describing several types of IPV, emphasizing the role of control as a distinguishing factor. *Intimate terrorism* is the type of IPV that may be encountered most often in justice-involved and shelter samples. It describes a combination of physical and sexual IPV with coercive control and violence that is primarily unidirectional and is used by men toward women. *Violent resistance* describes IPV that is bidirectional but undertaken out of self-defense by one of the partners. *Situational couple violence* is IPV that emerges out of arguments, does not include coercion or control, and can be unidirectional or bidirectional in nature. Johnson asserted that situational couple violence is the most common and variable type of IPV encountered.

Taken together, modern views of IPV suggest that it is not a singular construct with a one-size-fits-all solution, and therefore there may be couples for whom dyadic intervention is more appropriate than individual, gender-specific intervention. A consensus that has emerged in the literature is that couples treatment may be most appropriate for couples in stable relationships who do not fear each other, who report low to moderate levels of IPV, and who consider IPV in their relationship a problem that they are committed to resolving (LaTaillade, Epstein, & Werlinich, 2006). In Stith's work, couples are excluded if either partner is afraid that conjoint treatment may increase IPV, if a partner has been violent but does not believe he or she is responsible for ending IPV, and if there are mental health or substance abuse issues that might interfere with couples treatment if not addressed (Stith & McCollum, 2011). Others have emphasized the importance of a conjoint treatment format only when there is no ongoing husband-to-wife IPV (Heyman & Schlee, 2003). Conjoint treatment is also an option to consider after a course of group or individual treatment has been successfully completed by the violent partner and there has been an extended period (the usual recommendation is 6 months) with no physical assaults.

SOCIAL INFORMATION PROCESSING, TRAUMA, AND INTIMATE RELATIONSHIP DIFFICULTIES

Throughout this volume, we have discussed how social information processing biases and deficits may be affected by trauma and may confer risk for relationship difficulties and IPV. The work of Marshall and her colleagues may be particularly relevant in the couples context, especially research indicating that maladaptive trauma-related thoughts contribute to interpreting social situations as more threatening and partner behaviors as more rejecting, both increasing IPV risk (Marshall, Robinson, & Azar, 2011; Sippel & Marshall, 2011). This work suggests that helping couples recognize the impact of their trauma exposure on interpretations of their partners and working with them to better communicate and avoid such misinterpretations, should be a central focus in therapy.

Specific symptoms of posttraumatic stress disorder (PTSD) may also contribute to overall relationship difficulties that increase the risk for IPV (for reviews, see Dekel & Monson, 2010; and Monson, Taft, & Fredman, 2009). Drawing from the military literature that has examined this most closely, a number of studies have indicated that PTSD symptoms in general are associated with intimate relationship problems such as decreased relationship satisfaction, poorer relationship adjustment, and marital distress (Allen, Rhoades, Stanley, & Markman, 2010; Erbes, Meis, Polusny, & Compton, 2011; Goff, Crow, Reisbig, & Hamilton, 2007; Renshaw, Rodrigues, & Jones, 2008). The numbing symptoms of PTSD seem especially critical to intimate relationship functioning (Galovski & Lyons, 2004). Specifically, reduced emotional expression may impede communication and erode intimacy and may ultimately lead to a pattern of detachment, isolation, conflict, and withdrawal (Galovski & Lyons, 2004). Similarly, avoidance symptoms may make it difficult for couples to engage in social activities, and the way in which relationship partners respond to avoidance can inadvertently maintain avoidance behavior (Monson et al., 2009). For example, Monson et al. (2009) described a pattern in which intimate partners may accommodate avoidance behavior by facilitating "work-arounds" (e.g., agreeing not to drive a certain way to work) that reinforce PTSD symptoms and can erode relationship satisfaction. Hyperarousal symptoms such as anger, irritability, and hypervigilance may lead to constant tension in the household, and hyperarousal symptoms have been specifically associated with IPV use among Vietnam veteran samples (Savarese, Suvak, King, & King, 2001).

Up to this point, we have discussed trauma and PTSD as if it is primarily diagnosed in one partner. It is important to note, however, that both partners may have experiences with trauma. In a recent study, Alexander (2014) examined rates of IPV and trauma history in 473 couples in which the male partner was court-mandated to IPV intervention. Results revealed that in 46.3% of the couples, both partners endorsed a history of childhood trauma exposure. Whereas men in these dual-trauma couples reported significantly higher rates of psychological and physical IPV use compared with other groups of men (no-trauma or men-only trauma), women described them as less psychologically and no more physically violent then men in other groups. Women in dual-trauma couples were also less likely to report any help-seeking behaviors, suggesting they may be at particularly high risk for the negative physical and psychological correlates of IPV.

To understand how treatment needs may differ between single and dual-trauma couples, Nelson and colleagues (2002) completed a series of focus group discussions with both types of couples. Salient characteristics of both types of couples were extreme pursuer–distancer patterns accompanied by a high intensity level and potential for volatility and aggression. For dual-trauma couples, a risky time for such patterns was when partners were preoccupied with or dismissing of their traumatic experiences. For both types of couples, there was a negative impact of PTSD symptoms on couple functioning. These findings are echoed in Balcom's (1996) earlier suggestions that dual-trauma couples may be characterized by extreme boundaries (too rigid or fluid), intense emotional reactivity (too little or too much), and trauma responses that interfere with healthy relationship functioning. Thus, clinicians are encouraged to assess both partners for trauma exposure and PTSD symptoms and to include such data in case formulation.

In Chapter 1, we reviewed the ways in which core themes, or schemas, affected by trauma may have an impact on how one processes social information and thus may underlie relationship functioning difficulties and IPV. Such thought patterns likely affect intimate functioning on a daily basis in ways that are not limited to IPV. Thus, in some couples, dyadic intervention that focuses on the impact of trauma on relationship functioning including low-level IPV may be able to address problems related to these core themes and social information processing (see Fredman, Monson, & Adair, 2011).

ASSESSMENT WITHIN A COUPLE CONTEXT

If clinicians who are experienced in couples treatment undertake work with couples who report IPV, certain safety considerations should be at the forefront of assessment and treatment. Specifically, for every couple, all dimensions of IPV should be assessed using a multimethod and behaviorally specific approach, outlined in Chapter 4 (see also Schacht, Dimidjian, George, & Berns, 2009). To do so, both partners should complete self-report measures of IPV separately and privately (LaTaillade, Epstein, & Werlinich, 2006), followed by an interview. Key domains that should be covered in the interview include types, context, and consequences of IPV; justice involvement; presence and impact on children; and whether treatment seeking is voluntary for both members of the dyad (Bograd & Mederos, 1999; Schacht et al., 2009). Clinicians should inquire into the most severe episode of IPV as well as the most recent and frequent types of IPV (Heyman & Schlee, 2003). Lethality of violence must also be assessed, including inquiry into frequency and severity of IPV, weapons used, whether weapons are present in the home, injuries sustained, substance use, and any justice involvement (LaTaillade, Epstein, & Werlinich, 2006; Schacht et al., 2009). This assessment helps determine the severity and context of violence, whether either partner is afraid of the other, and whether the couple is appropriate for treatment. In her work, Stith emphasizes gaining an understanding of whether the partners take responsibility for violence of if they blame the other partner (Stith & McCollum, 2011). Such assessment should be repeated regularly to examine any changes in the couple's situation.

Clinicians must also be prepared to engage in crisis management when necessary (LaTaillade, Epstein, & Werlinich, 2006). Examples include offering immediate access to additional sessions if a violent incident occurs while couples are in treatment. The purpose of such a session is to help the couple with safety planning and stabilization that could include removing any weapons from the home, separating the couple physically, creating a no-harm contract, referring one partner to a shelter, and ultimately examining whether conjoint treatment is still appropriate. Similar procedures might be implemented during the intake assessment process if severe IPV is detected. Clinicians must be aware of local resources, including shelters and individual resources for treatment of IPV.

COUPLE-BASED TREATMENTS

In this section, we review several evidence-based treatments that have been developed specifically for use with couples to prevent or end IPV. We also review two relevant disorder-specific dyadic treatments for substance abuse or PTSD.

Physical aggression couples treatment (PACT) was developed by Heyman and Neidig (1997) to stop IPV among couples and is an adapted version of an earlier treatment (Neidig & Friedman, 1984). A key tenet of this 14 session cognitive behavioral group treatment is the principle that both members of a couple take responsibility for their anger and their own behavior by increasing awareness of aggression and acquiring skills in anger management and communication. The authors described PACT as taking a feminist-social learning approach to ending IPV by emphasizing both the couple context in which violence occurs as well as the larger societal context of the marriage, and they emphasize the importance of understanding the cyclical pattern in which violence can occur within a relationship (Heyman & Schlee, 2003). The first half of the program focuses on the acquisition of intrapersonal skills such as anger control and the cognitive behavioral model of anger; the second half emphasizes communication skills and conflict management.

An empirical study of the effectiveness of PACT found that, compared with a gender-specific treatment modality, it was equally effective in reducing physical IPV and improving marital quality (O'Leary et al., 1999). Longitudinal study of outcomes also indicated that reductions in physical and psychological IPV and improvement in marital quality were maintained at 1-year follow-up (O'Leary et al., 1999). The authors suggested that their findings indicate that PACT was as effective as gender-specific groups and may be appropriate for some intact couples, especially those who seek marital therapy but who do not identify IPV as a problem (Heyman & Schlee, 2003).

LaTaillade, Epstein, and Werlinich (2006) developed a cognitive behavioral couples treatment, the *Couples Abuse Prevention Program*, designed for couples who have experienced psychological IPV and low to moderate physical IPV but with no physically damaging IPV. The program emphasizes reduction of IPV risk and enhanced relationship quality through skills acquisition including anger and conflict management skills, communication and problem-solving skills, improved support and positive activities, and recovery from relationship trauma. The program also includes a psychoeducation component focused on IPV and the negative consequences of IPV (LaTaillade et al., 2006). An examination of this intervention compared with usual couples treatment revealed that although both types of treatment resulted in improved relationship functioning and reductions in the use of psychological IPV, neither resulted in changes in physical IPV (LaTaillade et al., 2006). The authors noted that the lack of a finding for physical IPV may be due to the low overall rate of physical IPV in the sample and concluded that conjoint treatments are feasible and effective for couples with low level physical and psychological IPV (LaTaillade et al., 2006).

Domestic violence focused couples treatment is a solution-focused couples treatment to end IPV and improve relationship quality that was developed and tested by Stith and colleagues (McCollum & Stith, 2008). In this treatment, intact couples who wish to stay together, have only used mild-to-moderate IPV, and want to end violence in their relationship receive 6 weeks of gender-specific treatment followed by 12 weeks of multicouple group treatment or individual couple treatment. As described by Stith, McCollum, Amanor-Boadu, and Smith (2012), the emphasis of the first phase of treatment is on goal setting for a healthy relationship, IPV education, safety planning, and skills building such as negotiated time-outs. In the second phase, couples work conjointly on issues or problems brought to the session (Stith, Rosen, McCollum, & Thomsen, 2004). To enhance and evaluate safety, each individual meets with a therapist separately before and after each session. Outcome data suggest that completion of the multicouple group format of the intervention resulted in significantly lower male recidivism rates compared with no-treatment controls (Stith, Rosen, et al., 2004). Additional positive improvements were found for marital satisfaction (Stith, Rosen, et al., 2004). Another study reported significant reductions in physical IPV for men who completed either the individual-couple or multigroup format (Stith, McCollum, Amanor-Boadu, & Smith, 2012).

The Strength at Home Couples Program (described in more detail in Chapter 10, this volume) is a 10-week cognitive behavioral dyadic group intervention designed to prevent IPV in returning male service members and their intimate female partners (Taft et al., 2014). This intervention is informed by a social information–processing model for IPV among military populations (Taft, Walling, Howard, & Monson, 2011) and draws on existing cognitive behavioral interventions, with intervention components tailored to be relevant for military couples. The program is intended for couples who are experiencing relationship difficulties but are not engaging in a pattern of physical IPV or coercive, controlling behavior. Further detail about this intervention and research results on its efficacy is presented in the next chapter.

RELEVANT DISORDER-SPECIFIC INTERVENTIONS

A number of studies examining IPV before and after behavioral couples therapy (BCT) for substance abuse have shown a positive impact on IPV in both men and women. In BCT, both members of a dyad attend sessions, and the treatment addresses abstinence as well as relationship functioning (O'Farrell & Clements, 2012). In two examinations of IPV prevalence and frequency before and after treatment in 88 male alcoholics, results indicated that IPV was reduced after treatment, and this was influenced by the level of abstinence. Specifically, when alcoholism was remitted, violence was no longer elevated compared with community norms (O'Farrell & Murphy, 1995). This effect was stable at a 2-year follow-up, suggesting that treatment for both substance abuse and relationship functioning may have lasting effects on reducing couples use of IPV (O'Farrell, Van Hutton, & Murphy, 1999; for reviews, see O'Farrell & Clements, 2012; and Murphy & Ting, 2010). Similar results have been found after BCT for women with alcohol problems (Schumm, O'Farrell, Murphy, & Fals-Stewart, 2009). Questions remain regarding the extent to which reductions in IPV can be induced through individual, versus couple, treatment approaches for substance use problems. Detailed data modeling suggests that improvements in relationship functioning and reduced drinking jointly contribute to the observed reductions in IPV after BCT (O'Farrell, Murphy, Stephan, Fals-Stewart, & Murphy, 2004). In a recent study comparing the efficacy of BCT to individual treatment among women with alcohol use disorder, Schumm, O'Farrell, Kahler, Murphy, and Muchowski (2014) found that IPV was reduced after treatment in both conditions, although the authors concluded that BCT overall was more effective in reducing substance abuse and improving relationships.

Cognitive-behavioral couple therapy for PTSD (CBCT) was developed by Monson and colleagues to address PTSD symptoms and intimate relationship problems simultaneously (Monson & Fredman, 2012). It is a 15-session treatment organized around three phases that build on one another (for a review, see Fredman et al., 2011). In Phase 1, couples receive psychoeducation about PTSD and relationship problems and complete exercises to improve positive interactions and acquire conflict management skills. In Phase 2, couples participate in behavioral interventions designed to improve their communication and address avoidance. Finally, in Phase 3, couples complete cognitive interventions to address maladaptive thought patterns that may have an impact on both PTSD and relationship problems. The treatment has been tested in a randomized clinical trial and resulted in decreased PTSD symptoms severity and improved relationship satisfaction for the CBCT group compared with a wait-list control group (Monson et al., 2012). Although CBCT does not specifically focus on IPV, aggression is addressed early in the intervention by including psychoeducation on anger regulation and conflict management skills.

SUMMARY

In this chapter, we reviewed different perspectives on working with couples who report IPV in their relationship. Evidence suggests that dyadic treatment for IPV may be most helpful in those couples who meet criteria for low-level IPV, including low-level situational couple violence and those who have experienced psychological IPV but no other kinds of violence. The ability to address trauma-related social information–processing deficits in the context of intimate relationship functioning may be particularly beneficial. Ongoing assessment of safety and each partner's voluntary willingness to participate in such treatment is paramount if it is to be undertaken, as is a strong connection with local resources such as shelters. We also reviewed a number of promising dyadic treatments that have been developed for use with IPV couples or that may be appropriate for some couples reporting problems with IPV.

10

EXAMPLE OF COUPLES INTERVENTION

In this chapter, we provide an example of a trauma-informed couples-based intimate partner violence (IPV) group prevention intervention, the Strength at Home Couples Program. As with our Strength at Home Men's Program, Strength at Home Couples and a similar adapted program (Strength at Home Friends and Families) have been shown to be efficacious in pilot studies and a randomized controlled clinical trial. In this chapter, we provide an overview of the program and a session-by-session description of the intervention with a particular focus on trauma-related issues. We then review the available research evidence for the Strength at Home Couples Program.

Just to make sure that the reader understands the differences between the two Strength at Home programs, the couples' intervention discussed in this chapter was designed for couples who report relationship concerns, relationship problems, or conflicts that place them at risk for IPV but do not report any current physical IPV in the relationship. That is, this intervention is not

http://dx.doi.org/10.1037/14918-011
Trauma-Informed Treatment and Prevention of Intimate Partner Violence, by C. T. Taft, C. M. Murphy, and S. K. Creech

an intervention for those engaging in physical IPV but rather is intended to prevent abusive patterns from developing.

Couples are considered ineligible for the program if they report physical IPV within the past 6 months on the Revised Conflict Tactics Scales (CTS2; Straus, Hamby, Boney-McCoy, & Sugarman, 1996). If they report psychological IPV and no fears of safety with respect to their partners, they remain eligible. In our previous work, we have recruited returning military couples to receive this intervention, described as a *relationship-enhancement* and *conflict-prevention* group. The program has yet to be used with civilian couples but could easily be adapted for this purpose, particularly if the population targeted reports high levels of trauma.

STRENGTH AT HOME COUPLES PROGRAM OVERVIEW

The Strength at Home Couples Program was designed to enhance intimate relationships and prevent IPV. The program is similar in content to the men's program described in Chapter 8 and draws on the same interventions for enhancing relationships, preventing violence, and treating posttraumatic stress disorder (PTSD). The program is tailored to couples who may or may not be new to psychotherapy. As is the case for the men's program, the couples' program is guided by a social information processing model of IPV to assist couples in identifying and correcting misappraisals and to develop effective communication and conflict resolution skills.

The Strength at Home Couples Program is a 10-week program conducted in a group format. It targets social information processing deficits and common themes that may underlie relationship difficulties and IPV. As with the men's program, it is trauma informed and is conducted in a supportive, nonconfrontational atmosphere by two coleaders. It follows a closed-group format involving weekly 2-hour sessions containing brief instructional material; couples-based activities to discuss, learn, and practice new behaviors; and flexible time to solve ongoing problems, enhance motivational readiness, and promote a positive therapy process.

It is common in the group for members to identify a relationship problem at home that is ongoing and that might represent risk for escalation of aggression (e.g., a partner who is verbally abusive or a need to discuss an emotion-laden situation). Group members are assisted in planning how to deal with the problem using the skills they have learned in group. For example, it is common to engage group members in a role-play for how a conversation might go or to create an action plan for how to regulate emotions, use time-outs, or remain nonabusive that is specific to the situation. Group members are supported and provided coaching, and group leaders follow up the next week.

In some situations, the group leader may directly provide feedback regarding concerns about risk, such as "I am concerned that the way you plan to resolve this problem is risky." Although all risk cannot be eliminated and these situations are not always resolved in a perfectly healthy way, we have found that providing support and resources to both members of the couple and obtaining and reminding group members of their commitment to remain nonviolent is an effective strategy. The need to be able to provide this type of specific coaching is why the group is conducted in 2-hour sessions that leave ample time for such discussions. In general, we have found that group members want to resolve conflict in nonabusive ways and that they are willing to engage in such problem solving. If a group member reports back that a situation did involve aggression, the therapist points this out directly and engages the group member in a discussion about how they would resolve the situation differently.

The phases of the Strength at Home Couples Program are similar to those of the men's program but with somewhat less of a focus on recognizing anger triggers and other anger management techniques and considerably greater focus on dyadic interventions and exercises. Couples complete in-session practice exercises throughout the group sessions, typically pairing off as dyads, and are provided assignments to practice the skills learned in group as a couple. Assignments also involve intimacy-enhancing exercises (e.g., self-monitoring of positive relationship behaviors) across sessions.

SESSION DESCRIPTION

Session 1. Introduction and Welcoming

This session introduces couples to the structure, expectations, and philosophy of the group. After initial introductions, the group leaders give participants insight into the rationale and goals for the group, explain the importance of practice assignments, and answer questions about the group. The main clinical tasks are to begin establishing a therapeutic alliance with each couple, to validate and address participants' concerns and reservations about counseling, and to model and encourage healthy group interactions. In addition, group leaders teach participants the skill of paraphrasing, which is the foundation of active listening and is key to reversing social information processing deficits related to trauma. Group leaders will refer to this skill and encourage participants to use it throughout the program.

As discussed in Chapter 8, group leaders should be mindful that some trauma-exposed group members may have a difficult time being in a room full of strangers for the first time. An overly active and faulty threat response in the presence of others is a hallmark problem among those exposed to severe interpersonal trauma. Furthermore, it is important to be mindful that often both partners will have experienced substantial trauma that affects their relationships. Thus, group members are sometimes relieved when they are informed that this is not an "exposure-based" group that requires they go into great detail about previous trauma. However, group members are expected to be able to discuss how their trauma has affected their relationship.

Session 1 is often quite emotional for couples. Hearing other couples who are struggling with similar issues and difficulties related to trauma can be a great relief for some group members. It is our experience that the simple sharing of difficulties during this session assists the group in developing strong group cohesion at the outset. Many of those exposed to trauma feel like they must be the only one who has certain trauma-related experiences or may feel like they are "going crazy." Our couples groups have notably higher attendance than our men-only groups or any other clinical activity, presumably because of the bonding that takes place at the outset.

During the first session, couples learn the skill of *paraphrasing* or putting something into one's own words. As noted, this skill is fundamental to correcting social information processing deficits that manifest in the form of relationship problems for couples. A reason this skill is so important is because it essentially forces couples to adopt a different mind-set, one in which they are focused on understanding the other person's perspective. This helps to avoid misinterpretations of one's partner that is so common for trauma-exposed clients. Learning to really focus on hearing the other person's perspective can be the most powerful skill couples learn during the entire group program.

At the end of Session 1, couples are given an assignment on healthy relationships as well as an assignment where each couple member is asked to note on a recording form the nice things that their partner does for them each day (Appendix K). These behaviors can range from a friendly look to a larger gesture. The point is for the couples not only to work on decreasing negative behaviors in their relationships but also to pay more attention to and increase positive behaviors. This is an important exercise for trauma-exposed couples because those exposed to trauma tend to focus on more negative aspects across a spectrum of situations and issues. This simple exercise of trying to view one's partner more positively and focus on more positive interpretations of behaviors is quite a powerful tool for combating social information processing deficits in couples.

Session 2. Trauma and Relationships I

Couples discuss healthy and unhealthy relationships and review assignments designed to enhance intimacy and solidify mutual treatment goals. Psychoeducational material on definitions of IPV and the impact of trauma and deployment separation on couples' relationship functioning are then reviewed. The main clinical tasks of the session are to enhance motivation, increase couple awareness about IPV and trauma, and help each couple gain insight into the effects of trauma on their own relationship.

Psychoeducation on trauma and its effects can be critically helpful for couples. Many of the couples entering our program have stated that their primary reason for entering therapy was to understand what their partner is going through with respect to trauma and associated difficulties. Thus, an important clinical task of this exercise is to increase understanding and to normalize the effects of trauma.

Group leaders should be aware that focusing on the consequences of trauma can be upsetting to some members. Leaders may need to reassure couples that this is a normal reaction, and it is an important part of the change process. It is important to understand the symptoms or problems one may be experiencing to change them. Group leaders are careful to acknowledge that it may be difficult to discuss the negative effects of trauma, but the good news is that the group will help teach strategies that have been shown to help relationships, prevent conflict and IPV, and lessen the effects of trauma.

Session 3. Trauma and Relationships II

This session begins with a discussion of the practice assignment focusing on understanding how trauma has affected the couples' relationships. Couples are asked to interview each other to learn about the effects of trauma. The group discussion then shifts to several themes related to trauma that can affect relationships, including trust, power and control, self- and other-esteem, and intimacy. Group material facilitates further contemplation of behavior change and treatment goals, building on psychoeducational material from Session 2.

Material focused on common trauma themes is covered to assist couples in communicating around common issues related to trauma that may be hindering closeness and intimacy (Appendix L). Through a better understanding of these issues, couples may be able to learn to more openly talk about their experience of trauma and how it affects them and their relationship. This material may also open the door for continued work outside the group sessions. For example, they may seek individual therapy to focus on issues related to trust.

Session 4. Conflict Management I: Assertiveness

This session focuses on conflict management and expressing anger assertively, with some material focusing on how conflict management styles were learned. The clinical goals are to continue to facilitate an understanding of the impact of trauma on relationships (and conflict management styles in particular) and to help group members identify positive (i.e., assertive) versus potentially harmful (i.e., aggressive, passive) communication styles during conflict.

Couples completed a practice assignment over the previous week to interview each other (paraphrasing responses) about how they have learned to handle conflict and express emotions. This is a modified "couples" version of the "Roots of Your Communication Style" handout described in Chapter 8 (Appendix H). Many men have been socialized to engage in passive or aggressive behavior rather than open expression of anger and other emotions in a healthier, assertive way. Group leaders should highlight this overarching theme in the group discussion and indicate that this is why we emphasize assertiveness and communication skills in this group. Group members are asked if they learned anything new about their partner by completing this exercise and how they might be able to negotiate differences in conflict management styles.

A number of themes are commonly discussed in this practice assignment review. In our work with veterans, they often indicate that they were taught either to follow or to give orders in the military and report that they learned to channel all emotions into anger and aggression. They indicate that, similarly, they were taught while growing up that "real men" do not talk about their feelings and do not discuss negative feelings. Partners of veterans also discuss how they have learned to be more passive with their partners because they feel like they are "walking on eggshells" for fear of upsetting the veteran or because they, too, were socialized to be passive in relationships.

These are important areas for discussion because to unlearn dysfunctional (passive and aggressive) communication styles, couples must first understand how they initially developed them. Group therapists may indicate that it is not surprising that some may experience difficulty in expressing feelings because they were never taught how to do so. This makes working on assertiveness skills particularly important, and the remainder of the session focuses on discussing assertiveness and how to be more assertive in relationships. At the end of the session, couples are provided a Conflict Analysis Sheet (Appendix M) as a practice assignment to help them analyze the strategies they currently use when confronted with an anger-provoking situation.

Session 5. Conflict Management II: Time-Outs

Group members review the self-monitoring assignment designed to assess group members' assertive, passive, and aggressive responses to conflict situations. The group discussion then focuses on developing strategies to deescalate conflict situations. Couples are asked to generate and put into practice a detailed "Time-Out Plan" to use during potential conflict situations. The development of these plans is an important crisis management tool that helps ensure safety for the couple and provides a skill that assists in laying the groundwork for future work on communication. Please refer to our discussion in Chapter 8 on Time-Outs, including their importance and how they can lessen the negative impact of trauma on social information processing abilities.

A fundamental key to successful Time-Outs is for couples to understand that they should not be used to avoid their partner. This is especially important in trauma-exposed clients because trauma-exposed individuals are much more likely to exhibit avoidance behaviors and respond passively to conflict situations. Thus, learning to take proper Time-Outs can be a first step in teaching couples to engage with each other in productive, respectful, assertive dialogue to resolve disagreements. At the conclusion of the Time-Out discussion, each couple collaboratively drafts their own unique Time-Out plan and is asked to put the plan into action and practice Time-Outs over the next week (Appendix N).

Session 6. Communication Skills I: Active Listening

This session begins with a discussion of the Time-Outs and self-monitoring practice assignments. The focus then shifts to discussing aspects of healthy and unhealthy communication. Active listening skills are the most important for developing a solid foundation for good communication and are critical for deescalating conflict and enhancing intimacy. The provision of listening skills for couples help to counter social information processing deficits that couples may exhibit.

As we have noted, active listening skills, including paraphrasing, are fundamental skills for combating the negative effects of social information processing deficits on relationships and IPV. Couples are encouraged not only to use the paraphrasing skills they have been taught but also to ask each other more questions rather than assuming they know how the other feels and to practice "validating" each other when having discussions and expressing feelings.

Session 7. Communication Skills II: Assertive Messages

After discussion of listening skills from the previous week and completion of communication self-monitoring practice assignments, the groups switches to a focus on how to give an assertive message, and group members participate in role-plays to practice these skills. These skills are intended to reduce the negative impact that trauma may have on communication and to further enhance intimacy, improve relationship problem solving, and facilitate the sharing of trauma-related material.

Couples are taught that assertive messages often have three parts, all of which are important for effective communication:

1. A clear and concise *description of the issue, concern, or behavior* that they would like their partner to change.
2. A statement of their *feelings* about the behavior and its *effects* on them. Group members are encouraged to use "I" statements when expressing their feelings.
3. A *suggestion or request* about what they would like their partner to do or how the problem might be resolved.

Session 8. Communication Skills III: Expressing Feelings

After discussing skills from the previous week and completion of self-monitoring forms, the group discussions focus on difficulties in identifying and expressing feelings, with a focus on how trauma can lead to the avoidance of expressing feelings. Strategies for expressing feelings are discussed, and couples are given an opportunity to practice these expression skills during the session. Specifically, couples are provided four tips on how best to share feelings:

1. *Practice identifying real feelings*. It is quite easy to express anger, but it may be more difficult to express the true feelings underneath the anger, such as embarrassment or hurt. We assist group members in learning to identify what they truly feel and to express that to their partners.
2. *Use "I" statements*. Use phrases such as "I feel . . .", or "I would like . . ." instead of "You make me feel . . . ," "You never . . . ," or "You always. . . ." This helps to avoid putting one's partner on the defensive and escalating a conflict situation.
3. *Be nonjudgmental*. Couples are taught not to judge how their partner feels or, in other words, not to be invalidating.
4. *Remember to listen*. Sometimes trauma-exposed individuals in particular have a difficult time just letting their partner "vent" when their partner expresses distress or concern. It is important for couples to understand that their partner does not always want their help to immediately "fix" the problem.

Following the discussion of group material, couples are given a form to use for practice assignment on which they are both asked to write down a feeling they expressed to their partner every day of the week (Appendix O). This exercise will be discussed every week for the remainder of the group and is intended to help couples practice more regularly sharing their feelings and to prevent avoidance of feelings expression.

Session 9. Communication Skills IV: Common Communication Traps

Couples first discuss the communication and feelings expression self-monitoring assignments. Then the group material focuses on four communication traps that undermine assertive communication. These traps are particularly salient for those who have experienced trauma, so it is important to discuss strategies to avoid falling into these traps. The communication traps discussed include the following:

1. *Generalizing*: making statements such as "you never" or "you always" instead of discussing one specific situation.
2. *Mind-reading*: assuming one knows what his or her partner is thinking or feeling. This is common in trauma-exposed couples because those who experience trauma often assume the worst when guessing their partner's intentions or feelings.
3. *The dump*: saving up all negative emotions and hurts and dumping them on one's partner all at once. This is more likely to occur in trauma-exposed couples when one or both couple members is avoidant and "stuffs" feelings until an explosion occurs.
4. *Dwelling on the negative*: focusing on only the negative aspects of one's partner and dwelling on his or her mistakes or weaknesses. Again, this negative focus is more common among those with trauma histories.

Session 10. Reviewing Treatment Gains and Planning for the Future

The final session focuses on processing changes made over the course of the group, potential barriers to continued change, and saying goodbye to the other couples. The goal of this session is to help couples to develop a realistic appraisal of the changes they have made and to help them identify areas needing continued attention and strategies for continuing this work after the group ends.

EVIDENCE FOR THE STRENGTH AT HOME COUPLES PROGRAM

We recently completed a research program funded by the Centers for Disease Control and Prevention (CDC) to examine the efficacy of Strength at Home Couples Program versus a supportive prevention group in returning male service members/veterans and their partners. During the first phase of this project, we finalized the manual for this intervention and piloted the intervention with couples. Results from nine couples suggested the effectiveness of Strength at Home Couples Program in preventing IPV relative to supportive prevention, although findings were tempered by low sample size. None of the participants engaged in physical IPV toward their female partner during the 3-month follow-up assessment after receiving the Strength at Home Couples intervention. Female partners receiving the intervention also evidenced reductions in physical IPV use, whereas female partners participating in the supportive prevention groups evidenced large increases in their physical IPV. Findings for psychological IPV were even stronger for the Strength at Home Couples intervention. There was a statistical trend suggesting that mild psychological IPV by both partners decreased more in the Strength at Home groups than the supportive prevention groups, and the effect sizes for these trends was large. Respectively, reductions in severe psychological IPV by both partners were moderate and large.

The second phase of the CDC project, the clinical trial phase, compared couples who participated in the Strength at Home Couples intervention with those who participated in supportive therapy. A total of 69 couples, or 138 individuals, participated in the clinical trial across two study sites. Analyses of data from the CTS2 (Straus et al., 1996) and the Multidimensional Measure of Emotional Abuse (Murphy & Hoover, 1999) showed lower psychological IPV at 6-month follow-up among those receiving Strength at Home Couples intervention relative to those receiving the supportive group intervention. Further, and importantly, both service members/veterans and partners in the supportive condition reported considerably more physical IPV relative to those in the Strength at Home Couples condition.

The Strength at Home Couples Program also evidenced superior outcomes when examining the proportion of service members/veterans (see Figure 10.1) and female partners (see Figure 10.2) who were classified as physically violent or nonviolent. The proportion of physically violent service members/veterans was similar in both conditions at Time 2 and Time 3, but at Time 4, the relative risk of physical violence by men assigned to Strength at Home Couples was .53 compared with those assigned to supportive prevention. The results were more pronounced when examining the proportion of physically violent female partners, which was lower in the Strength at Home Couples condition at every time point. The relative risk of physical violence at T4 for female partners assigned to Strength at Home Couples was .43 compared with those assigned to supportive prevention. The "number needed to treat" (NNT) to prevent physical violence at T4 was 5.26 for service members/veterans and 4.02 for female partners, which suggests that

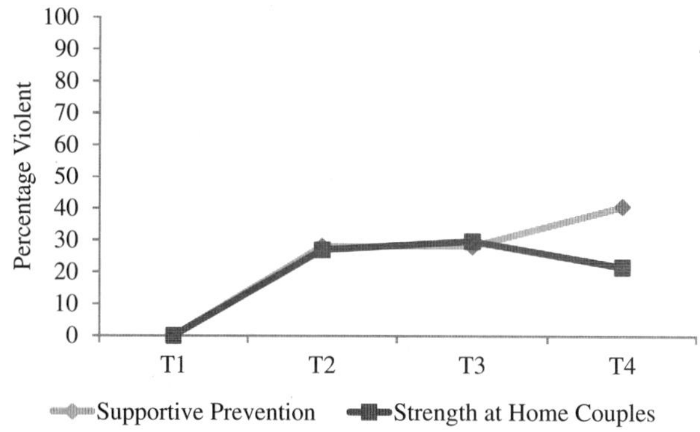

Figure 10.1. Percentage of physically violent veterans across time by treatment condition.

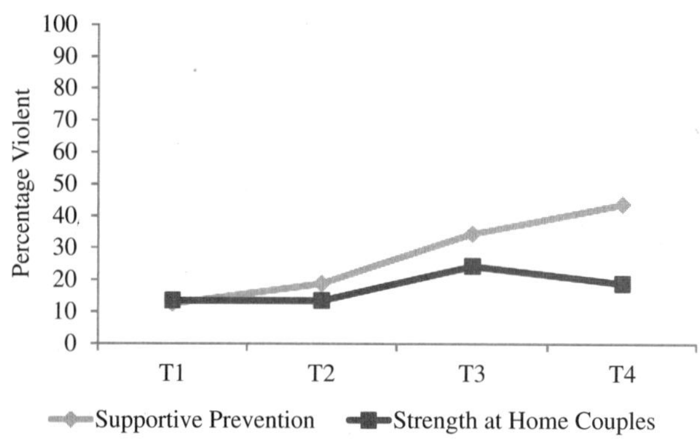

Figure 10.2. Percentage of physically violent partners across time by treatment condition.

Strength at Home Couples may provide a relatively efficient intervention strategy for preventing violence in both members of military dyads. Results from this study are available at the *Journal of Clinical Psychiatry* (Taft, Macdonald, Creech, Monson, & Murphy, 2015).

Finally, we recently published a study based on data from 70 veterans and their loved ones in a community-based implementation study using an adapted version of Strength at Home Couples to include friends and family members, funded by Blue Shield California Foundation (Hayes et al., 2015). Psychological IPV between dyads decreased significantly from baseline to postintervention and was sustained through follow-up. Interestingly, we also found reductions in depressive and PTSD symptoms for both veterans and their loved ones.

SUMMARY

The Strength at Home Couples group IPV prevention program is a 10-session cognitive behavioral intervention to prevent IPV before abusive patterns develop. This prevention program is based on a social information processing model of IPV and works to assist couples in enhancing their communication, improving their intimacy, and preventing the escalation of conflict situations through use of psychoeducational, skills-based, and dyadic strategies. Groups consist of couples and are therapy focused. We discussed the intervention session by session with a particular emphasis on trauma-relevant elements. Pilot studies and findings from a recent randomized controlled trial (Taft, Macdonald, et al., 2015) indicate that this program is effective in preventing and reducing IPV in relationships.

11

INDIVIDUAL INTERVENTIONS

Remarkably little has been written about individual treatments for individuals who engage in intimate partner violence (IPV) or about the ways in which trauma and traumatic stress reactions can be addressed in these treatments. For example, a recent review of the state of knowledge regarding interventions for partner-violent individuals identified 30 published studies that contained one or more intervention condition and a comparison or control group (Eckhardt et al., 2013). With the exception of three studies that delivered brief (1–2 session) motivational interventions in a one-on-one format (Kistenmacher & Weiss, 2008; Mbilinyi et al., 2011; Musser, Semiatin, Taft, & Murphy, 2008), none of the published studies provided individual treatment to IPV offenders. Despite the absence of research on the topic, our clinical experience indicates that individual (one-on-one) strategies can provide a useful tool in comprehensive efforts to treat individuals who engage in IPV.

http://dx.doi.org/10.1037/14918-012
Trauma-Informed Treatment and Prevention of Intimate Partner Violence, by C. T. Taft, C. M. Murphy, and S. K. Creech

MODELS OF INDIVIDUAL TREATMENT FOR INTIMATE PARTNER VIOLENCE

Sequential Treatment Models

Individual treatment can be delivered in several modalities—as an add-on to group treatment or as an alternative. Sequential models involve delivery of individual sessions before or after a standard group intervention in an effort to supplement, enhance, or extend the effects of group work. As a pregroup preparation approach, brief (1–2 session) motivational interventions delivered in a one-on-one format have been shown to reduce external responsibility attributions for aggression (Kistenmacher & Weiss, 2008), increase positive group behavior, enhance compliance with structured home assignments, and improve the therapeutic alliance in subsequent group treatment (Musser et al., 2008). These brief interventions use the principles and techniques of motivational interviewing (W. R. Miller & Rollnick, 2002). Therapists provide a high level of reflective listening to diffuse initial resistance and hostility toward treatment, give feedback on structured assessments, and facilitate client change planning. The primary goal is to help clients identify and articulate personal motivations for change and to facilitate a self-directed change process.

Individual sessions can also be delivered after the completion of group treatment. For some clients approaching the end of their time in group, the therapist may believe that further services are necessary to achieve or maintain nonviolence. In addition, some clients themselves express a need for ongoing treatment to continue work begun in group or to alleviate problems and concerns that were not sufficiently addressed in group. Individual treatment can provide an excellent context for continued work to consolidate, extend, and maintain the changes initiated during group. Some clients face considerable challenges in maintaining behavior change, including multiple life stressors and unresolved relationship conflicts. Although group interventions address a variety of concerns, some clients need additional assistance with specific problems that maintain elevated risk of abusive behavior. A brief case example appears in Exhibit 11.1.

In addition, some clients have more problems that are identified during group but that are not sufficiently addressed in the group context. Ongoing struggles with mood and emotion regulation, social anxiety, panic attacks, or persistent posttraumatic stress disorder (PTSD) symptoms, for example, may not be clearly understood or expressed prior to treatment. As clients develop closer bonds with group members and therapists, they often reveal difficulties that warrant continued treatment or active referral to adjunctive treatments after group. A brief case example is discussed in Exhibit 11.2.

EXHIBIT 11.1
Brief Case Example (John)

John was a friendly and engaged group member who often joked during sessions that he would like to fix his ex-partner up with another guy so she would leave him alone. In group, he reported significant violence around the time of their separation, including a conflict in which he punched her and one in which she attempted to run him over with her car. Near the end of group, John asked to meet individually with the therapist and requested help with panic attacks. Subsequent individual assessment revealed that John was experiencing anxiety and panic symptoms in response to (and anticipation of) frequent phone calls from his ex-partner. During these calls, she asked John to reunite and threatened to kill him if he refused. John was often denigrating, putting her down and calling her "crazy." Individual sessions focused on helping John to end his denigrating behavior, limit the duration and frequency of interactions with his ex-partner, and manage his anxiety through applied relaxation and cognitive restructuring.

Postgroup individual work usually begins with a review of the helpful components of group work, changes made, and targets for continued growth and change. One advantage of offering these services within the same context as group work for IPV is the ability to focus on the relationship-relevant manifestations of difficulties that require additional treatment. For example, a client may have panic symptoms that arise exclusively during interactions with an estranged relationship partner; suicidal thinking that arises from guilt, remorse, and rumination about one's abusive actions; or generalized problem avoidance in both relationship and non-relationship contexts.

For some clients with traumatic histories, postgroup work involves a shift from a trauma-informed care approach to providing trauma-specific services to directly address the trauma and its impact (Fallot & Harris, 2001). The psychoeducation and support provided in group can help some clients enhance their motivation to address posttraumatic stress reactions. In a number of such cases, we have observed favorable responses to the use of cognitive processing therapy (CPT) strategies (Resick & Schnicke, 1992), described in more detail later. As with other emotional and behavioral difficulties, this work can be done with enhanced sensitivity to relationship-relevant manifestations of posttraumatic stress.

Simultaneous Treatment Models

In contrast to sequential models, a less commonly used approach involves the simultaneous delivery of individual and group treatment sessions, typically through separate contacts each week. Our clinical experience indicates that this approach can be helpful for certain cases. Most notably, it is often prudent to increase supportive contact for individuals who present a high risk of danger to self or others. For such individuals, weekly group therapy may be helpful, but not fully sufficient, to address imminent concerns and resolve crises (e.g., acute responses to relationship separation or discovery of a partner's affair). These individual sessions typically involve provision of empathic support, a focus on helping the client to access or enhance social support from friends and family, and efforts to identify and change underlying catastrophic thinking and hopelessness. In

EXHIBIT 11.2
Brief Case Example (Julio)

Near the end of a standard community-based group intervention program, Julio indicated to his therapist that there were some important details of his life situation that he had not felt comfortable revealing in sessions. The therapist offered additional individual sessions after the completion of group. Julio described traumatic events behind his decision, 12 years earlier, to immigrate to the United States. Julio's family owned a successful business in a highly conflictual region in Latin America, and the family had become embroiled in an escalating conflict with corrupt local authorities. This situation eventuated in an armed confrontation that left Julio traumatized and racked with guilt and fear as he narrowly escaped being murdered and fled the country with his wife.

Although Julio continued to have intrusive memories, nightmares, and hyperarousal symptoms, other aspects of his life had been going well since he moved to the United States. However, he continued to avoid all contact with people from his home country. One day he came home early from work and heard his wife speaking on the phone using familiar slang from their home region. He confronted her angrily and became enraged on learning that she had been maintaining contact with old friends. Before the neighbors called the police, he smashed her phone and some personal belongings that she kept as reminders of their past.

Subsequent treatment used cognitive processing therapy (CPT) techniques to address Julio's PTSD symptoms and abusive behavior. These efforts began with an iterative review of Julio's trauma narrative and progressed to identify and reevaluate key themes related to his traumatic stress reactions and recent marital problems. Prominent themes relating to safety, security, betrayal, and mistrust were linked to the ongoing desire to control his wife's behavior and to avoid reminders of his traumatic past. Julio's PTSD symptoms declined substantially in response to these CPT interventions. He concluded that his wife's actions were not dangerous and accepted her efforts to maintain contact with old friends.

---

some instances, voluntary or involuntary hospitalization may be necessary to address imminent danger.

In addition to individual sessions to address danger and resolve crises, some clients need supportive case management to address problems that are not a focus of group work or that may be disruptive to group treatment. For example, a group therapist may not be able to effectively manage and monitor adjunctive service referrals for clients who require medication for a psychotic condition, bipolar disorder, or severe depression; clients who need intensive treatment for substance use disorders; or those who need assistance with housing, education, or employment support. Additional individual treatment sessions usually focus on structured problem solving to facilitate active service referrals, to identify and alleviate barriers to treatment, and to help clients maintain health behaviors (e.g., medication compliance) to promote stability. These efforts are not only helpful to the individual but also promote the integrity of group therapy by limiting distractions from the primary focus on trauma, relationships, and IPV.

Individual Treatment as an Alternative to Group

In addition to sequential or simultaneous treatment models, individual therapy is sometimes delivered as an alternative to group treatment for IPV. An individualized version of cognitive behavior therapy (CBT) for those who engage in IPV has been developed (Murphy & Eckhardt, 2005) and investigated in a preliminary trial that demonstrated similar outcomes to group CBT (Murphy, Meis, Clifford, Persampiere, & Eckhardt, 2008). This approach emphasizes case formulation to identify specific change targets and select intervention strategies for each client. Aspects of this treatment model and its application to trauma survivors are presented in the subsequent chapter.

GUIDELINES FOR RECOMMENDING INDIVIDUAL VERSUS GROUP TREATMENT

The controlled research to date on interventions for IPV use has almost exclusively used group-based treatment formats (Eckhardt et al., 2013). The main reasons for this involve presumed advantages of the group format that can be challenging to replicate in individual treatment. Although there are no hard-and-fast guidelines for recommending individual versus group treatment, both practical and clinical concerns can influence this decision. Practical concerns include work schedules that conflict with group meeting times and insufficient case flow to initiate or sustain group treatment. In addition, individual treatment can be provided on a short-term basis while clients are waiting for a group to form.

The provision of some individual sessions while clients are awaiting group is strongly encouraged in treating individuals who are at high risk of violence or have acute problems warranting immediate attention. It is also important to note that motivation to change may be relatively high when clients first present for services. While a client awaits group assignment, treatment motivation may be reduced by intervening changes in relationship status (i.e., separating or reuniting), legal disposition (e.g., dismissed charges or deferred prosecution), or levels of personal distress (e.g., reduction of acute shame associated with a recent incident of IPV). For some clients, the provision of individual sessions during this gap may help maintain treatment motivation by establishing a collaborative alliance. In addition, problems with group wait time can be largely circumvented by offering open-ended groups; however, most published treatment models and research studies use closed-ended formats to deliver interventions in a logical order.

In addition to practical concerns, individual treatment is sometimes recommended for clients with disruptive behavior or severe comorbid conditions that may threaten the integrity of a treatment group and may negatively affect others' treatment. One example involves the suspected use of alcohol or drugs prior to treatment sessions, including, in some cases, use of prescription drugs, such as opiate painkillers, that produce sedation and difficulty with attention and participation in group treatment. In addition, participants with psychotic symptoms, manic symptoms, or severe depression (especially if notable suicidal thinking is present) often require careful management in individual treatment to promote stabilization and determine appropriateness for group.

Depending on the specific concerns, individual treatment strategies can provide a constructive alternative for those who are not sufficiently stabilized to work well in a standard IPV group. As noted earlier, some require careful case management and referral to receive or adjust medications. If their condition stabilizes, these individuals may be good candidates for group. Others can benefit from supportive feedback and focused work to address behavioral concerns such as disruptive communication. Individual sessions can provide an in vivo context to identify problematic communication and teach and shape alternatives.

On occasion, a client will have to be switched from group to individual work because of an inability to stop talking, to pay sufficient attention to others in the group, or to inhibit frequent negative or disruptive behavior in the group. We recommend giving clients a few sessions to "settle in" to group before making this determination. Before removing a client from group, therapists should try both indirect strategies to deflect and redirect the group's attention away from disruptive group behavior and direct approaches to label and address disruptive group behavior. Some clients who are disruptive in group are more productive in individual therapy, although many continue to present significant interpersonal challenges in individual sessions.

In addition to potential group disruptions, individual work is sometimes indicated by specific clinical concerns. For example, some clients report areas of high sensitivity that they want to address in therapy but feel unable to discuss in a group setting. For male clients, histories of childhood sexual abuse or military sexual assault often fall into this category. In making such determinations, it is important to distinguish a focused need for individual treatment from a general desire to avoid group therapy, which many clients convey. Clients who request individual over group treatment are often avoiding the shame that may arise from public disclosure of their abusive actions. Some clients have distorted views about other group members, including exaggerated expectations about the level and nature of violence that others have engaged in (sometimes accompanied by minimization of the level and nature of one's abusive actions). These beliefs produce an assumption of difference and an expectation that it will be difficult to bond with and relate to other members of the group. Such expectations are rarely sustained once individuals can be encouraged to enter a group, especially if the therapist acknowledges that initial discomfort is normal and to be expected and gives clients permission not to self-disclose in group until they feel comfortable doing so. Thus, clients who are initially unwilling to disclose their difficulties and those who presume that they will not be able to identify with other group members should be distinguished from those who report problematic personal experiences of victimization that they feel unable to discuss in a group setting.

A final area of consideration for recommending individual treatment involves motivation and readiness to change. As noted earlier, clients who are initially unmotivated or resistant to change appear to benefit from brief individual work using motivational interviewing strategies (Murphy, Linehan, Reyner, Musser, & Taft, 2012; Musser et al., 2008). However, it is our clinical experience that such individuals can benefit greatly from subsequent opportunities for positive peer influence in group, and also that extended individual treatment without clear change goals is unproductive and frustrating for both therapist and client.

With clients who have more sufficient motivation to change, in contrast, individual treatment has some potential advantages to consider. Most notably, the individual therapist has flexibility to allocate considerably more time and attention to specific client problems (Murphy & Eckhardt, 2005). It is common in individual work to spend many sessions, or a portion of many sessions, focused on a specific change target. For example, many clients have specific problems with communication and problem solving, such as persistent avoidance of relationship problems; an arrogant, condescending, or judgmental tone of voice; or a paternalistic and overbearing style of interaction. Although such individuals are likely to receive feedback and encouragement to change such behaviors in group, an individual therapist can devote intense and sustained attention to such concerns, addressing them through in vivo examples that arise in sessions, repetitive role plays, and frequent review of life situations.

SUMMARY

Individual approaches to the treatment of IPV may be clinically indicated for some cases and may be necessary from a practical standpoint in some situations. Results from a small-scale randomized clinical trial suggested that structured group CBT may be more efficacious than a flexible, one-on-one version of CBT that relies on individualized case formulation (Murphy, Eckhardt, Clifford, LaMotte, & Meis, 2015). However, individuals with significant mental health or substance use problems, arguably the most likely to require individual treatment, were excluded from that trial. One-on-one treatment allows the therapist to provide interventions that are more specifically tailored to the individual client's concerns and problems, including the possibility of shifting from a trauma-informed care approach to provision of trauma-specific services. Individual treatment may be most helpful for clients who are motivated to change and need assistance with co-occurring disorders, specific relationship problems, and significant posttrauma reactions. In light of the potential for positive peer influence, the challenges presented by one-on-one therapy with treatment-resistant clients, and favorable initial data on the Strength at Home Men's group program (presented in Chapter 8, this volume), our general recommendations are to use a structured group approach as the primary treatment option for IPV among trauma survivors and to rely on individual strategies to supplement and extend group treatment. One-on-one treatment provides an alternative approach for individuals whose problems are not well addressed in the group format, those who display disruptive behavior in group, and those who have personal or clinical concerns that may distract fellow group members from productive work.

12

EXAMPLES OF INDIVIDUAL INTERVENTION

Given that clients vary substantially in the nature and severity of intimate partner violence (IPV), relationship problems, difficulties with emotion regulation, histories of trauma, posttraumatic symptoms, other life problems, and motivation to change, individual treatment does not follow a highly specified session-by-session format. The approach described here relies on case formulation of the individual's problems and flexible selection and implementation of common intervention strategies tailored to the client's specific needs.

The conceptual foundation for trauma-informed individual therapy for IPV relies on the social information–processing model described throughout this book. Treatment uses similar cognitive- and behavior-change strategies to promote relationship skill development. The group intervention strategies outlined elsewhere in the book can be selected and adapted to meet the client's most significant concerns and limitations. As in group work, the individual is provided education about the role of trauma in relationship problems

http://dx.doi.org/10.1037/14918-013
Trauma-Informed Treatment and Prevention of Intimate Partner Violence, by C. T. Taft, C. M. Murphy, and S. K. Creech

and is helped to identify relevant cognitive themes and behavioral difficulties. In addition to these trauma-informed intervention strategies, individual treatment can also provide trauma-focused therapy involving the analysis of trauma narratives and cognitive change strategies adapted from cognitive processing therapy (Monson, Resick, & Rizvi, 2014; Resick & Schnicke, 1992).

TREATMENT PHASES

Individual treatment with those who engage in IPV proceeds in phases that vary in length for different clients. An awareness of treatment phases can help the clinician to maintain clear goals and priorities. The phases are not rigidly distinct. There is often a gradual transition from one phase to the next. In a typical course of treatment lasting 4 to 6 months (roughly 16–25 sessions), not all clients progress through all of these treatment phases. For some clients, notably those with extensive life difficulties or comorbid conditions, such as borderline personality disorder, individual treatment may have to be extended well beyond the typical duration to promote lasting change in relationship functioning.

The first phase focuses on enhancing motivation to change, engaging the client into treatment, establishing a therapeutic alliance, and clarifying change goals. The primary intervention strategies involve empathic reflection, motivational interviewing to evoke client change talk, collaborative goal setting, and change planning. During assessment and this early phase of treatment, the therapist develops a case formulation to identify key targets for change. Important elements are shared with the client to promote a treatment alliance characterized by agreement on change goals and strategies to achieve and maintain behavior change.

The second phase focuses on safety and stabilization. Together, the therapist and client establish clear safety plans and strategies to prevent physical assault by managing reactions to difficult relationship events. The therapist and client engage in detailed review and analysis of relationship conflicts and moment-by-moment events associated with conflict escalation and IPV. Self-monitoring of ongoing relationship events and other emotional challenges and retrospective analysis of relationship conflicts and past abusive incidents are used to identify points of intervention. These key change points are used to help the client devise and implement alternative behaviors to prevent conflict escalation and abusive behavior. During this phase of treatment, many clients develop a safety and time-out plan, which is practiced and shared with the relationship partner. However, clinicians must be mindful that trauma survivors often use avoidance strategies to deal with relationship difficulties, and therefore, some clients may co-opt safety and time-out plans in the service of conflict avoidance. The therapist has to identify these tendencies and help the client develop clear alternatives, including the distress tolerance skills needed to hear and validate the partner's concerns. Typically, these relationship skills are addressed at length during the subsequent phase of treatment.

In addition to addressing strategies to maintain safety and promote nonviolent responses to relationship conflicts, during this early phase of treatment the therapist may also assist the client with problems that create instability in his or her life situation. Unemployment, work-related conflicts, problems with extended family, unstable housing arrangements, inconsistencies in medical care or medical compliance, and a variety of similar life problems often require clinical attention during the early phase of treatment. The most common intervention involves structured problem solving. The therapist helps the client to create a constructive mindset for approaching problems, to define problems accurately and constructively, to generate possible solutions, to evaluate and select alternatives, and to enact solutions and analyze their effectiveness (Nezu, Nezu, & D'Zurilla, 2012). Ideally, through this process, the client not only makes progress in addressing current life problems but also develops better problem solving for future challenges.

Clinical judgment is needed at this stage regarding problems that should be addressed immediately and problems that can be set aside to maintain focus on IPV and relationship enhancement. The general principle is to address problems that have a direct impact on relationship functioning and life instabilities that confer risk of conflict escalation. For example, serious challenges with housing or employment often create a high level of relationship stress that provides a frequent topic of conflict. The client's active efforts to resolve such problems can reduce tension, allowing for more productive relationship behavior change. In addition, the therapist's expressions of concern, encouragement of effective problem solving, and affirmation of client efforts and successes often enhance the therapeutic alliance and can promote client engagement and openness to change in other areas.

The third phase of treatment focuses on enhancement of relationship functioning. The therapist promotes cognitive change and the development of skills to support effective communication and problem solving. Whereas the strategies in Phase 2 focus on establishing safety and nonviolence in the immediate short term, the relationship skills addressed during Phase 3 are designed to provide a long-term antidote to IPV. Within the context of an individualized case formulation (discussed later), common treatment targets at this phase include increasing basic knowledge about intimate relationships, altering beliefs and assumptions that promote abusive behavior, altering other problematic relationship beliefs, and enhancing communication skills including listening, validation, emotional expression, assertiveness, negotiation, and compromise (Murphy & Eckhardt, 2005).

Finally, the fourth phase of individual treatment focuses on trauma recovery and relapse prevention. At this phase, therapy often shifts from a trauma-informed approach to a trauma-focused approach. Some clients make important changes in relationship functioning yet remain troubled by posttraumatic stress symptoms or stymied by entrenched posttraumatic beliefs that exert a negative impact on their relationships. For others, initial attempts to alter relationship beliefs and develop relationship skills are significantly impeded by posttraumatic stress symptoms, producing a need to shift to a trauma-focused approach before returning to address relationship skill development. Trauma-focused strategies are used to identify and alter beliefs that reflect over-accommodation to trauma, described in more detail next. In addition, at this later phase of treatment, all clients can benefit from relapse prevention strategies to consolidate gains and identify potential risks for a return to abusive behavior.

CASE FORMULATION

Whereas standard group treatment uses a general formulation of trauma-informed therapy for abusive clients, individual approaches lend themselves to more specific case formulation (Murphy & Eckhardt, 2005). Case formulation relies on careful assessment of the client's problems and strengths, identification of cognitions that promote or maintain abusive behavior, and development of hypotheses about the functions of abusive behavior.

The process of case formulation begins by assessing the forms, patterns, and frequency of emotional and physical IPV that the individual has used; the situational conditions under which IPV has occurred; and the immediate (short-term) and delayed (longer term) interpersonal consequences of IPV (both functional and problematic). This assessment of IPV is complemented by identifying the main areas or topics of conflict in the relationship and notable difficulties in communication and problem solving. In addition, other life difficulties are identified, which may include problems at work, difficulties with employment or housing, extended family issues, childrearing or co-parenting concerns, ongoing legal complications, health problems, mood and anxiety symptoms, substance use issues, and other emotional or psychological difficulties.

Through initial assessment and early treatment dialogues, the therapist also identifies cognitive factors, including attributions, assumptions, standards, and beliefs that are linked to controlling and abusive behavior, as well as cognitions associated with more general relationship difficulties and other life problems. Commonly, these cognitive factors include negatively biased assumptions about the partner's intentions (e.g., "She does those things just to piss me off"), unrealistic standards for the partner's behavior or relationship (e.g., "She should never do things that make me mad"; "We should never disagree"), and problematic underlying assumptions and beliefs (e.g., "Women [or men] cannot be trusted"; "I should be in control of my family"). Following the social information processing model, the therapist also evaluates the client's ability to generate nonabusive alternative behaviors—for example, by inquiring about different ways that someone might behave or respond in difficult relationship situations described by the client. These discussions also address the client's appraisal of the likely outcomes of different responses to relationship challenges, including unrealistic positive beliefs about the effects of controlling and abusive behaviors.

It is also important in case formulation to evaluate the client's strengths and resources. These often include personal motivations to change, previous successes in personal growth or behavior change, positive relationship behaviors, positive characteristics of the partner or relationship, constructive coping strategies, positive social supports, and other personal strengths and resources (e.g., resilience in the face of trauma). It is important to both affirm client strengths directly and to use them as a springboard for change. Clients are likely to experience initial success in therapy by building on existing strengths.

An initial case formulation typically includes hypotheses about the associations among various identified problems, hypotheses about the apparent functions of abusive behavior, and hypotheses about how cognitive factors influence the presenting problems. For example, a client's underlying belief that he must rely solely on himself and not trust others may be prominently manifested in relationship difficulties (e.g., failure to disclose feelings, hostile attributions about the partner's intentions, rejection of the partner's attempts to help), as well as other life difficulties (e.g., work problems due to an inability to trust that others will do their job, failure to seek needed health care). A situational analysis may reveal abusive behaviors (e.g., monitoring the partner's phone calls and e-mails, attempts to isolate the partner from other social contacts) and short-term consequences of IPV (e.g., the partner's attempts at reassurance that she is not cheating or interested in other guys). Together, this information supports a functional hypothesis that abusive and controlling behaviors are a problematic approach to maintain connection and prevent rejection in light of pervasive mistrust. This example case formulation links observed problem behaviors, both within and outside the relationship, to presumed functions and underlying schemas.

The next step is to develop a list of key intervention targets for behavioral and cognitive change. In the earlier example, these might include enhancement of specific skills in emotion regulation (e.g., distress tolerance associated with feelings of jealousy), communication (e.g., noncontrolling expression of emotions), reappraisal (e.g., reframing the partner's and coworkers' attempts to help), and response generation and selection (e.g., shift in the relative valuing of controlling vs. nonabusive responses to difficult emotions and relationship situations).

Case formulation also requires the therapist to select, adapt, and devise clinical change strategies, in consultation with the client, that are likely to alter the key change targets. For example, in the case outlined earlier, the therapist might use strategies such as self-monitoring, step-by-step review and analysis of difficult relationship events, mindfulness exercises to enhance tolerance of negative emotions, and carefully designed behavioral experiments to test out alternative behaviors. The therapist's goals are varied, but one key intention is to help the client become more aware of the underlying schemas driving the mistrust and controlling behaviors and to challenge and ultimately change these beliefs. Such work can also involve supportive exploration of the ways in which traumatic experiences helped to shape these beliefs and assumptions.

Finally, it is important to note that case formulation is an ongoing and dynamic process. New information is derived from ongoing client revelations and from observation and review of both successful and unsuccessful change efforts. The therapist and client work collaboratively to evaluate the effects of interventions and to adjust and alter change strategies when necessary. As treatment progresses, the client is encouraged to take more responsibility for prioritizing goals and applying the concepts and skills learned in treatment whereas the therapist provides less direction and more supportive coaching to refine these change efforts.

INITIAL TREATMENT PRIORITIES

Safety Concerns

In individual therapy it is helpful to prioritize treatment targets. Safety issues always take top priority. Individual sessions should begin with a quick check-in regarding any adverse relationship incidents that occurred following the previous session and, when relevant for the individual, any ongoing suicidal thinking or intentions to harm others. A careful analysis of adverse interactions is used to identify points at which the client could exercise self-control strategies and to generate and discuss alternative response options. These discussions typically also use cognitive strategies to identify and alter problematic beliefs associated with conflict escalation. When necessary, more extensive safety planning is conducted to help the client commit to a nonviolent course of action, which may include contacting help lines and going to an emergency room if necessary. For such cases, it is usually helpful to schedule one or more phone check-ups between treatment sessions to follow up on the safety plan.

Behaviors That Undermine Treatment

Following the logic and strategies developed for dialectical behavior therapy (Linehan, 1993), the second priority for treatment is the identification and labeling of client behaviors that are likely to undermine treatment or preclude the client from receiving much-needed services. Logically, a therapist is unable to help a client who cannot maintain the treatment relationship. Common problems include practical barriers (e.g., work schedules, child care, transportation), problems with fees, and complicating issues such as untreated substance use problems. Some clients frequently show up late or at the wrong time for sessions, have no strategy for organizing their schedules (e.g., no calendar), or display a general tendency to prioritize other activities over treatment. The latter pattern is surprising yet relatively common among clients who are court mandated and who may face significant legal consequences for noncompliance.

In an effort to be supportive, many therapists are insufficiently proactive in identifying and addressing treatment-undermining behaviors. When these problems are eventually addressed, such therapists often invoke rules or punishments and may appear frustrated or critical of the client. The better approach is to address attendance and collaborative work explicitly from the outset of treatment and to let clients know in advance that the therapist will be attentive to any client decisions or actions that may prevent clients from getting the help they need, and to promote open discussion and problem solving, the therapist will address such concerns with clients as soon as they are identified. For example, we have found that many clients are unwilling to discuss their schedule challenges with work supervisors and, therefore, miss treatment sessions because of unscheduled overtime or other unpredictable work demands. However, with encouragement and support from the therapist to address these issues, we have found that many clients report that their work supervisors were supportive and willing to make adjustments to help them complete treatment.

Life Stabilization

Many clients have unstable residential, work, relationship, or other life situations that make it challenging to initiate or sustain the focus on personal behavior change. Focused problem solving can be helpful in the early stages of therapy to facilitate progress in these areas. Such efforts also convey the therapist's concern for the client's well-being and can be important in the effort to establish a strong therapeutic alliance. Typically, the clinical focus on life-stabilization concerns will not require all the time or attention of individual sessions but may require some intense focus at the outset of treatment followed by regular updates and check-ins to assist in these areas.

Some clients need assistance with education, employment, or housing. The therapist may help by discussing cognitive barriers, specifically beliefs that limit the client's perceived options. For example, some clients are unwilling to consider a wider range of employment or career options despite their challenges in maintaining a specific type of employment. Traditional strategies to uncover and explore underlying cognitive assumptions can be helpful. For example, clients may believe that their personal worth or value is compromised if they take a lower paying job after an extended period of unemployment, or they may lack self-efficacy for undertaking a new educational or career opportunity. These problems, particularly extended unemployment, often contribute significantly to relationship distress and may be a frequent topic of conflict.

In addition to exploration and focused problem solving around life challenges, therapists often refer clients for assistance with these problems. It is essential for therapists to be aware of key community resources. Examples include career counseling (which may be offered for free at community colleges), employment support, temporary shelter, food assistance, housing assistance, low-cost health care, and assistance obtaining health insurance. Low-cost options for psychiatric evaluation, substance use services, and self-help groups such as Alcoholics Anonymous and Narcotics Anonymous are also important resources for some clients. Many who engage in IPV have considerable difficulty asking for or receiving help. Therefore, it is essential for the clinician to go beyond simply providing referral information to also assist the client in creating a feasible plan to seek and obtain assistance and to explore potential barriers that may arise. For example, it is often helpful to have a willing client make a phone call with the therapist present or for the therapist to facilitate direct contact with other providers.

Clients often have difficulty requesting emotional or material support from family members or friends. In some cases, clients are estranged from relatives because of long-standing family dysfunction or the client's own expressions of anger and hostility. In addition, many abusive clients have isolated their partners from family and friends through controlling expressions of jealousy and insecurity or by creating rifts and loyalty conflicts when others attempt to help or question the partner's decision to remain in the abusive relationship. In many instances, however, family and friends are willing to assist a client who is unwilling to ask for help. It is important for the clinician to explore relevant details with the client to determine whether and how others might be willing and able to assist with life instabilities.

For example, one client was out of work and needed $100 to renew a driver's license that had lapsed while he was in jail. After discussing the situation with the therapist, the client decided to ask his mother for the money and learned that she was much happier providing a loan than constantly driving him to appointments and job interviews. Another client was ashamed to tell his family that his wife had obtained a protection order and that he was sleeping in his car rather than asking to stay at his brother's house. As noted earlier, life challenges often contribute to therapy-interfering behaviors, such as when a client is unwilling to discuss mandatory treatment attendance with a work supervisor or is unwilling to ask for assistance with transportation to attend sessions.

For many clients, instabilities in various areas of life trace back to their abusive relationship behaviors. Time in jail causes loss of employment. A criminal record makes it difficult to get job interviews. A stay-away order creates housing challenges. Knowledge or observation of abuse alienates friends and family. It can be helpful for clients to acknowledge these negative consequences in light of a long-term commitment to end IPV and establish healthier relationship patterns.

One of the most common areas of concern that affects both life stabilization and safety involves relationship separations. Some clients need assistance to accept the partner's request for separation, to avoid pressuring the partner to reunite, to identify and alter monitoring or stalking behaviors, or to ultimately accept the fact that a relationship has ended. To address such concerns, the therapist has to maintain empathic attention to the client's distress while remaining firm in promoting safety. It is common for clients to verbalize problematic perspectives on relationship separation, including highly catastrophic views. In addition to jealousy, these cognitions may contain cultural beliefs about gender roles (e.g., "Only the man has a right to decide whether or not to end a relationship"), religious beliefs (e.g., "Divorce is a sin, and I am trying to prevent my wife from being punished by God"), a fantasized view of the relationship (e.g., "She's the only one for me"; "We are soul mates"), and personal inadequacies (e.g., "I'll never find another partner"; "This means she never loved me"). Pursuit and stalking behaviors are often driven by obsessional thinking, and many clients dismiss or minimize the threatening nature of these acts and the fact that they often backfire and push partners further away.

COMMON FEATURES OF INDIVIDUALIZED RELATIONSHIP SKILL TRAINING FOR TRAUMA SURVIVORS

Among the most common problem areas identified in case formulation involves a lack of assertive self-expression. Trauma is often associated with an avoidant pattern of coping, which leads clients to favor unassertive options. As a result, clients perceive only two choices to relationship disagreements: passive avoidance or aggressive dominance. Many fear assertive handling of problems because they believe that any effort at self-assertion will lead to conflict escalation and the potential for violence. Negative assumptions about the need for, and value of, assertive self-expression must be addressed before other communication and relationship skills can make any sense to clients. For example, negotiation, compromise, and even active listening and validation will be distorted and often ineffective outside of a relational context in which both partners have a role in finding solutions to their disagreements and problems.

Thus, this phase of treatment often begins with psychoeducation about relationships. As a common homework assignment, we ask clients to list common qualities of healthy and unhealthy relationships, along with personal challenges and barriers to healthy relationships. Some clients provide fantasized views in which partners rarely disagree, one partner always goes along with the others' wishes, or love conquers all challenges. Many clients provide a list of desired relationship qualities, such as love, trust, caring, and support, but have limited experience with these relationship qualities and limited understanding of the relationship processes that promote (or erode) positive qualities. Interestingly, relatively few clients consider factors such as the importance of give and take, the need for compromise, and the ability to openly discuss differences and negotiate solutions as key features of a healthy relationship. Through exploration and education, clients often develop motivation to learn and practice these new ways of relating.

In working with trauma survivors, relationship skills training is typically interwoven with efforts to enhance emotion regulation. Many clients need enhanced distress tolerance skills to engage productively in problem discussions with a partner. In these cases, intervention strategies can be used to promote emotion labeling and emotional awareness and to reduce emotional avoidance through acceptance and mindfulness exercises. In addition, the logic of exposure therapy is often part of relationship skill training for trauma survivors. For example, the therapist and client may design exposure exercises that involve listening to a partner's concerns without tuning out, leaving the conversation, or dominating the conversation. This approach is particularly helpful for clients who are struggling to tolerate reminders of their own abusive actions and how they have hurt the partner or other loved ones.

Relationship skill training is also interwoven with cognitive restructuring of problematic assumptions and beliefs. Many of the hostile attributions described elsewhere in this volume, for example, make it difficult if not impossible to engage in active listening or to validate a partner's feelings. Trauma survivors often interpret any negative expression by a partner as intentional and harmful and need assistance reframing these expressions as concerns or requests with benign or positive intentions. A common example occurs when a partner's negative view of a client's dangerous or risky behaviors (e.g., excessive drinking) is interpreted as control rather than concern. Another common example is the belief that outcomes and choices have to go one person's way. Efforts to compromise make little sense if this view is not changed to allow for give and take and the possibility of solutions that are not entirely determined by one partner.

TRAUMA-FOCUSED INDIVIDUAL THERAPY STRATEGIES

The later phase of individual treatment for some clients involves a shift to a trauma-focused approach. Cognitive processing therapy (CPT; Monson et al., 2014; Resick & Schnicke, 1992) provides an excellent conceptual foundation for addressing traumatic reactions in clients who engage in IPV. This approach focuses on the cognitive responses to trauma, specifically the problems that arise from efforts to create consistency between traumatic experiences and important beliefs about self, others, and the world. In earlier chapters we illustrated how trauma-induced alterations in information processing can be manifested as difficulties in intimate relationships that increase risk of IPV. CPT provides important intervention strategies to focus treatment on cognitive distortions about traumatic events and distorted interpersonal beliefs that arise from traumatic exposures. These interventions are consistent with the trauma-informed group strategies outlined in Chapter 8. However, the individual treatment format allows the therapist to provide more extensive trauma-focused interventions that are specifically tailored to the client's unique cognitive manifestations of trauma and the negative effects of these beliefs on their intimate relationships.

Addressing Posttraumatic Anger and Guilt

Although the diagnostic formulation of posttraumatic stress disorder (PTSD) focuses primarily on anxiety-based symptoms (hyperarousal, avoidance, and reexperiencing), many trauma survivors experience significant anger and anger-related shifts in cognition. In addition, significant guilt, shame, and unrealistic appraisals of personal responsibility are also common.

Partner-abusive clients often display posttraumatic anger and guilt in the relative absence of anxiety-based symptoms that form the diagnostic framework for PTSD. Histories of witnessed and/or experienced abuse in childhood, in particular, often produce complex reactions involving anger, mistrust, guilt, and fears of abandonment. These intense relationship experiences are typically linked to assimilated distortions of traumatic childhood memories and over-accommodated beliefs that justify coercion, manipulation, and aggression in relationships.

The cognitive underpinnings of these reactions can be subtle and complex. For example, many abusive clients with a history of childhood victimization reinterpret these traumatic experiences as discipline, expressing the belief that the caregiver was responding in a justifiable way to the client's misbehavior and negative attitude. At the outset, many such clients will express ideas such as "I deserved it," "I learned my lesson not to do that again," or "All kids need to get whipped once in a while." Closer inspection of events through detailed recollection or through the analysis of written or oral trauma narratives often reveals that these appraisals reflect distorted memories and distorted interpretations of childhood experiences. For example, the adult's aggression was not always disciplinary in nature, was far more intense than normal punishment, occurred at nonnormative ages (e.g., when the client was very young or adolescent), was part of a general pattern of aggression and violence in the household, caused negative emotional reactions that have nothing to do with discipline, and/or was not actually effective in altering misbehavior. In addition, these appraisals of normalcy and disciplinary intent may function to protect against feelings of vulnerability, powerlessness, and betrayal by providing the client with a sense that the traumatic events were under their personal control and preventable.

Similar distortions are also often found with respect to histories of witnessed abuse. For example, it is common for clients to express the belief that they should have been able to stop or prevent the abuse of their mother, even though a more objective analysis may reveal that the client was very small, afraid, and entirely ill-equipped to stop one adult from harming another. It is also relatively common for clients to claim that they did, in fact, stop the abuse of their mother by threatening or beating up a father figure and to claim that this effort was completely effective in ending the abuse. Such events are typically recalled with a sense of righteous indignation and with little or no recollection of the other complex emotions and events that preceded and ensued from this traumatic scene. Once again, these assimilated memories and interpretations help to maintain a sense of controllability and predictability over traumatic aspects of one's family history.

Many assimilated recollections of traumatic childhood events also support positive appraisals of interpersonal aggression. A common belief among abusive clients is that people get what they deserve or what they have coming to them (i.e., the belief in a just world). This notion is strongly linked to the idea that one's own maltreatment, or the maltreatment of others in the family, was justifiable and effective. In turn, these beliefs are used to justify aggressive and violent reactions to interpersonal situations in which someone is judged to have wronged the abusive client. Thus, aggression is deemed important for teaching the other person a lesson, preventing future wrongs, and correcting a perceived injustice. From the perspective of social information processing (Crick & Dodge, 1994), these abuse-justifying schemas and scripts play a prominent role in the database of stored social knowledge that is referenced during ongoing social information processing. These beliefs heighten the suspicious appraisal of others' negative and harmful intentions, shift the response generation and selection processes toward aggressive options, and promote a favorably distorted appraisal of the correctness and effectiveness of aggressive responses to interpersonal problems.

It is important to note that these themes paint complex relationship-relevant reactions to trauma with broad brushstrokes. Some clients have idiosyncratic and unexpected interpretations of traumatic experiences, along with unique resulting beliefs that are manifested in relationship problems and abusive actions. For example, one individual expressed the belief that he was not abused because he spent most of his childhood locked in a basement with a sibling. He indicated that his parents had little opportunity to harm him because they almost never interacted with him. Another client who was sexually abused as a child by an older married woman in the neighborhood developed the belief that women need sex constantly or they will wander. As a result, he made coercive demands for sex from his partner in a misguided attempt to prevent her from cheating on him. A client who emigrated from his home country after a violent confrontation with corrupt police officers developed intense suspicions about his partner's communications, spent a lot of time monitoring her interactions, and smashed her computer when he learned that she had been e-mailing friends from their home country.

Clients often surprise the therapist with their selection of the most traumatic event to use as the subject of a trauma narrative. For example, a client who experienced and witnessed severe physical abuse over an extended period selected the moment when he was removed from the home by child protective services as the index traumatic event. Careful analysis revealed core themes of betrayal because the client was removed for attacking an abusive parent who the rest of the family protected by lying to the authorities. Another client who had experienced years of neglect from drug-dependent parents identified as an index trauma the moment when he discovered his teenage girlfriend smoking pot with his parents. Further analysis revealed how this event was related to intense guilt and anger over his girlfriend's subsequent addiction to heroin and cocaine and to the many years during which the client used supportive, coercive, and abusive strategies in an attempt to get her to stop using drugs.

Addressing Traumatic Reactions to One's Own Violent Actions

Quite often, clients identify their own violent or criminal behavior as an important traumatic event. Some display notable posttraumatic symptoms, including intrusive memories, nightmares, and extensive efforts to avoid cues that stimulate recollection of these events. In such cases, the violent act is experienced as highly inconsistent with core beliefs about the self, creating dissonance between positive self-appraisals and the realities of one's own harmful behavior. Clients often struggle to resolve these incongruences by creating distorted recollections of events that place blame on others (e.g., the partner) for one's own abusive and violent actions and/or by altering self-appraisals to acknowledge that one is a dangerous, harmful, and bad person. These experiences are also often confounded by the sense of loss, guilt, and anger that result when the partner ended the relationship in response to the IPV. In fact, struggles with personal responsibility, shame, anger, blame, and positive versus negative self-beliefs are common cognitive themes for many partner-abusive clients and are highly notable when individuals display posttraumatic reactions to their own violent behavior.

Cognitive Behavioral Interventions to Address Posttraumatic Beliefs and Behaviors

The identification, clarification, and exploration of cognitive consequences of trauma and their manifestations in relationship problems provide important first steps in trauma-focused work with partner-abusive individuals. Many clients initiate cognitive and behavioral change as they uncover the links between traumatic events and relationship problems. However, these insights are not always sufficient to guide change, and therefore, additional cognitive and behavioral strategies are needed to alter IPV-maintaining beliefs and to shape nonabusive alternative behaviors. Thus, analysis of trauma narratives, more general clinical dialogue about traumatic exposures, and/or focused consideration of common relationship-relevant posttraumatic cognitions produce targets for further cognitive and behavior change efforts, with further efforts based on intervention strategies detailed elsewhere in this and other sources (e.g., Murphy & Eckhardt, 2005).

Once they are uncovered and clarified, the restructuring of problematic beliefs proceeds within a collaborative process involving rational and logical analysis, comparison of assumptions to evidence and data, appraisal of alternative interpretations and beliefs, and construction of behavioral experiments to test assumptions (Murphy & Eckhardt, 2005). Judicious use of humor, self-disclosure, and metaphor are often helpful in these efforts. In addition, the functional consequences of various beliefs are often used as a heuristic guide—for example, the functional consequences of assuming that a relationship partner engaged in an ambiguous act with good versus bad intentions.

These cognitive change efforts typically uncover behavioral deficits that require clinical attention. For example, a client may lack the emotion language and communication skill needed to express gratitude, concern, desires, personal vulnerabilities, or remorse in a nonthreatening and noncoercive fashion. Traumatic childhood events are often accompanied by invalidation experiences that produce manipulative and dramatic efforts to communicate needs and emotions (Linehan, 1993). Conflict avoidance, poor problem solving, or an obsessive need for organization and control are common targets of exposure and behavior change in individual treatment of abusive clients. A brief case example is provided in Exhibit 12.1.

SUMMARY

Individual strategies can be used before or after standard group interventions. Pregroup one-on-one sessions can be helpful in enhancing motivation to change and engagement in subsequent group work. Motivational interviewing can be delivered in a brief (1–3 session) format and may benefit from the inclusion of structured assessment feedback to help clients identify difficulties with PTSD symptoms, anger, emotional and physical IPV, and relationship difficulties. After group treatment, individual strategies can be used to address problems that were not sufficiently ameliorated by the group treatment experience, to provide additional trauma-focused work, and to extend and maintain gains established during group treatment.

In addition, individual treatment can be delivered as an alternative to group. There are practical reasons why this may be necessary, including inadequate case flow to form groups and client work schedules that preclude group attendance. In addition, there are clinical reasons to consider recommending individual services. Some clients have other disorders or disruptive behaviors that require careful management in individual treatment. Others request assistance dealing with traumatic experiences that they are not currently able or willing to discuss in a group context. Some may need assistance with educational services, employment support, or housing. For many such clients, individual sessions focused on supportive case management can be provided in addition to group to help address these difficulties.

EXHIBIT 12.1
Brief Case Example

Background
Glenn, a 30-year-old African American man, indicated during the initial treatment session that he was experiencing a high level of stress in his family situation. Glenn had been married for 4 years and had two young daughters. He reported that his wife had a history of prescription drug abuse and, after a lengthy period of sobriety, had relapsed several months before his referral incident. Glenn expressed serious concerns about the well-being of their young children and the future of his marriage. He had been arrested after locking his wife in their bedroom for 2 days and assaulting a man who had been supplying her with drugs. Although he reported mixed feelings about assaulting the man, Glenn conveyed remorse about his controlling behavior toward his wife and expressed a desire to find more constructive ways to deal with the challenges in his family situation.

Establishing Treatment Goals
Early sessions focused on motivation to change and collaborative goal setting. Glenn consistently emphasized the importance of being a responsible father, a committed husband, and a provider for his family. The therapist affirmed these strongly held values and used a high level of empathic reflection to convey understanding of Glenn's stress level and the challenges posed by his partner's substance abuse. The initial goals for treatment included helping Glenn to formulate and enact noncoercive strategies to cope with his partner's substance use, improving Glenn's ability to manage stress and enhancing his supportive communication skills, including assertive communication. In addition, the therapist agreed to help Glenn enhance his positive parenting skills and increase his work attendance to maintain employment.

Trauma-Informed Elements of Case Conceptualization
Treatment began with a detailed analysis of conflict situations and Glenn's use of controlling and coercive strategies, examining the associated contextual factors, thoughts, emotions, behaviors, and behavioral consequences. The therapist provided an overview of assertive communication and nonabusive strategies for emotion expression and reviewed supportive behavioral strategies to encourage help-seeking in substance-dependent spouses (W. R. Miller, Meyers, & Tonigan, 1999). As is common in individual treatment for this population, the intervention focus shifted between behavioral skill development and cognitive restructuring. Glenn's efforts to enact supportive communication strategies were often impeded by intense and complex emotions, including anger at his wife, fear regarding the safety of his wife and children, and anxiety about losing his family. The therapist helped Glenn articulate these emotions while affirming his deep investment in maintaining his marriage and family.

During this process, Glenn revealed that his parents had been addicted to drugs throughout his childhood, leading to many adversities and several traumatic experiences, including witnessed assaults in his home. Despite these early adversities, Glenn reported that the most painful experience was being removed from the home after his father left the family and his mother was deemed unfit to care for him. His mother's functioning had continued to decline after that, and Glenn reported intense guilt over not having been present to help her. The therapist helped Glenn explore how his early experiences produced cognitive themes related to safety and trust and helped him draw connections to his controlling relationship behaviors. These interventions were intended to help him identify and reduce trauma-related cognitive distortions, including catastrophic thinking (e.g., "If my marriage ends, my children will have no father"), and a desire for control (e.g., "I have to force my wife to stop using drugs").

We recommend the use and adaptation of CPT strategies as the primary means to conduct trauma-focused work with survivors who engage in IPV. Although the specific experiences and cognitive responses to trauma are unique to each individual, there are also some common themes related to posttraumatic anger, guilt, and the justification of aggression that are observed in this population. Treatment may include the use of trauma narrative analysis and identification of cognitive assimilations and accommodations to resolve inconsistencies between traumatic experiences and the client's belief system. In addition, traditional cognitive restructuring approaches are used to address trauma-influenced beliefs associated with relationship problems. These cognitive efforts typically also uncover behavioral deficits in communication, problem solving, and conflict avoidance that can be addressed using behavioral skills training.

13

ADJUNCTIVE INTERVENTIONS

Some concomitant mental health and behavioral problems, or comorbidities, may complicate treatment for intimate partner violence (IPV) and limit success in efforts to end the violence. To most effectively prevent and treat IPV, it is important to consider the client's full psychosocial picture. This may include their housing status, occupational status, literacy and education, parenting, injury and physical health status, and psychiatric status. Perhaps the most challenging professional service needs for community IPV programs involve major psychiatric disorders, substance abuse, and traumatic brain injury (TBI), which are discussed in the following sections. Although no comorbid problem can be thought of as a "cause" of IPV, a number of comorbidities appear to be associated with increased IPV risk and may require intervention beyond the IPV intervention.

http://dx.doi.org/10.1037/14918-014
Trauma-Informed Treatment and Prevention of Intimate Partner Violence, by C. T. Taft, C. M. Murphy, and S. K. Creech

In examining services for comorbid problems, it is important to distinguish between adjunctive and concomitant service approaches (Murphy, Meis, & Eckhardt, 2009). We encourage providers to distinguish between difficulties that are likely to impede or prevent the success of IPV treatment from difficulties that warrant advice for adjunctive help but are unlikely to affect treatment success. In a *concomitant service approach*, the individual or team providing the IPV treatment uses additional treatment strategies and/or additional treatment sessions to address the comorbid condition. In an *adjunctive approach*, the IPV treatment provider refers the individual to a different treatment provider to address the comorbid condition. In some instances, both approaches are used—for example, by providing assessment and brief motivational treatment for substance use problems as a concomitant service and then referring individuals with severe problems for more thorough substance use services as an adjunctive treatment.

For court-mandated intervention, with conditions that are likely to impede the success of IPV counseling, it may be helpful to require that individuals receive services for these problems to remain eligible for participation in IPV intervention (Murphy et al., 2009). Providers should either offer such services directly, if possible, or actively facilitate appropriate referrals and monitoring compliance and progress. With comorbid problems that may impede functioning but may not directly hinder IPV intervention effectiveness, adjunctive services can be recommended but not required.

Intervention for comorbid problems can also vary in intensity (Murphy et al., 2009). Some clients may benefit from reasonable but more moderate clinical attention for problems that do not pose serious risk of IPV recidivism or other major impairment. For example, when unhealthy or risky patterns of substance use are present although the individual does not meet criteria for substance abuse or dependence, a brief intervention to facilitate motivational readiness for change may invoke less resistance than a more extensive treatment program.

Trauma is associated with a range of problems, and discussion of adjunctive interventions for all of them is beyond the scope of this book. We focus on the primary problems that may co-occur and that may need adjunctive intervention. Specifically, we discuss adjunctive interventions for posttraumatic stress disorder (PTSD), depression, substance use problems, and TBI. In addition to these problems, evidence of psychotic thought processes, including paranoid delusions or disorganized thinking, should be addressed carefully prior to initiation of IPV intervention services. Similarly, symptoms of bipolar disorder are important to assess and address because IPV sometimes occurs in the context of manic agitation.

ADJUNCTIVE INTERVENTIONS FOR POSTTRAUMATIC STRESS DISORDER

A question that we are often asked is whether effectively treating PTSD in trauma-exposed individuals would lead to a cessation of their violent behavior because PTSD and IPV are so highly correlated. To date, no research that we are aware of has examined this question, so we can only offer our best educated guess based on our clinical experience with this population. It is likely that for some individuals, once they have fully processed their trauma and worked through stuck points in the areas of trust, power and control, intimacy, and self-esteem, their relationships will improve and IPV risk will decrease. However, it is extremely difficult to successfully treat and end IPV in those with PTSD without directly addressing the abusive behavior itself and working with the client to promote accountability and become more skillful in identifying and correcting negative thinking styles. Often the most treatment resistant clients are those with severe trauma histories and PTSD that require greater attention; that is, it is challenging to assist a client in ending their hostile attributions of ambiguous events if they have severe PTSD that is triggered across a range of stimuli in their natural environment.

Trauma-focused IPV intervention often serves as an entry point for PTSD intervention in our clients. Clients in IPV intervention who explore links between their traumatic experiences in childhood and adulthood and their links with their anger and relationship problems often realize that they have to delve deeper into their issues to truly get relief. If done well, trauma-focused IPV intervention can assist clients in recognizing the role that trauma has played in their lives and uncovers specific areas that require more intensive clinical focus than may be possible in the IPV intervention context.

Adjunctive interventions for PTSD may be delivered in multiple formats and take different approaches, though cognitive behavioral interventions for PTSD have been demonstrated to be the most effective, and psychological treatments are more efficacious than drug therapies (Keane, Marshall, & Taft, 2006). Basic anxiety management therapy uses cognitive and behavioral strategies to enhance client capacity to manage emotions associated with PTSD. Such skills might include relaxation training, breathing retraining, trauma education, guided self-dialogue, and cognitive restructuring.

Exposure therapies have been widely studied and disseminated and are highly effective (Taylor, 2004). At its most basic level, exposure therapy for PTSD involves guiding the client through a vivid remembering of the trauma until extinction of the traumatic memory occurs. These exposures can be directly connected to the situation or place that evokes the anxiety or imaginally by presenting cues and imagery to evoke the event to the greatest degree possible. The goal of exposures in PTSD intervention is to reduce avoidance and promote mastery of the memory.

Cognitive processing therapy (Resick & Schnicke, 1992) uses elements of exposure therapy and also incorporates a cognitive component that focuses on *stuck points*, or core themes for which the client may be experiencing difficulties working through. The exposure component of the intervention involves writing and reading about the traumatic event. The cognitive therapy component involves addressing key cognitive distortions resulting from the trauma, particularly in the areas of safety, trust, power and control, self-esteem, and intimacy. As discussed throughout this volume, these are core themes or schemas that may be affected by trauma and that may underlie trauma difficulties. Moreover, difficulties in each of these areas may underlie relationship difficulties and problems with anger and IPV. For this reason, cognitive processing therapy may be especially useful for working with trauma-exposed individuals with PTSD who engage in IPV (Murphy & Eckhardt, 2005). Interestingly, a recent study of this therapy found that the cognitive component of the treatment alone worked as well in treating PTSD as the full treatment package, suggesting that working through these stuck points may be the key to the effectiveness of this intervention (Resick et al., 2008).

ADJUNCTIVE INTERVENTIONS FOR DEPRESSION

Depressive symptoms are common in trauma-exposed individuals who engage in IPV, and our research shows that there is considerably greater risk of IPV when one has both PTSD and depression than when one has only one of these diagnoses (Taft et al., 2005). Abusive clients should be assessed for suicidal ideation and other common aspects of depression at every initial assessment and periodically thereafter. Men in treatment for IPV often display mild to moderate depressive symptoms associated with relationship conflict and real or feared separation from the partner. When these depressive experiences are clearly linked to the relationship problems, treatment addressing IPV and relationship skill enhancement often alleviates these temporary depressive reactions. Participation in a supportive group atmosphere may also be an important aspect of this process.

It is also important to note that treatment with SSRI medications has shown some initial promise in reducing IPV (George et al., 2011) and anger problems (Kamarck et al., 2009). Common cognitive behavioral strategies to treat depression and stress-related symptoms can be helpful as a concomitant (or integrated) feature of treatment for abusive men. Cognitive interventions designed to target social information processing deficits and cognitive distortions can assist clients in viewing their situations and others in a more positive light. Strategies to identify negative or hostile thought patterns and replace them with more positive interpretations are vital to effective IPV prevention from a social information processing perspective and are also key to cognitive behavioral treatment for depression (Beck, 1979).

Behavioral activation to promote daily functioning, participation in pleasurable activities, and a sense of mastery can also be helpful for men who are acutely deactivated by their negative mood state (Dimidjian et al., 2006). In addition, problems accepting that a relationship has ended or difficult and inhibited grieving for other losses are also common targets for supportive interventions with this population.

ADJUNCTIVE INTERVENTIONS FOR SUBSTANCE USE PROBLEMS

Findings suggest a co-occurrence rate of substance use problems and IPV in clinical populations of over 50% (see Thomas, Bennett, & Stoops, 2013), and this rate is likely even higher among those exposed to significant trauma. Those who engage in IPV and also have substance use problems are more violent (Thomas et al., 2013) and present a challenge to those working to prevent and end the IPV.

Social information processing models have been used and evaluated to explain associations between substance use and IPV. For example, the empirically supported alcohol myopia model (Steele & Josephs, 1990) holds that effortful cognitive processes are impaired during acute alcohol consumption, resulting in attention biases that negatively affect one's ability to perceive and process relevant social cues (see Giancola, Josephs, Parrott, & Duke, 2010). Laboratory studies have likewise indicated that intoxicated individuals are more likely to negatively interpret ambiguous social stimuli as threatening, to infer hostile intent, and to respond aggressively to perceived threats (Ogle & Miller, 2004; Schmutte, Leonard, & Taylor, 1979; Taylor & Leonard, 1983).

Problems with alcohol and/or drugs, in particular, have received attention in IPV treatment research, and those with trauma histories have increased rates of substance use problems (Semiatin, 2012). In general treatment for partner-abusive men, those with substance use problems have poorer engagement in treatment and are less likely to end their violence with standard services for IPV (Hamberger & Hastings, 1990a, 1990b; Ting, Jordan-Green, Murphy, & Pitts, 2009). In one large-scale study of abusive men in treatment in four cities, those who reported frequent drinking during a quarterly follow-up were over 3 times more likely than other men to have reassaulted a partner (Jones & Gondolf, 2001). On the positive side, successful treatment of alcohol problems has been associated with substantial reductions in both physical and psychological IPV for both men and women seeking substance use treatment (O'Farrell & Murphy, 1995; O'Farrell, Murphy, Stephan, Fals-Stewart, & Murphy, 2004; Schumm, O'Farrell, Murphy, & Fals-Stewart, 2009; Stuart et al., 2002). Other more coordinated interventions integrating IPV and substance use intervention have shown favorable treatment effects for both problems (Easton et al., 2007), though challenges arise in addressing substance use problems for those seeking IPV treatment because they often display limited motivation to change their patterns of drinking or drug use. Taken in sum, these research findings provide strong support for the need to assess and treat substance use problems as part of trauma-informed therapy for IPV.

A brief overview of how one of the authors (CMM) handles substance use issues in a general IPV clinic illustrates this type of approach. First, all individuals who come to the clinic are screened using common tools, including the Alcohol Use Disorders Identification Test (Saunders, Aasland, Babor, de la Fuente, & Grant, 1993), Drug Abuse Screening Test (Skinner, 1982), and interview questions about the quantity and frequency of alcohol and drug use, frequency of binge drinking (defined as five or more standard drinks on one occasion), and any instances of physical IPV while under the influence of alcohol or drugs (including evidence from police reports when available). A low threshold is set for detection of potential concerns, including regular binge drinking, drinking beyond levels considered healthy by the medical community (i.e., average consumption of more than two standard drinks per day), and any evidence of IPV under the influence.

Those who screen positive for potential concerns are then asked to participate in a brief substance use intervention (typically three sessions). They first complete additional assessments that inquire about dependence symptoms, common negative effects of alcohol and drugs (e.g., legal, health, occupational), negative affects of substance use on their relationship, motivations for use, any concerns they have about alcohol and drug use, and their readiness to change. Clients are then given feedback on their assessment results and are provided with two to three follow-up sessions of motivational enhancement therapy to discuss their substance use in a supportive, open, and empathic framework. When possible, a change plan is negotiated, which may include harm- and risk-reduction strategies, sobriety sampling (e.g., a period of 1 week, 2 weeks, or a month of abstinence as a personal awareness and growth experiment), attendance at an Alcoholics Anonymous or Narcotics Anonymous meeting, or reaching out to others in one's social network to discuss relevant issues. Individuals who display more evidence of dependence and loss of control are referred to more extensive services, such as medical detoxification (if needed) and outpatient treatment, and are encouraged to use self-help resources in the community. Case management and follow-up, including coordination with probation agents when appropriate, are important in promoting these treatment activities.

ADJUNCTIVE INTERVENTIONS FOR TRAUMATIC BRAIN INJURY

The past 2 decades of research on the relationship between TBI and neuropsychological functioning and IPV have provided a consistent set of results. Rates of TBIs among those who engage in IPV, ranging from 40% to 61%, have been significantly higher than those found in the general population (Pinto et al., 2010). Such high rates have been maintained regardless of how the injury was determined—that is, by either a physician diagnosing a concussion or a study participant reporting a loss of consciousness. Neuropsychological studies also have consistently found that individuals who engage in IPV demonstrate poor performance on measures of verbal intellectual ability, executive functioning, attention, impulsivity, learning, and memory (Pinto et al., 2010). Thus, it is quite clear that presence of TBI and associated deficits increase risk of IPV.

Some evidence also suggests that TBI may strengthen negative personality traits that underlie aggressive behavior. In a previous study of a clinical sample receiving assessments at the PTSD clinic at VA Boston, we found that presence of TBI potentiated the relationship between antisocial features and IPV (Taft et al., 2012). In other words, the risk of engaging in IPV increased more intensely for those with antisocial features who also experienced head contact events. There are currently no treatment protocols available to address the multiple cognitive and neuropsychiatric deficits in TBI, and no treatment programs specifically targeting IPV in those who have experienced such an injury. The lack of an available model for integrating TBI and IPV intervention is unfortunate given the high co-occurrence of these two problems. The treatment of combined TBI and associated comorbidities is extremely challenging because traditional cognitive behavioral therapy relies on executive functions, which are impaired in head injury. Patients with brain injuries and attendant executive function deficits are especially challenging to rehabilitate because of poor insight into their problems, lack of mental flexibility, impoverished planning ability and impulse control, and poor motivation. Some of these same attributions are also commonly made for those who engage in IPV (Lila, Herrero, & Gracia, 2008). However, interventions focused on social information processing deficits may serve to improve executive function abilities to help patients recover across multiple functional domains, reducing aggression and impulsivity, and thus decreasing risk of IPV.

Cognitive rehabilitation efforts for clients with head injuries have been shown to be effective across a number of studies (Bogdanova & Verfaellie,

2012; Cicerone et al., 2011). These interventions focus on developing cognitive strategies for restoring, reorganizing, or compensating for impaired cognitive functioning (Harley et al., 1992). Recommendations from the Cognitive Rehabilitation Task Force include training on learning and executive functioning and developing awareness of limitations through self-monitoring and awareness exercises (Cicerone et al., 2011).

Effective cognitive behavioral work with those who engage in IPV must necessarily use many of these same strategies used in cognitive rehabilitation. Helping clients to develop self-awareness of their faulty cognitive patterns, to engage in self-monitoring exercises to understand their limitations, to recognize and anticipate difficult situations, and to practice responses to these situations are critical for successful intervention. Also consistent with cognitive rehabilitation approaches, we believe that it is critical to help clients prepare for potential future difficulties by writing down their thoughts and actively rehearsing responses to different situations. Practicing these strategies over time, often escalating the difficulty of practice situations, plays an important role in mastery of potentially challenging situations. How IPV interventions are structured may also make a difference for those who have experienced a head injury or who experience learning and memory difficulties. We believe that it is important to keep the number of concepts covered in any particular session low so as not to overwhelm and confuse clients. Repetition of core concepts across most or all treatment sessions, such as understanding the client's specific cognitive difficulties, taking time-outs to deescalate situations, listening to the partner's concerns, and expressing one's feelings more effectively, will likely be more successful than discussing a completely new concept for each individual session. It is also important to provide clients with homework assignments to give more thought to and practice material and skills covered in group.

SUMMARY

Several comorbid issues present a challenge for IPV intervention and may have to be addressed either as an adjunctive or concomitant intervention. To effectively prevent and treat IPV, the provider may have to consider factors such as housing and occupational status, literacy and education, parenting, injury and health status, and psychiatric status. It is important to consider whether these potential difficulties are likely to impede the success of treatment versus whether they may warrant advice and referrals but are unlikely to affect intervention outcome. Such interventions may vary in the level of intensity that is required. In this chapter, we discussed adjunctive or concomitant interventions for several of the most common comorbidities observed in IPV treatment for populations that have experienced trauma, namely, PTSD, depression, substance use problems, and TBI.

AFTERWORD: CONCLUSIONS, FUTURE DIRECTIONS, AND CHALLENGES

We have outlined the importance of trauma-informed intimate partner violence (IPV) intervention, discussed research that supports such interventions, and given practical guidance on effective intervention strategies to use with this population. Before we implement trauma-informed treatment, there are some potential barriers, pitfalls, and considerations that should receive attention. In this chapter, we focus on some of these, including challenges in the coordination of care, state IPV intervention standards, a lack of programs for self-referred individuals who engage in IPV, issues related to stigma, and overall resistance to breaking from the status quo in this area of intervention.

http://dx.doi.org/10.1037/14918-015
Trauma-Informed Treatment and Prevention of Intimate Partner Violence, by C. T. Taft, C. M. Murphy, and S. K. Creech

COORDINATION OF CARE

It is axiomatic in the IPV field that when working with those who experience IPV, the most effective approach is to develop collaboration between mental health services, social work services, legal services, and case management (Goodman & Smyth, 2011). Research has also shown that a coordinated approach to IPV use is important, including coordination among the court and prosecution system, probation oversight, and the counseling program (Murphy, Musser, & Maton, 1998). In the broader community context, IPV intervention coordination typically involves effective police practices, vigorous case prosecution, mandated intervention, and sustained legal supervision, usually probation monitoring. There are others who should be involved in this coordination of care who are not typically part of a "treatment plan" for the individual engaging in IPV, however. Specifically, there is often little or no coordination between these entities and others providing trauma-focused intervention, mental health services, or treatment for substance use problems.

If we are to try to understand why trauma-informed intervention has yet to be emphasized in the IPV intervention field and why there is little coordination between IPV intervention programs and mental health providers, we can look back at the political history of these programs as well as current state intervention standards. Since the shelter movement began and programs for those who engage in IPV began to spring up in the late 1970s, programs and guidelines have been developed and shaped according to a model of IPV that has downplayed the relevance of personal and mental health factors because they could be viewed as justifications for abusive behavior (Pence & Paymar, 1993). Identified risk factors such as substance abuse, posttraumatic stress disorder (PTSD), and trauma exposure do not fit neatly within such conceptualizations and thus have been de-emphasized in traditional approaches to IPV intervention.

We appreciate the perspective of many early activists in this field who were concerned that mental health providers had ignored IPV, minimized its negative effects, blamed victims, or interpreted IPV as a symptom of an underlying condition. At times, it may appear as if efforts to understand the social and psychological causes of IPV perpetration conflict with efforts to get police, prosecutors, and judges to treat IPV as a serious crime and hold individuals who use violence accountable for their actions. Ironically, however, the goal of promoting accountability in those who engage in violence may be undermined by the use of punitive, shaming, or confrontational intervention strategies and facilitated by the provision of understanding and support, particularly with respect to these individuals' histories of trauma and victimization.

STATE INTIMATE PARTNER VIOLENCE INTERVENTION STANDARDS

Currently, 45 states have mandated intervention standards for IPV offenders (Maiuro & Eberle, 2008). Many state guidelines promote or require core elements of the Duluth model, which uses a psychoeducational framework focused on abuse as a gender-based expression of power and control (Pence & Paymar, 1993). To date, however, no randomized controlled trials have shown such interventions to be more effective than legal monitoring alone (Dutton & Corvo, 2006; Rosenbaum, 2010), and less adequate evaluation designs suggest modest benefits, at best, from these widespread intervention approaches (Babcock, Green, & Robie, 2004). Most guidelines also proscribe couples-based approaches despite evidence of their success in addressing noninjurious and less severe forms of IPV and couples problems, in addition to PTSD (Monson et al., 2011; Stith & McCollum, 2011). Given the large research base showing that trauma and PTSD are robust risk factors for IPV, it is also problematic that many state guidelines caution against interventions emphasizing mental health factors.

In addition to mandating IPV program content and focus, most state guidelines also specify program length—up to 52 weeks—despite empirical evidence showing that longer programs are no more effective at reducing IPV recidivism postintervention than shorter programs (Maxwell, Davis, & Taylor, 2010). This poses real barriers to implementing state-approved trauma-informed IPV intervention for this population. Trauma-informed interventions are typically cognitive–behavioral in nature, conducted by clinical psychologists or other mental health professionals, and time-limited. Other than treatment for severe personality disorders (e.g., Linehan, Armstrong, Suarez, Allmon, & Heard, 1991), we are aware of no cognitive behavioral therapy for any other problem, mental health or otherwise, that is standardly delivered as a yearlong intervention. It may appear reasonable to assume that if a more time-limited approach is not having intended effects in reducing IPV, a longer program is needed. However, it is perhaps more sound to experiment with alternative approaches rather than simply providing more of a treatment that is not achieving its intended effects. In addition, our goal should not be to "punish" the client by imposing long treatment "sentences," but rather to deliver the most effective intervention possible using the ideal number of sessions needed to promote safety and end the violence.

Not only do state standards hinder program implementation, they also hinder intervention innovation and development. For example, whereas a small number of states allow experimentation in a research context with novel interventions or approaches that do not fit within existing state guidelines, many state standards preclude conducting randomized controlled clinical trials to test relative efficacy of alternative approaches. Thus, efforts to develop community-based trauma-informed IPV interventions are virtually nonexistent, and controlled research on such interventions may be seriously hindered by legal program requirements in a number of states and jurisdictions.

We believe strongly that practice guidelines should be based on research, not simply on the opinion of well-intentioned advocates and policymakers. Ideally, guidelines that restrict practice should only be developed and implemented on the basis of solid evidence from randomized controlled clinical trials or similarly rigorous intervention studies. To force programs to be conducted in a specific format using a specific intervention model and a specified program length when there is virtually no empirical evidence for the effectiveness of these requirements seems at best counterintuitive and at worst reckless and dangerous to the ultimate goal of promoting safety and ending IPV.

It is important for practitioners who are working to provide trauma-informed services in this arena to reach out to groups and organizations in their states and local communities that oversee practice guidelines or program certification and to make reasoned arguments for the value of expanding treatment options for individuals who engage in partner violence. A number of helpful suggestions for how researchers and practitioners can work together to promote effective IPV intervention standards have been suggested, including active partnership on state or local standards committees, recognition of shared goals, respectful acknowledgment of differences in perspective, and recognition of the challenging and sensitive nature of the work we do and its effect on IPV survivors (Hamberger, 2001; Murphy, 2001).

Policymakers in some states and local jurisdictions have begun reexamining restrictive aspects of IPV practice guidelines, and many have begun raising questions about the efficacy and cost-effectiveness of existing IPV intervention programs. Data from carefully designed and well-conducted research studies may prove helpful in efforts to expand service options for this population and to maintain community programming for IPV offenders. Finally, it is important to note that most practice guidelines apply only to services for court-mandated clients. We discuss next the importance of developing additional pathways and strategies, beyond the criminal justice system, to engage individuals who use IPV in trauma-informed services.

PROVIDER TRAINING

Another difficulty in providing quality trauma-informed intervention for those who use IPV is that providers in some community-based programs have little or no training related to trauma and traumatic stress. Our Strength at Home Men's Program clients sometimes tell us that they left community IPV intervention programs because the group leaders did not seem to care or attempt to understand their traumatic experiences. In fact, the available IPV treatment literature contains notable examples in which providers are instructed to downplay or ignore psychological factors, such as the individual's trauma history, because psychological explanations are seen as antithetical to the goal of holding offenders accountable for their actions (e.g., Pence & Paymar, 1993). This perspective is reflected in some state guidelines that restrict the use of mental health change targets, such as stress, anger, or communication skills, in IPV offender services (Maiuro & Eberle, 2008).

Training standards for community-based IPV programs and educational standards for providers are highly variable across jurisdictions. Typical training requirements may focus more on the social dimensions of IPV to the exclusion of individual psychological factors. It is also common in such training programs to highlight mental health issues and substance use problems as either irrelevant to the social dynamics of power and control or as excuses for engaging in abuse. Naturally, if one does not have prior training and hands-on supervised clinical experience with trauma-exposed clients, he or she will have a much harder time delivering effective services, helping clients feel understood, and establishing a treatment alliance to promote change.

Increasing the standards for clinical training may do more to enhance program effectiveness than lengthening programs. The Strength at Home Men's program approach is to deliver more intense therapy of shorter duration with highly trained (masters or doctoral level) clinicians who have a background in treating trauma-related problems. Delivering such intervention is likely to be no less cost effective (and perhaps more cost effective) than delivering longer programs with less well-trained providers.

This is not to say that providers for clients who engage in IPV can only deliver effective intervention if they have advanced degrees; prior experience and training with trauma-exposed individuals is a great benefit and helps achieve a minimum level of competence. We believe that any provider, however, can work to become more educated about trauma and its impacts and more competent in delivering services to this population. A willingness to learn and seek out training experiences is key to the development of competency in working with trauma-exposed individuals. Unfortunately, the existing systems and standards for the provision of IPV services may actually hinder the development of these competencies and the implementation of trauma-informed programs.

LACK OF SERVICES FOR SELF-REFERRED CLIENTS

Another barrier to effective trauma-informed intervention is a general lack of adequate services for self-referred clients. One can see why a client might avoid voluntarily entering state-approved community IPV programs simply by noting that these programs are almost always called a "batterer program." A trauma-informed perspective would not place labels such as *batterer* on our clients, and we certainly would not think that using such stigmatizing labels does any service to the client or those they abuse. In fact, the opposite is more likely: Men will not voluntarily step forward for help with IPV, and they will feel stigmatized and shamed when being labeled in this manner.

The program length issue and lack of provider training also make it far less likely that an individual will voluntarily present for IPV services or will stick with the services after initial contacts. Few clients will enter a program knowing that they will have to remain in the program for a year, and some clients may also be reluctant to voluntarily seek counseling with providers who lack requisite clinical training. Thus, it is our experience that most clients who want help for their anger and abusive behavior will seek care in mental health clinics and with individual providers who may or may not be well-equipped to deliver IPV intervention. It is worth noting that models outside the United States exist for successful voluntary IPV intervention with highly trained mental health providers. For example, voluntary IPV intervention is the standard of care in Scandinavian countries (Askeland & Heir, 2013), and recent research has identified favorable outcomes from cognitive behavioral therapy groups for IPV in this context (Palmstierna, Haugan, Jarwson, Rasmussen, & Nøttestad, 2012).

SCREENING FOR INTIMATE PARTNER VIOLENCE USE

Related to the issue of the lack of self-referred IPV interventions is the issue of screening for those who engage in IPV. Although routine screening for IPV is becoming a common practice across health care disciplines, including primary care, mental health, substance abuse, as well as prenatal care clinics (H. Thompson, 2012), procedures and policies for screening for those who engage in IPV lag far behind. This systemic pattern allows violence to remain undetected until the violence escalates in severity to the point of arrest, significant injuries, or other serious negative consequences. Again, if there are not inviting programs from which self-referred abusive individuals can seek intervention, the effectiveness of screening may be limited. However, beyond that in state IPV programs, screening for use of IPV in a number of settings can trigger referrals to local counselors or clinics trained to deliver effective trauma-informed care.

ATTITUDES

What we are suggesting in this chapter is that we have to make a shift in our attitudes if we are going to deliver more trauma-informed services in IPV intervention. This change in attitude may also be necessary for some who view such interventions as a "way out" or escape from personal responsibility for the individual engaging in IPV. Acknowledging and processing trauma and holding clients responsible for their actions are not mutually exclusive; both can and must be done for effective IPV intervention to occur. In fact, it is considerably easier to promote the taking of responsibility on the client's part if their personal experiences are recognized and acknowledged within the context of an empathic relationship focused on motivating change. This is not an "either–or" proposition, but a "both–and" approach that involves acknowledging the effects of trauma while promoting personal accountability for ending abusive behavior.

OVERCOMING BARRIERS

If we are to truly move toward a more trauma-informed, empirically supported approach, we should examine how to modify existing intervention programs to be more sensitive to the traumatic experiences and posttraumatic reactions of individuals who engage in IPV. At the very least, we believe this should involve an initial assessment of traumatic experiences and PTSD symptoms among all individuals seeking services for IPV, along with staff training in understanding the effects of trauma and traumatic stress on interpersonal relationships and help seeking. In addition, these changes should include opportunities for supportive clinical dialogue regarding the effects that trauma has had on the client's interpersonal and romantic relationships and psychoeducation about common themes linking traumatic stress to relationship problems and abuse. A review of physical space may also be helpful in promoting feelings of safety and security in survivors of trauma. Example recommendations are to hold group sessions in a room with more than one exit and to have a safe space where trauma survivors can take a break if they become uncomfortable in session. These efforts may require a careful review and revision of the intake, assessment, and intervention processes used by existing IPV programs to create a supportive and welcoming environment to promote healing and change.

If such innovations are not possible within existing community IPV programs, we believe that it is time to consider replacing them with alternatives, particularly in light of the limited empirical data supporting the efficacy of existing approaches. As we discussed in this chapter, the fundamental barriers to implementing supportive trauma-informed interventions that have demonstrated efficacy in controlled research may place recipients of IPV at greater risk of revictimization. It will take bold leadership to supplant long-standing intervention practices that have been largely ineffective in reducing IPV. The Veterans Affairs system may play a key role in these efforts, in light of its long-standing focus on reducing the negative effects of trauma and posttraumatic stress. At the very least, whatever guidelines are in place at the state and local level should encourage innovation and research on program efficacy and should not prevent empirically supported programs from operating (Maiuro & Eberle, 2008).

What is also needed is a change in the way that we view IPV programs. A shift to a more trauma-informed approach that avoids placing stigmatizing labels on our clients should encourage more people to voluntarily seek services. We cannot have nearly the impact we should have in combating the IPV problem if we are only seeing abusive individuals after they are court mandated to intervention. With a less stigmatizing trauma-informed approach that is more welcoming, clients may seek treatment for their trauma-related problems and aggressive behavior on their own before the violence escalates. We know that it is difficult to treat IPV once abusive patterns have been deeply ingrained over many years—we can more effectively prevent the IPV in the first place or end it during the early stages of escalation if we create a supportive environment that brings people through the door and engages them in responsible self-change.

We also should keep in mind that much of the work in preventing IPV and working with this population is conducted outside of established domestic violence centers or "batterer programs." Individual providers and clinics, pastoral counselors, social workers, medical providers, and a host of others may be the primary clinical contact for the abusive individual, and it is our hope that this book will help them engage with their abusive clients effectively to prevent and end IPV.

Perhaps most important, those who provide services to this population should understand that showing understanding for trauma-related problems is not the same thing as excusing abusive behavior. Too often we have heard critics of trauma-informed approaches confuse the issue of personal responsibility. Acknowledging that trauma experiences and trauma-related problems are important risk factors that contribute to IPV does not excuse individuals from the responsibility to change their abusive behavior patterns, nor does this perspective ignore other potential causes and contributing factors. None of us would argue that anyone should be held less accountable for abusive behavior because they have experienced severe trauma. A provider can recognize the devastating impact of trauma on clients while also holding them accountable and responsible for their abusive behavior. If we listen to our clients and truly hear their stories of trauma, and if clients feel heard and understood, they will respond more favorably when we hold them accountable for their behavior and encourage them to change. We know of no more basic principle of behavior change than the fact that others will be more likely to listen to us if they feel heard and understood themselves.

APPENDIX A: GROUP PHILOSOPHY

Some simple principles summarize the group philosophy:

1. Many factors can contribute to conflict in relationships, including prior traumatic or stressful experiences, anger, poor communication, difficulties trusting others, low self-esteem, feelings of powerlessness, insecurity, and substance abuse. All of these things can be addressed without resorting to violence.
2. For you to get the most out of the program, you will need to make a firm commitment to change and work on better managing your anger.
3. You cannot change your partner, but you can change yourself. You will be asked to try new behaviors and practice them at home.
4. Many physical health and emotional health benefits can result from managing anger better.
5. Violence and aggression in relationships is learned behavior, and it can be unlearned.

APPENDIX B: COMMON REACTIONS TO TRAUMA

Trauma and negative life events can change the way one sees the world and have an impact on relationships. This handout describes some common reactions people have after trauma.

1. **Reexperiencing the trauma.** A traumatized person often has **unwanted thoughts** of the trauma. Partners may sometimes think that the person is not paying attention to what he or she is saying, when in fact the person is distracted with trauma memories.
2. Some people have **flashbacks,** or very vivid images that feel as if the trauma is occurring again. **Nightmares** are also common. Couples may find it hard to sleep in the same bed due to disturbed sleep and restlessness. This occurs because a traumatic experience is so shocking and so different from everyday experiences that they cannot fit it into what they know about the world. So to understand what happened, their mind keeps bringing the memory back, as if to better digest it and fit it in.
3. **Increased arousal** includes feeling jumpy, being easily startled, and having trouble concentrating or sleeping. The person may see the world as filled with danger, so their bodies are on constant alert. These physical reactions are due to the fight-or-flight response, which causes our bodies to pump out extra adrenaline.
4. Continuous arousal can lead to **impatience** and **irritability,** especially if the person is not getting enough sleep. High levels of irritability and impatience can erode the happiness in relationships and lead to problems with anger.
5. **Avoidance** is a common way of managing trauma-related pain. The most common is avoiding reminders of the trauma and trying to push away painful thoughts and feelings. This can lead to **emotional numbness,** in which people find it difficult to have and express feelings. Emotional numbness is especially difficult for relationships, because emotions help couples feel close to one another.
6. **Depression** is also a common reaction to trauma. It can include feeling sad and hopeless and crying more often. The person may lose interest in people and activities they used to enjoy. At times, the relationship may feel "depressed" as well, because the

traumatized person has withdrawn and is not very interested in doing things as a couple.

7. **Self-image** and **views of others** often become more negative after a trauma. Many people see themselves as more negative overall. It is also common to feel that others cannot be trusted. Relationships become tense when trust decreases.
8. People who experience trauma may try to have **complete control** in relationships and have a tough time letting the other person have any control. This leads to controlling behavior and difficulties with anger.
9. On the other hand, some exposed to trauma may feel completely helpless. They become **overly passive** and easily give in to the demands of others because they feel like they have no control over their lives. They keep their feelings to themselves and may become resentful of others who do not understand what they are going through.

If you're experiencing these problems, there are effective treatments available. Also keep in mind that although trauma can contribute to relationship problems, you're ultimately responsible for your behavior.

APPENDIX C: TRAUMA IMPACT QUESTIONS

This assignment asks you to write about how trauma has affected your relationship with your partner. Please bring this with you to your next group session.

1. How has trauma affected your relationship? For example, has it contributed to your anger or arguments with your partner? Has it affected your ability to trust your partner or feel close to her? Has it led to power struggles in your relationship?

2. What has been the most difficult consequence of trauma for your relationship that you have had to deal with?

APPENDIX D: ANGER ANALYSIS FORM

Briefly describe a recent anger situation.

____

____

____

____

What were your physical reactions during this anger episode? (Please circle or add your own).

muscles tight	**teeth clenched**	**blood rushing**	**rapid breathing**	**sweating**
heart racing	**adrenaline rush**	**headache**	**stomach pain**	**trembling**

Add your own ____

____

____

What were your feelings during this anger episode? (Please circle or add your own).

mad	**disgusted**	**rageful**	**jealous**	**ashamed**	**hurt**
sad	**glad**	**depressed**	**embarrassed**	**lonely**	**frustrated**
scared	**irritable**	**anxious**	**humiliated**	**guilty**	**horrified**

Add your own ____

____

____

What were your thoughts during this anger episode? (Please circle or add your own).

"If I don't stuff my anger, I'll blow up."

"She/he is trying to push my buttons."

"I'll show her/him who they are dealing with."

"She/he is not listening to me, and I need to make her/him understand my side."

"She/he is not on my side."

"I'm going to get my way no matter what."

Add your own ____

____

____

How did you respond to this situation? Check off your behaviors.

ASSERTIVE:

____Asked clarifying questions instead of making accusations

____Communicated your needs without demeaning or being sarcastic to the other person

____Expressed your feelings about the issue

____Took a Time-Out

____Used "I" statements (e.g., "I am upset" instead of "You make me upset")

____Used polite language (e.g., no swearing or insults)

____Approached problem with a constructive attitude and tone

____Set limits (e.g., explain that you will not tolerate certain behaviors)

____Suggested a compromise to a disagreement

____Controlled your display of anger despite the other person's reaction

Add your own ____

AGGRESSIVE:

____Made verbal threats

____Used inflammatory language (e.g., swearing and/or insults)

____Raised voice or used a sarcastic/demeaning tone

____Glared at or "stared down" the other person

____Broke or threw something

____Became physically aggressive

Add your own ____

PASSIVE:

____Did not communicate your thoughts and feelings

____Withdrew or walked away in an attempt to avoid addressing the problem

____Dwelled on feelings of anger and defeat without attempting to solve the problem

____Used a form of negative distraction (e.g., drinking or other substance, risky behaviors)

____Used sarcasm

Add your own ____

COOLING DOWN BEHAVIORS:

____Worked off your anger through physical activity or exercise

____Spoke to a friend or professional

____Used positive distraction (e.g., favorite hobby or activity)

____Created a soothing environment (e.g., put on music, took a warm bath)

____Treated yourself to something special (e.g., a nice lunch, a massage)

____Wrote down your feelings

____Did a deep breathing or relaxation exercise

Add your own ____

APPENDIX E: WHAT TO DO DURING TIME-OUT

It is important to keep in mind that the goal of Time-Out is to give yourself some time to calm down so you can think more clearly and express yourself in a nonaggressive way. It can be helpful to keep in mind a few basic tips to follow during Time-Out.

1. *Be aware of negative thoughts.* When we are angry or upset, we can make ourselves even more upset by our ways of thinking. For example, we often focus on the most negative aspects of the situation, on how we have been wronged by the other person, and about how we will get back at him or her. In the heat of the moment, we also have a tendency to assume the worst in our partners.
2. *Replace negative thoughts with more positive thoughts.* Once you are aware of your negative thoughts while angry or upset, you can do something about them. It can be helpful to tell yourself something positive during Time-Out, such as "She didn't mean what she said," "She's just having a bad day," or "I probably didn't help the situation very much myself."
3. *Think about what you want to communicate to your partner once the Time-Out has ended.* This doesn't mean to try to think of ways to win the argument or to get back at your partner. Rather, think about what it is that you really want to say and practice saying it in a nonaggressive, nonhostile way. It can be helpful to write your thoughts down on paper.
4. *Be aware of feelings other than anger.* With most arguments, anger isn't the only feeling present. Usually, there are other feelings, such as sadness, hurt, and rejection. These feelings can cause both you and your partner to say things that you don't mean. It's important to talk about these feelings once the Time-Out has ended.
5. *Use relaxation strategies.* Your main focus during Time-Out should be to relax so you can think more clearly. People differ in how they relax. Going for a walk, reading, going for a drive, and watching a movie or television are some examples of activities that some people find relaxing. There are also a number of relaxation strategies that have been shown to work for those with PTSD or problems with stress, such as deep breathing and progressive muscle relaxation.

APPENDIX F: "SURVIVAL MODE" AND ALTERNATIVE THOUGHTS

Spending time in dangerous places such as a war zone can have a major impact on the way that you sense threats. When you are in a dangerous area, you have to be extremely alert at all times and constantly scan your environment for danger. You are trained to see threats that others can't see. Noticing threats can be a matter of life or death for you and those you are serving with.

You may have also been trained to respond aggressively to threats in the military. Your fight-or-flight response kicks in to help you deal with the threat in a fast, often aggressive, way. This is sometimes known as the "survival mode" of functioning.

Survival mode is an obvious benefit in a war zone. It can help you and your buddies stay alive. However, going into survival mode at home can be harmful. Your sensitivity to possible threats may be exaggerated. You may misread a facial expression as angry or threatening, when in fact the person is not angry at all. You may enter into survival mode and act aggressively in a situation where you are not really threatened. Even though you are no longer in a war zone, you have not been trained to turn off this survival mode reaction.

Survival mode can have an impact on other aspects of life. You may be more likely to see other people's intentions as negative. For example, if someone cuts you off on the highway, you may assume that the person did it on purpose.

Can you think of a civilian situation in which you went into survival mode?

Unfortunately, survival mode can cause problems in relationships as well. When you function in survival mode, you may assume that your partner is being hostile when it may not necessarily be the case. Thoughts such as, "She's just trying to manipulate me," "She's just trying to push my buttons," "She's trying to make me jealous," or "She's trying to control me" are common among veterans who have experienced trauma.

How does one unlearn survival mode?

- The first step is to recognize your ways of thinking about situations and search for other possibilities.
- One strategy is to not assume that you know what others are thinking. It is helpful to ask instead of guess.
- Another strategy is to try to assume the best in others. Try to assume that your partner has good intentions. This approach leads to less problems and conflict than assuming the worst in every situation.

APPENDIX G: ANGER METER

RATE YOURSELF ON THE ANGER METER

1	3	5	7	10
Completely Relaxed				Completely Angry

CHECK THE BODY SIGNALS THAT YOU ARE EXPERIENCING

Shallow or rapid breathing	Relaxed breathing
Rapid heartbeat	Slow heartbeat
Tense muscles	Relaxed muscles
Sweaty palms or clenched hands	Relaxed hands
Restlessness or trembling	Calm and relaxed
Hot flashes or chills	No hot flashes or chills
Tense stomach	Relaxed stomach
Chest tension	Chest relaxed

....

FOLD AT THE DOTTED LINE

RATE YOURSELF ON THE ANGER METER

1	3	5	7	10
Completely Relaxed				Completely Angry

CHECK THE BODY SIGNALS THAT YOU ARE EXPERIENCING

Shallow or rapid breathing	Relaxed breathing
Rapid heartbeat	Slow heartbeat
Tense muscles	Relaxed muscles
Sweaty palms or clenched hands	Relaxed hands
Restlessness or trembling	Calm and relaxed
Hot flashes or chills	No hot flashes or chills
Tense stomach	Relaxed stomach
Chest tension	Chest relaxed

APPENDIX H: ROOTS OF YOUR COMMUNICATION STYLE

LESSONS LEARNED AS A CHILD:
How did your parents and other family members express anger?

____

____

____

What did your family teach you about how to handle other feelings such as fear, sadness, and helplessness?

____

____

____

Did your childhood experiences affect how you communicate now? Describe.

____

____

____

LESSONS LEARNED IN THE MILITARY:
What did your military experience teach you about how to handle anger?

____

____

____

What did the military teach you about how to handle other feelings such as fear, sadness and helplessness?

____

____

____

Did your experience in the military affect how you communicate now? Describe.

____

____

____

APPENDIX I: IDENTIFYING FEELINGS HANDOUT

	Feelings (intensity)	**Thought**
	0 50 100	
Mad	*Irritated* ➔ *annoyed* ➔ *angry* ➔ *hostile* ➔ *rageful*	Unfairness
Sad	*Down* ➔ *glum* ➔ *depressed* ➔ *miserable* ➔ *despondent*	Loss
Scared	*Cautious* ➔ *apprehensive* ➔ *anxious* ➔ *terrified*	Danger
Disgusted	*A little turned off* ➔ *appalled* ➔ *revolted*	Contamination/violation
Shame	*Embarrassed* ➔ *disgraced* ➔ *humiliated* ➔ *mortified*	Self as bad
Glad	*Contented* ➔ *pleased* ➔ *happy* ➔ *delighted* ➔ *ecstatic*	Self, others, or world as positive
Horrified	*Scared + Disgusted*	Danger + Contamination
Jealous	*Mad + Scared*	Unfairness + Danger
Disappointed	*Mad + Sad*	Unfairness + Loss

APPENDIX J: DAILY FEELINGS EXPRESSION—INDIVIDUAL

At least once a day, share a feeling with your partner or with somebody else if you are not currently in a relationship. Record the feelings that you shared in the chart below. Notice the effects of sharing your feelings. You may wish to use your Session 10 handouts to help identify and express your feelings.

Sunday	
Monday	
Tuesday	
Wednesday	
Thursday	
Friday	
Saturday	

APPENDIX K: YOU'VE BEEN CAUGHT DOING SOMETHING NICE

	Person Caught: ________	Person Caught: ________
Sunday		
Monday		
Tuesday		
Wednesday		
Thursday		
Friday		
Saturday		

Write down **why** you liked what your partner did (what thought is going through your mind at the time you notice this). For example, "my partner brought me breakfast in bed. He or she must really care about me."

APPENDIX L: COMMON THEMES RELATED TO TRAUMA

Various common themes or issues are more likely to develop among those who have experienced deployments and possible trauma. These themes can affect relationships.

TRUST

Trust in others is often disrupted following trauma. A trauma may have been caused by someone who was supposed to be trustworthy. In other cases, a trauma may occur because other people made poor decisions or mistakes. One example is a combat trauma in which fellow service members made unwise or risky decisions. Sometimes feelings of mistrust and betrayal can carry over into relationships. People who have experienced this sort of trauma may feel like they can't trust anyone or that all people are out to hurt or betray them.

POWER AND CONTROL

People who experience trauma may try to have complete control in relationships and have a tough time letting the other person have any control. As a result, controlling behaviors may develop. This can also lead to difficulty controlling anger and occurrences of relationship abuse.

In contrast, some people exposed to trauma may feel completely helpless. They might become overly passive in relationships and easily give in to the demands of others because they feel like they have no control over their lives. They keep their feelings to themselves and may become resentful of others who do not understand what they are going through.

SELF-ESTEEM AND OTHER-ESTEEM

Self-esteem is the acceptance and appreciation of one's basic worth. Being understood, respected, and taken seriously is basic for developing self-esteem. People who have experienced trauma often have poor opinions of themselves because they harshly judge themselves whenever they make a mistake or they unfairly blame themselves for what happened to them. Low self-esteem can lead to depression, insecurity in relationships, and abusive behavior.

INTIMACY

Our desire for intimacy, connection, and closeness is one of the most basic human needs. Many people who experience trauma withdraw from people and avoid being close to others. They may withdraw from the very people who could be most supportive as a way of protecting themselves from possible rejection, blame, or further harm.

APPENDIX M: CONFLICT ANALYSIS SHEET

Please complete this practice assignment **together as a couple.** Use this form to track the different strategies that you used during a specific disagreement or conflict. In the blank space, indicate whether the man ("M"), woman ("W"), or both ("B") members of the couple engaged in that behavior.

Describe a recent disagreement or conflict in your relationship with each other: ____

How did you respond to this situation? Write in all the blank spaces that apply.

ASSERTIVE:

____Asked clarifying questions instead of making accusations

____Communicated your needs without demeaning or being sarcastic to the other person

____Took a time-out

____Used "I" statements (e.g., "I am angry" instead of "You make me angry")

____Used polite language (e.g., no swearing or insults)

____Approached problem with a constructive attitude and tone

____Set limits (e.g., explain that you will not tolerate certain behaviors)

____Suggested a compromise to a disagreement

____Controlled your display of anger despite the other person's reaction

Add your own:

____

AGGRESSIVE:

____Made verbal threats

____Used inflammatory language (e.g., swearing and/or insults)

____Approached problem with the goal of "showing who is boss"

____Raised voice or used a sarcastic/demeaning tone

____Glared at or "stared down" the other person

Add your own:

____

PASSIVE:

____Did not communicate your thoughts and feelings

____Withdrew or walked away in an attempt to avoid addressing the problem

____Dwelled on feelings of anger and defeat without attempting to solve the problem

____Used a form of negative distraction (e.g., drinking, other substance abuse, risky behaviors)

Add your own:

____

COOLING-DOWN BEHAVIORS:

____Worked off your anger through physical activity or exercise

____Spoke to a friend or professional

____Used positive distraction (e.g., favorite hobby or activity)

____Created a soothing environment (e.g., put on music, took a warm bath)

____Treated yourself to something special (e.g., a nice lunch, a massage)

____Wrote down your feelings

____Did a deep breathing or relaxation exercise

Add your own:

____

APPENDIX N: TIME-OUTS—PLANNING, PREPARING, AND PRACTICING

Step I: Developing a Time-Out Plan

Together as a couple, answer the following questions to develop your personal Time-Out plan:

1. Who will have the right to call a Time-Out?

   ____

   ____

2. What will each of you use as the signal or signals for a Time-Out?

   ____

   ____

3. Where will each of you go, and what will each of you do when a Time-Out is called?

   ____

   ____

4. How long will your Time-Out last?

   ____

   ____

5. What will be used to signal the end of a Time-Out?

   ____

   ____

6. What will you do when the Time-Out has ended?

   ____

   ____

Step II: Practicing Time-Outs

Take two or three practice Time-Outs during situations that are anger provoking. **Do not wait until the last minute** to take a Time-Out. Take Time-Outs at the earliest signs of anger.

Briefly describe one situation in which you used your Time-Out plan.

____

____

____

How did you recognize that it was time to take a Time-Out? What thoughts, feelings, and physical reactions served as a cue that you needed a Time-Out?

____

____

____

What did you do to calm down during the Time-Out?

____

____

____

Were you able to stick to your Time-Out plan during this situation?

____

____

____

Did you talk about the situation that led to your Time Out after it was over? Were each of you able to express your feelings about the issue? Did you listen to the other person without arguing?

____

____

____

APPENDIX O:
DAILY FEELINGS EXPRESSION

	Partner: ____________	Partner: ____________
Sunday		
Monday		
Tuesday		
Wednesday		
Thursday		
Friday		
Saturday		

At least once a day, **share one or more of your feelings** with your partner. Record your feeling above. Place this form somewhere that is convenient and visible to the two of you. Notice the effects of sharing your feelings with each other.

REFERENCES

Alexander, P. C. (2014). Dual-trauma couples and intimate partner violence. *Psychological Trauma: Theory, Research, Practice, and Policy*, 6, 224–231. http://dx.doi.org/10.1037/a0036404

Alexander, P. C., Morris, E., Tracy, A., & Frye, A. (2010). Stages of change and the group treatment of batterers: A randomized clinical trial. *Violence and Victims*, *25*, 571–587. http://dx.doi.org/10.1891/0886-6708.25.5.571

Allen, E. S., Rhoades, G. K., Stanley, S. M., & Markman, H. J. (2010). Hitting home: Relationships between recent deployment, posttraumatic stress symptoms, and marital functioning for Army couples. *Journal of Family Psychology*, *24*, 280–288. http://dx.doi.org/10.1037/a0019405

American Psychiatric Association. (2013). *Diagnostic and statistical manual of mental disorders* (5th ed.). Washington, DC: Author.

Anglin, K., & Holtzworth-Munroe, A. (1997). Comparing the responses of maritally violent and nonviolent spouses to problematic marital and nonmarital situations: Are the skill deficits of physically aggressive husbands and wives global? *Journal of Family Psychology*, *11*, 301–313. http://dx.doi.org/10.1037/0893-3200.11.3.301

Archer, J. (2000). Sex differences in aggression between heterosexual partners: A meta-analytic review. *Psychological Bulletin*, *126*, 651–680.

Ascione, F. R., Weber, C. V., Thompson, T. M., Heath, J., Maruyama, M., & Hayashi, K. (2007). Battered pets and domestic violence: Animal abuse reported by women experiencing intimate violence and by nonabused women. *Violence Against Women*, *13*, 354–373. http://dx.doi.org/10.1177/1077801207299201

Askeland, I. R., & Heir, T. (2013). Early dropout in men voluntarily undergoing treatment for intimate partner violence in Norway. *Violence and Victims*, *28*, 822–831. http://dx.doi.org/10.1891/0886-6708.VV-D-12-00137

Babcock, J. C., Green, C. E., & Robie, C. (2004). Does batterers' treatment work? A meta-analytic review of domestic violence treatment. *Clinical Psychology Review*, *23*, 1023–1053. http://dx.doi.org/10.1016/j.cpr.2002.07.001

Balcom, D. (1996). The interpersonal dynamics and treatment of dual trauma couples. *Journal of Marital & Family Therapy*, *22*, 431–442. http://dx.doi.org/10.1111/j.1752-0606.1996.tb00218.x

Bandura, A. (1977). *Social learning theory*. Oxford, England: Prentice-Hall.

Barbour, K. A., Eckhardt, C. I., Davison, G. C., & Kassinove, H. (1998). The experience and expression of anger in maritally violent and maritally discordant-nonviolent men. *Behavior Therapy*, *29*, 173–191. http://dx.doi.org/10.1016/S0005-7894(98)80001-4

Beck, A. T. (1979). *Cognitive therapy and the emotional disorders*. New York, NY: Penguin.

Beckham, J. C., Feldman, M. E., & Kirby, A. C. (1998). Atrocities exposure in Vietnam combat veterans with chronic posttraumatic stress disorder: Relationship to combat exposure, symptom severity, guilt, and interpersonal violence. *Journal of Traumatic Stress, 11*, 777–785. http://dx.doi.org/10.1023/A:1024453618638

Begun, A. L., Brondino, M. J., Bolt, D., Weinstein, B., Strodthoff, T., & Shelley, G. (2008). The Revised Safe at Home instrument for assessing readiness to change intimate partner violence. *Violence and Victims, 23*, 508–524. http://dx.doi.org/10.1891/0886-6708.23.4.508

Begun, A. L., Murphy, C., Bolt, D., Weinstein, B., Strodthoff, T., Short, L., & Shelley, G. (2003). Characteristics of the Safe at Home instrument for assessing readiness to change intimate partner violence. *Research on Social Work Practice, 13*, 80–107. http://dx.doi.org/10.1177/1049731502238758

Bell, K. M., & Orcutt, H. K. (2009). Posttraumatic stress disorder and male-perpetrated intimate partner violence. *JAMA, 302*, 562–564. http://dx.doi.org/10.1001/jama.2009.1126

Bender, K., & Roberts, A. R. (2007). Battered women versus male batterer typologies: Same or different based on evidence-based studies? *Aggression and Violent Behavior, 12*, 519–530. http://dx.doi.org/10.1016/j.avb.2007.02.005

Birkley, E. L., & Eckhardt, C. I. (2015). Anger, hostility, internalizing negative emotions, and intimate partner violence perpetration: A meta-analytic review. *Clinical Psychology Review, 37*, 40–56. http://dx.doi.org/10.1016/j.cpr.2015.01.002

Bogdanova, Y., & Verfaellie, M. (2012). Cognitive sequelae of blast-induced traumatic brain injury: Recovery and rehabilitation. *Neuropsychology Review, 22*, 4–20. http://dx.doi.org/10.1007/s11065-012-9192-3

Bograd, M., & Mederos, F. (1999). Battering and couples therapy: Universal screening and selection of treatment modality. *Journal of Marital & Family Therapy, 25*, 291–312. http://dx.doi.org/10.1111/j.1752-0606.1999.tb00249.x

Boira, S., del Castillo, M. F., Carbajosa, P., & Marcuello, C. (2013). Context of treatment and therapeutic alliance: Critical factors in court-mandated batterer intervention programs. *The Spanish Journal of Psychology, 16*, E40. http://dx.doi.org/10.1017/sjp.2013.43

Bordin, E. S. (1979). The generalizability of the psychoanalytic concept of the working alliance. *Psychotherapy: Theory, Research & Practice, 16*, 252–260. http://dx.doi.org/10.1037/h0085885

Bowen, E. (2011). An overview of partner violence risk assessment and the potential role of female victim risk appraisals. *Aggression and Violent Behavior, 16*, 214–226. http://dx.doi.org/10.1016/j.avb.2011.02.007

Breiding, M. J., Black, M. C., & Ryan, G. W. (2008). Prevalence and risk factors of intimate partner violence in eighteen U.S. states/territories, 2005. *American Journal of Preventive Medicine, 34*, 112–118. http://dx.doi.org/10.1016/j.amepre.2007.10.001

Brown, P. D., & O'Leary, K. D. (2000). Therapeutic alliance: Predicting continuance and success in group treatment for spouse abuse. *Journal of Consulting and Clinical Psychology, 68,* 340–345. http://dx.doi.org/10.1037/0022-006X.68.2.340

Brown, P. D., O'Leary, K. D., & Feldbau, S. R. (1997). Dropout in a treatment program for self-referring wife abusing men. *Journal of Family Violence, 12,* 365–387. http://dx.doi.org/10.1023/A:1021906825073

Budman, S. H., Soldz, S., Demby, A., Feldstein, M., Springer, T., & Davis, M. S. (1989). Cohesion, alliance and outcome in group psychotherapy. *Psychiatry, 52,* 339–350.

Cadsky, O., Hanson, R. K., Crawford, M., & Lalonde, C. (1996). Attrition from a male batterer treatment program: Client–treatment congruence and lifestyle instability. *Violence and Victims, 11,* 51–64.

Campbell, J. C. (2001). Safety planning based on lethality assessment for partners of batterers in intervention programs. *Journal of Aggression, Maltreatment & Trauma, 5,* 129–143. http://dx.doi.org/10.1300/J146v05n02_08

Campbell, J. C., Glass, N., Sharps, P. W., Laughon, K., & Bloom, T. (2007). Intimate partner homicide: Review and implications of research and policy. *Trauma, Violence, & Abuse, 8,* 246–269. http://dx.doi.org/10.1177/1524838007303505

Campbell, J. C., & Lewandowski, L. A. (1997). Mental and physical health effects of intimate partner violence on women and children. *Psychiatric Clinics of North America, 20,* 353–374. http://dx.doi.org/10.1016/S0193-953X(05)70317-8

Campbell, J. C., Webster, D. W., & Glass, N. (2009). The Danger Assessment: Validation of a lethality risk assessment instrument for intimate partner femicide. *Journal of Interpersonal Violence, 24,* 653–674. http://dx.doi.org/10.1177/0886260508317180

Campbell, J. C., Webster, D., Koziol-McLain, J., Block, C., Campbell, D., Curry, M. A., . . . Laughon, K. (2003). Risk factors for femicide in abusive relationships: Results from a multisite case control study. *American Journal of Public Health, 93,* 1089–1097. http://dx.doi.org/10.2105/AJPH.93.7.1089

Carlson, B. E. (2000). Children exposed to intimate partner violence: Research findings and implications for intervention. *Trauma, Violence, & Abuse, 1,* 321–342. http://dx.doi.org/10.1177/1524838000001004002

Carney, M., Buttell, F., & Dutton, D. (2007). Women who perpetrate intimate partner violence: A review of the literature with recommendations for treatment. *Aggression and Violent Behavior, 12,* 108–115. http://dx.doi.org/10.1016/j.avb.2006.05.002

Cattaneo, L. B., & Goodman, L. A. (2003). Victim-reported risk factors for continued abusive behavior: Assessing the dangerousness of arrested batterers. *Journal of Community Psychology, 31,* 349–369. http://dx.doi.org/10.1002/jcop.10056

Chaney, E. F., O'Leary, M. R., & Marlatt, G. A. (1978). Skill training with alcoholics. *Journal of Consulting and Clinical Psychology, 46,* 1092 1104. http://dx.doi.org/10.1037/0022-006X.46.5.1092

Chemtob, C. M., Novaco, R. W., Hamada, R. S., & Gross, D. M. (1997). Cognitive–behavioral treatment for severe anger in posttraumatic stress disorder. *Journal of Consulting and Clinical Psychology, 65*, 184–189. http://dx.doi.org/10.1037/0022-006X.65.1.184

Chemtob, C. M., Novaco, R. W., Hamada, R. S., Gross, D. M., & Smith, G. (1997). Anger regulation deficits in combat-related posttraumatic stress disorder. *Journal of Traumatic Stress, 10*, 17–36. http://dx.doi.org/10.1002/jts.2490100104

Cicerone, K. D., Langenbahn, D. M., Braden, C., Malec, J. F., Kalmar, K., Fraas, M., . . . Ashman, T. (2011). Evidence-based cognitive rehabilitation: Updated review of the literature from 2003 through 2008. *Archives of Physical Medicine and Rehabilitation, 92*, 519–530. http://dx.doi.org/10.1016/j.apmr.2010.11.015

Clements, K., Holtzworth-Munroe, A., Schweinle, W., & Ickes, W. (2007). Empathic accuracy of intimate partners in violent versus nonviolent relationships. *Personal Relationships, 14*, 369–388. http://dx.doi.org/10.1111/j.1475-6811.2007.00161.x

Clements, K., & Schumacher, J. A. (2010). Perceptual biases in social cognition as potential moderators of the relationship between alcohol and intimate partner violence: A review. *Aggression and Violent Behavior, 15*, 357–368. http://dx.doi.org/10.1016/j.avb.2010.06.004

Cloitre, M., Miranda, R., Stovall-McClough, K. C., & Han, H. (2005). Beyond PTSD: Emotion regulation and interpersonal problems as predictors of functional impairment in survivors of childhood abuse. *Behavior Therapy, 36*, 119–124. http://dx.doi.org/10.1016/S0005-7894(05)80060-7

Coker, A. L., Davis, K. E., Arias, I., Desai, S., Sanderson, M., Brandt, H. M., & Smith, P. H. (2002). Physical and mental health effects of intimate partner violence for men and women. *American Journal of Preventive Medicine, 23*, 260–268. http://dx.doi.org/10.1016/S0749-3797(02)00514-7

Coker, A. L., Smith, P. H., McKeown, R. E., & King, M. J. (2000). Frequency and correlates of intimate partner violence by type: Physical, sexual, and psychological battering. *American Journal of Public Health, 90*, 553–559. http://dx.doi.org/10.2105/AJPH.90.4.553

Constans, J. I. (2005). Information-processing biases in PTSD. In J. J. Vasterling & C. R. Brewin (Eds.), *Neuropsychology of PTSD: Biological, cognitive, and clinical perspectives* (pp. 105–130). New York, NY: Guilford Press.

Coronado, V. G., Thurman, D. J., Greenspan, A. I., & Weissman, B. M. (2009). Epidemiology. In J. Jallo & C. M. Loftus (Eds.), *Neurotrauma and critical care: Brain* (pp. 3–19). New York, NY: Thieme.

Crenshaw, D. A., & Mordock, J. B. (2005). *Understanding and treating the aggression of children: Fawns in gorilla suits*. Lanham, MD: Jason Aronson.

Crick, N. R., & Dodge, K. A. (1994). A review and reformulation of social information-processing mechanisms in children's social adjustment. *Psychological Bulletin, 115*, 74–101. http://dx.doi.org/10.1037/0033-2909.115.1.74

Daniels, J. W., & Murphy, C. M. (1997). Stages and processes of change in batterers' treatment. *Cognitive and Behavioral Practice*, *4*, 123–145. http://dx.doi.org/10.1016/S1077-7229(97)80015-6

Davison, G. C., Robins, C., & Johnson, M. K. (1983). Articulated thoughts during simulated situations: A paradigm for studying cognition in emotion and behavior. *Cognitive Therapy and Research*, *7*, 17–39. http://dx.doi.org/10.1007/BF01173421

Deffenbacher, J. L., Oetting, E. R., Lynch, R. S., & Morris, C. D. (1996). The expression of anger and its consequences. *Behaviour Research and Therapy*, *34*, 575–590. http://dx.doi.org/10.1016/0005-7967(96)00018-6

de Hooge, I. E., Zeelenberg, M., & Breugelmans, S. M. (2007). Moral sentiments and cooperation: Differential influences of shame and guilt. *Cognition and Emotion*, *21*, 1025–1042. http://dx.doi.org/10.1080/02699930600980874

Dekel, R., & Monson, C. M. (2010). Military-related post-traumatic stress disorder and family relations: Current knowledge and future directions. *Aggression and Violent Behavior*, *15*, 303–309. http://dx.doi.org/10.1016/j.avb.2010.03.001

DiClemente, C. C., & Scott, C. W. (1997). Stages of change: Interactions with treatment compliance and involvement. *NIDA Research Monograph*, *165*, 131–156.

DiGiuseppe, R., Tafrate, R., & Eckhardt, C. (1994). Critical issues in the treatment of anger. *Cognitive and Behavioral Practice*, *1*, 111–132. http://dx.doi.org/10.1016/S1077-7229(05)80089-6

Dimidjian, S., Hollon, S. D., Dobson, K. S., Schmaling, K. B., Kohlenberg, R. J., Addis, M. E., . . . Jacobson, N. S. (2006). Randomized trial of behavioral activation, cognitive therapy, and antidepressant medication in the acute treatment of adults with major depression. *Journal of Consulting and Clinical Psychology*, *74*, 658–670. http://dx.doi.org/10.1037/0022-006X.74.4.658

Dodge, K. A., Coie, J. D., & Lynam, D. (2006). Aggression and antisocial behavior in youth. In N. Eisenberg, W. Damon, & R. M. Lerner (Eds.), *Handbook of child psychology: Vol. 3. Social, emotional, and personality development* (6th ed., pp. 719–788). Hoboken, NJ: Wiley.

Dodge, K. A., Godwin, J., & The Conduct Problems Prevention Research Group. (2013). Social-information-processing patterns mediate the impact of preventive intervention on adolescent antisocial behavior. *Psychological Science*, *24*, 456–465. http://dx.doi.org/10.1177/0956797612457394

Dodge, K. A., Pettit, G. S., Bates, J. E., & Valente, E. (1995). Social information-processing patterns partially mediate the effect of early physical abuse on later conduct problems. *Journal of Abnormal Psychology*, *104*, 632–643. http://dx.doi.org/10.1037/0021-843X.104.4.632

Doss, B. D., Simpson, L. E., & Christensen, A. (2004). Why do couples seek marital therapy? *Professional Psychology: Research and Practice*, *35*, 608–614. http://dx.doi.org/10.1037/0735-7028.35.6.608

Dutton, D. G. (1995). Trauma symptoms and PTSD-like profiles in perpetrators of intimate abuse. *Journal of Traumatic Stress*, *8*, 299–316. http://dx.doi.org/10.1002/jts.2490080210

Dutton, D. G. (1998). *The abusive personality: Violence and control in intimate relationships*. New York, NY: Guilford Press.

Dutton, D. G., & Corvo, K. (2006). Transforming a flawed policy: A call to revive psychology and science in domestic violence research and practice. *Aggression and Violent Behavior*, *11*, 457–483. http://dx.doi.org/10.1016/j.avb.2006.01.007

Dutton, D. G., van Ginkel, C., & Starzomski, A. (1995). The role of shame and guilt in the intergenerational transmission of abusiveness. *Violence and Victims*, *10*, 121–131.

Easton, C. J., Mandel, D. L., Hunkele, K. A., Nich, C., Rounsaville, B. J., & Carroll, K. M. (2007). A cognitive behavioral therapy for alcohol-dependent domestic violence offenders: An integrated substance abuse-domestic violence treatment approach (SADV). *The American Journal on Addictions*, *16*, 24–31. http://dx.doi.org/10.1080/10550490601077809

Eckhardt, C. I. (2007). Effects of alcohol intoxication on anger experience and expression among partner assaultive men. *Journal of Counseling and Clinical Psychology*, *75*, 61–71. http://dx.doi.org/10.1037/0022-006X.75.1.61

Eckhardt, C. I., Babcock, J., & Homack, S. (2004). Partner assaultive men and the stages and processes of change. *Journal of Family Violence*, *19*, 81–93. http://dx.doi.org/10.1023/B:JOFV.0000019839.98858.5c

Eckhardt, C. I., Barbour, K. A., & Davison, G. C. (1998). Articulated thoughts of maritally violent and nonviolent men during anger arousal. *Journal of Consulting and Clinical Psychology*, *66*, 259–269. http://dx.doi.org/10.1037/0022-006X.66.2.259

Eckhardt, C., Holtzworth-Munroe, A., Norlander, B., Sibley, A., & Cahill, M. (2009). Readiness to change, partner violence subtypes, and treatment outcomes among men in treatment for partner assault. In C. M. Murphy & R. D. Maiuro (Eds.), *Motivational interviewing and stages of change in intimate partner violence* (pp. 89–131). New York, NY: Springer.

Eckhardt, C. I., & Jamison, T. R. (2002). Articulated thoughts of male dating violence perpetrators during anger arousal. *Cognitive Therapy and Research*, *26*, 289–308. http://dx.doi.org/10.1023/A:1016045226185

Eckhardt, C. I., & Kassinove, H. (1998). Articulated cognitive distortions and cognitive deficiencies in maritally violent men. *Journal of Cognitive Psychotherapy*, *12*, 231–250.

Eckhardt, C. I., Murphy, C. M., Whitaker, D. J., Sprunger, J., Dykstra, R., & Woodard, K. (2013). The effectiveness of intervention programs for perpetrators and victims of intimate partner violence. *Partner Abuse*, *4*, 196–231. http://dx.doi.org/10.1891/1946-6560.4.2.196

Eckhardt, C. I., & Utschig, A. C. (2007). Assessing readiness to change among perpetrators of intimate partner violence: Analysis of two self-report measures. *Journal of Family Violence*, *22*, 319–330. http://dx.doi.org/10.1007/s10896-007-9088-9

Edleson, J. L. (1999). Children's witnessing of adult domestic violence. *Journal of Interpersonal Violence*, *14*, 839–870. http://dx.doi.org/10.1177/088626099014008004

Elbogen, E. B., Beckham, J. C., Butterfield, M. I., Swartz, M., & Swanson, J. (2008). Assessing risk of violent behavior among veterans with severe mental illness. *Journal of Traumatic Stress*, *21*, 113–117. http://dx.doi.org/10.1002/jts.20283

Elbogen, E. B., Johnson, S. C., Wagner, H. R., Newton, V. M., Timko, C., Vasterling, J. J., & Beckham, J. C. (2012). Protective factors and risk modification of violence in Iraq and Afghanistan War veterans. *Journal of Clinical Psychiatry*, *73*, e767–e773. http://dx.doi.org/10.4088/JCP.11m07593

Ellis, C. C., Peterson, M., Bufford, R., & Benson, J. (2014). The importance of group cohesion in inpatient treatment of combat-related PTSD. *International Journal of Group Psychotherapy*, *64*, 208–226. http://dx.doi.org/10.1521/ijgp.2014.64.2.208

Ellsberg, M., Jansen, H. A., Heise, L., Watts, C. H., Garcia-Moreno, C., & The WHO Multi-country Study on Women's Health and Domestic Violence against Women Study Team. (2008). Intimate partner violence and women's physical and mental health in the WHO multi-country study on women's health and domestic violence: An observational study. *The Lancet*, *371*, 1165–1172. http://dx.doi.org/10.1016/S0140-6736(08)60522-X

Erbes, C. R., Meis, L. A., Polusny, M. A., & Compton, J. S. (2011). Couple adjustment and posttraumatic stress disorder symptoms in National Guard veterans of the Iraq war. *Journal of Family Psychology*, *25*, 479–487. http://dx.doi.org/10.1037/a0024007

Evans, L., McHugh, T., Hopwood, M., & Watt, C. (2003). Chronic posttraumatic stress disorder and family functioning of Vietnam veterans and their partners. *Australian & New Zealand Journal of Psychiatry*, *37*, 765–772. http://dx.doi.org/10.1080/j.1440-1614.2003.01267.x

Evers, K. E., Paiva, A. L., Johnson, J. L., Cummins, C. O., Prochaska, J. O., Prochaska, J. M., . . . Gökbayrak, N. S. (2012). Results of a transtheoretical model-based alcohol, tobacco and other drug intervention in middle schools. *Addictive Behaviors*, *37*, 1009–1018. http://dx.doi.org/10.1016/j.addbeh.2012.04.008

Fallot, R. D., & Harris, M. (2001). A trauma-informed approach to screening and assessment. *New Directions for Mental Health Services*, *89*, 23–31. http://dx.doi.org/10.1002/yd.23320018904

Faul, M., Xu, L., Wald, M. M., & Coronado, V. G. (2010). *Traumatic brain injury in the United States: Emergency department visits, hospitalizations and deaths 2002–2006*. Atlanta, GA: Centers for Disease Control and Prevention, National Center for Injury Prevention and Control.

Fenton, B., & Rathus, J. H. (2010). Men's self-reported descriptions and precipitants of domestic violence perpetration as reported in intake evaluations. *Journal of Family Violence, 25*, 149–158. http://dx.doi.org/10.1007/s10896-009-9278-8

Finkel, E. J. (2007). Impelling and inhibiting forces in the perpetration of intimate partner violence. *Review of General Psychology, 11*, 193–207. http://dx.doi.org/10.1037/1089-2680.11.2.193

Finkelhor, D., & Browne, A. (1985). The traumatic impact of child sexual abuse: A conceptualization. *American Journal of Orthopsychiatry, 55*, 530–541. http://dx.doi.org/10.1111/j.1939-0025.1985.tb02703.x

Finn, S. E. (2005). How psychological assessment taught me compassion and firmness. *Journal of Personality Assessment, 84*, 29–32. http://dx.doi.org/10.1207/s15327752jpa8401_07

Finn, S. E., & Tonsager, M. E. (1997). Information-gathering and therapeutic models of assessment: Complementary paradigms. *Psychological Assessment, 9*, 374–385. http://dx.doi.org/10.1037/1040-3590.9.4.374

Fite, J. E., Bates, J. E., Holtzworth-Munroe, A., Dodge, K. A., Nay, S. Y., & Pettit, G. S. (2008). Social information processing mediates the intergenerational transmission of aggressiveness in romantic relationships. *Journal of Family Psychology, 22*, 367–376. http://dx.doi.org/10.1037/0893-3200.22.3.367

Foran, H. M., & O'Leary, K. D. (2008). Alcohol and intimate partner violence: A meta-analytic review. *Clinical Psychology Review, 28*, 1222–1234. http://dx.doi.org/10.1016/j.cpr.2008.05.001

Fredman, S. J., Monson, C. M., & Adair, K. C. (2011). Implementing cognitive–behavioral conjoint therapy for PTSD with the newest generation of veterans and their partners. *Cognitive and Behavioral Practice, 18*, 120–130. http://dx.doi.org/10.1016/j.cbpra.2009.06.007

Friedlander, M. L., Escudero, V., Heatherington, L., & Diamond, G. M. (2011). Alliance in couple and family therapy. *Psychotherapy, 48*, 25–33. http://dx.doi.org/10.1037/a0022060

Funk, J. L., & Rogge, R. D. (2007). Testing the ruler with item response theory: Increasing precision of measurement for relationship satisfaction with the Couples Satisfaction Index. *Journal of Family Psychology, 21*, 572–583. http://dx.doi.org/10.1037/0893-3200.21.4.572

Gallagher, M. E., Tasca, G. A., Ritchie, K., Balfour, L., & Bissada, H. (2014). Attachment anxiety moderates the relationship between growth in group cohesion and treatment outcomes in group psychodynamic interpersonal psychotherapy for women with binge eating disorder. *Group Dynamics: Theory, Research, and Practice, 18*, 38–52. http://dx.doi.org/10.1037/a0034760

Galovski, T., & Lyons, J. A. (2004). Psychological sequelae of combat violence: A review of the impact of PTSD on the veteran's family and possible interventions. *Aggression and Violent Behavior, 9*, 477–501. http://dx.doi.org/10.1016/S1359-1789(03)00045-4

Gauthier, L. M., & Levendosky, A. A. (1996). Assessment and treatment of couples with abusive male partners: Guidelines for therapists. *Psychotherapy: Theory, Research, Practice, Training, 33*, 403–417. http://dx.doi.org/10.1037/0033-3204.33.3.403

George, D. T., Phillips, M. J., Lifshitz, M., Lionetti, T. A., Spero, D. E., Ghassemzedeh, N., . . . Rawlings, R. R. (2011). Fluoxetine treatment of alcoholic perpetrators of domestic violence: A 12-week, double-blind, randomized, placebo-controlled intervention study. *Journal of Clinical Psychiatry, 72*, 60–65. http://dx.doi.org/10.4088/JCP.09m05256gry

Giancola, P. R., Josephs, R. A., Parrott, D. J., & Duke, A. A. (2010). Alcohol myopia revisited: Clarifying aggression and other acts of disinhibition through a distorted lens. *Perspectives on Psychological Science, 5*, 265–278. http://dx.doi.org/10.1177/1745691610369467

Gil, E. (2011). Family play therapy: Igniting creative energy, valuing metaphors, and making changes from the inside out. In C. E. Schaefer (Ed.), *Foundations of play therapy* (2nd ed., pp. 207–226). Hoboken, NJ: Wiley.

Gilligan, J. (1997). *Violence: Reflections on a national epidemic*. New York, NY: Vintage.

Gilligan, J. (2003). Shame, guilt, and violence. *Social Research, 70*, 1149–1180.

Gimbel, C., & Booth, A. (1994). Why does military combat experience adversely affect marital relations? *Journal of Marriage and Family*, 56, 691–703. http://dx.doi.org/10.2307/352879

Goff, B. S. N., Crow, J. R., Reisbig, A. M., & Hamilton, S. (2007). The impact of individual trauma symptoms of deployed soldiers on relationship satisfaction. *Journal of Family Psychology, 21*, 344–353. http://dx.doi.org/10.1037/0893-3200.21.3.344

Goldner, V. (1999). Morality and multiplicity: Perspectives on the treatment of violence in intimate life. *Journal of Marital & Family Therapy, 25*, 325–336. http://dx.doi.org/10.1111/j.1752-0606.1999.tb00251.x

Goodman, L. A., & Smyth, K. F. (2011). A call for a social network-oriented approach to services for survivors of intimate partner violence. *Psychology of Violence, 1*, 79–92. http://dx.doi.org/10.1037/a0022977

Goodyear-Brown, P. (2009). Theraplay approaches for children with autism spectrum disorders. In E. Munns (Ed.), *Applications of family and group Theraplay* (pp. 69–80). Lanham, MD: Jason Aronson.

Grace, M., Niles, B., Quinn, S., & Taft, C. T. (n.d.). *Anger management manual*. Unpublished manuscript.

Gutjahr, H., Portnoy, G., & Murphy, C. M. (2014, November). *Coping differences and posttraumatic stress symptoms among partner-violent men*. Paper presented at the meeting of the Association for Behavioral and Cognitive Therapies, Philadelphia, PA.

Haller, M., & Chassin, L. (2014). Risk pathways among traumatic stress, posttraumatic stress disorder symptoms, and alcohol and drug problems: A test of four hypotheses. *Psychology of Addictive Behaviors, 28*, 841–851. http://dx.doi.org/10.1037/a0035878

Hamberger, L. K. (2001). Musings of a state standards committee chair. *Journal of Aggression, Maltreatment & Trauma, 5*, 265–286. http://dx.doi.org/10.1300/J146v05n02_16

Hamberger, L. K., & Hastings, J. E. (1990a, November). Different routes to mandated spouse abuser counseling: II. A cross validation study. In C. Rasche (Chair), *Current studies of perpetrators and victims of spousal violence*. Symposium conducted at the meeting of the American Society of Criminology, Baltimore, MD.

Hamberger, L. K., & Hastings, J. E. (1990b). Recidivism following spouse abuse abatement counseling: Treatment program implications. *Violence and Victims, 5*, 157–170.

Harley, J. P., Allen, C., Braciszeski, T. L., Cicerone, K. D., Dahlberg, C., & Evans, S. (1992). Guidelines for cognitive rehabilitation. *NeuroRehabilitation, 2*, 62–67.

Harper, F. W. K., Austin, A. G., Cercone, J. J., & Arias, I. (2005). The role of shame, anger, and affect regulation in men's perpetration of psychological abuse in dating relationships. *Journal of Interpersonal Violence, 20*, 1648–1662. http://dx.doi.org/10.1177/0886260505278717

Hart, S. D., Dutton, D. G., & Newlove, T. (1993). The prevalence of personality disorder among wife assaulters. *Journal of Personality Disorders, 7*, 329–341. http://dx.doi.org/10.1521/pedi.1993.7.4.329

Hayes, M. A., Gallagher, M. W., Gilbert, K. S., Creech, S. K., DeCandia, C. J., Beach, C. A., & Taft, C. T. (2015). Targeting relational aggression in veterans: The Strength at Home Friends and Family intervention. *Journal of Clinical Psychiatry, 76*, e774–e778. http://dx.doi.org/10.4088/JCP.14m09155

Heather, N., Hönekopp, J., Smailes, D., & The UKATT Research Team. (2009). Progressive stage transition does mean getting better: A further test of the transtheoretical model in recovery from alcohol problems. *Addiction, 104*, 949–958. http://dx.doi.org/10.1111/j.1360-0443.2009.02578.x

Heckert, D. A., & Gondolf, E. W. (2000a). Assessing assault self-reports by batterer program participants and their partners. *Journal of Family Violence, 15*, 181–197. http://dx.doi.org/10.1023/A:1007594928605

Heckert, D. A., & Gondolf, E. W. (2000b). Predictors of underreporting of male violence by batterer program participants and their partners. *Journal of Family Violence, 15*, 423–443. http://dx.doi.org/10.1023/A:1007562431410

Heckert, D. A., & Gondolf, E. W. (2004). Battered women's perceptions of risk versus risk factors and instruments in predicting repeat reassault. *Journal of Interpersonal Violence, 19*, 778–800. http://dx.doi.org/10.1177/0886260504265619

Herrenkohl, T. I., Sousa, C., Tajima, E. A., Herrenkohl, R. C., & Moylan, C. A. (2008). Intersection of child abuse and children's exposure to domestic violence. *Trauma, Violence, & Abuse, 9*, 84–99. http://dx.doi.org/10.1177/1524838008314797

Heyman, R. E., & Neidig, P. H. (1997). Physical aggression couples treatment. In W. K. Halford & H. J. Markman (Eds.), *Clinical handbook of marriage and couples interventions* (pp. 589–617). Hoboken, NJ: Wiley.

Heyman, R. E., & Schlee, K. (2003). Stopping wife abuse via physical aggression couples treatment. *Journal of Aggression, Maltreatment & Trauma, 7*, 135–157. http://dx.doi.org/10.1300/J146v07n01_07

Heyman, R. E., & Slep, A. M. S. (2002). Do child abuse and interparental violence lead to adulthood family violence? *Journal of Marriage and Family, 64*, 864–870. http://dx.doi.org/10.1111/j.1741-3737.2002.00864.x

Heyman, R. E., Taft, C. T., Howard, J. M., Macdonald, A., & Collins, P. S. (2012). Intimate partner violence. In D. K. Snyder & C. M. Monson (Eds.), *Couple-based interventions for military and veteran families: A practitioner's guide* (pp. 122–146). New York, NY: Guilford Press.

Hilton, N. Z., Harris, G. T., Rice, M. E., Lang, C., Cormier, C. A., & Lines, K. J. (2004). A brief actuarial assessment for the prediction of wife assault recidivism: The Ontario Domestic Assault Risk Assessment. *Psychological Assessment, 16*, 267–275. http://dx.doi.org/10.1037/1040-3590.16.3.267

Hoge, C. W., McGurk, D., Thomas, J. L., Cox, A. L., Engel, C. C., & Castro, C. A. (2008). Mild traumatic brain injury in U.S. soldiers returning from Iraq. *The New England Journal of Medicine, 358*, 453–463. http://dx.doi.org/10.1056/NEJMoa072972

Holtzworth-Munroe, A. (1992). Social skill deficits in maritally violent men: Interpreting the data using a social information processing model. *Clinical Psychology Review, 12*, 605–617. http://dx.doi.org/10.1016/0272-7358(92)90134-T

Holtzworth-Munroe, A. (2005). Male versus female intimate partner violence: Putting controversial findings into context. *Journal of Marriage and Family, 67*, 1120–1125. http://dx.doi.org/10.1111/j.1741-3737.2005.00203.x

Holtzworth-Munroe, A., & Anglin, K. (1991). The competency of responses given by maritally violent versus nonviolent men to problematic marital situations. *Violence and Victims, 6*, 257–269.

Holtzworth-Munroe, A., & Hutchinson, G. (1993). Attributing negative intent to wife behavior: The attributions of maritally violent versus nonviolent men. *Journal of Abnormal Psychology, 102*, 206–211. http://dx.doi.org/10.1037/0021-843X.102.2.206

Holtzworth-Munroe, A., Meehan, J. C., Herron, K., Rehman, U., & Stuart, G. L. (2000). Testing the Holtzworth-Munroe and Stuart (1994) batterer typology. *Journal of Consulting and Clinical Psychology, 68*, 1000–1019. http://dx.doi.org/10.1037/0022-006X.68.6.1000

Holtzworth-Munroe, A., & Stuart, G. L. (1994). Typologies of male batterers: Three subtypes and the differences among them. *Psychological Bulletin, 116*, 476–497. http://dx.doi.org/10.1037/0033-2909.116.3.476

Hoyt, T., Wray, A. M., Wiggins, K. T., Gerstle, M., & Maclean, P. C. (2012). Personality profiles of intimate partner violence offenders with and without PTSD. *Journal of Offender Rehabilitation, 51*, 239–256. http://dx.doi.org/10.1080/10509674.2011.650349

Hughes, F. M., Stuart, G. L., Gordon, K. C., & Moore, T. M. (2007). Predicting the use of aggressive conflict tactics in a sample of women arrested for domestic violence. *Journal of Social and Personal Relationships, 24*, 155–176. http://dx.doi.org/10.1177/0265407507075406

Hundt, N. E., & Holohan, D. R. (2012). The role of shame in distinguishing perpetrators of intimate partner violence in U.S. veterans. *Journal of Traumatic Stress, 25*, 191–197. http://dx.doi.org/10.1002/jts.21688

Jankowski, M. K., Leitenberg, H., Henning, K., & Coffey, P. (1999). Intergenerational transmission of dating aggression as a function of witnessing only same sex parents vs. opposite sex parents vs. both parents as perpetrators of domestic violence. *Journal of Family Violence, 14*, 267–279. http://dx.doi.org/10.1023/A:1022814416666

Jennings, J. L. (1987). History and issues in the treatment of battering men: A case for unstructured group therapy. *Journal of Family Violence, 2*, 193–213. http://dx.doi.org/10.1007/BF00976539

Johnson, M. P. (2011). Gender and types of intimate partner violence: A response to an anti-feminist literature review. *Aggression and Violent Behavior, 16*, 289–296. http://dx.doi.org/10.1016/j.avb.2011.04.006

Jones, A. S., & Gondolf, E. W. (2001). Time-varying risk factors for reassault among batterer program participants. *Journal of Family Violence, 16*, 345–359. http://dx.doi.org/10.1023/A:1012268725273

Jordan, B. K., Marmar, C. R., Fairbank, J. A., Schlenger, W. E., Kulka, R. A., Hough, R. L., & Weiss, D. S. (1992). Problems in families of male Vietnam veterans with posttraumatic stress disorder. *Journal of Consulting and Clinical Psychology, 60*, 916–926. http://dx.doi.org/10.1037/0022-006X.60.6.916

Joyce, A. S., Piper, W. E., & Ogrodniczuk, J. S. (2007). Therapeutic alliance and cohesion variables as predictors of outcome in short-term group psychotherapy. *International Journal of Group Psychotherapy, 57*, 269–296. http://dx.doi.org/10.1521/ijgp.2007.57.3.269

Kachadourian, L. K., Taft, C. T., O'Farrell, T. J., Doron-Lamarca, S., & Murphy, C. M. (2012). Correlates of intimate partner psychological aggression perpetration in a clinical sample of alcoholic men. *Journal of Family Psychology, 26*, 206–214. http://dx.doi.org/10.1037/a0027436

Kalmuss, D. (1984). The intergenerational transmission of marital aggression. *Journal of Marriage and Family, 46*, 11–19. http://dx.doi.org/10.2307/351858

Kamarck, T. W., Haskett, R. F., Muldoon, M., Flory, J. D., Anderson, B., Bies, R., . . . Manuck, S. B. (2009). Citalopram intervention for hostility: Results of a randomized clinical trial. *Journal of Consulting and Clinical Psychology, 77*, 174–188. http://dx.doi.org/10.1037/a0014394

Keane, T. M., Marshall, A. D., & Taft, C. T. (2006). Posttraumatic stress disorder: Etiology, epidemiology, and treatment outcome. *Annual Review of Clinical Psychology, 2*, 161–197. http://dx.doi.org/10.1146/annurev.clinpsy.2.022305.095305

Kendra, R., Bell, K. M., & Guimond, J. M. (2012). The impact of child abuse history, PTSD symptoms, and anger arousal on dating violence perpetration among college women. *Journal of Family Violence, 27*, 165–175. http://dx.doi.org/10.1007/s10896-012-9415-7

King, D. W., Taft, C. T., King, L. A., Hammond, C., & Stone, E. R. (2006). Directionality of the association between social support and posttraumatic stress disorder: A longitudinal investigation. *Journal of Applied Social Psychology, 36*, 2980–2992. http://dx.doi.org/10.1111/j.0021-9029.2006.00138.x

Kistenmacher, B. R., & Weiss, R. L. (2008). Motivational interviewing as a mechanism for change in men who batter: A randomized controlled trial. *Violence and Victims, 23*, 558–570. http://dx.doi.org/10.1891/0886-6708.23.5.558

Kivlighan, D. M., & Shaughnessy, P. (1995). Analysis of the development of the working alliance using hierarchical linear modeling. *Journal of Counseling Psychology, 42*, 338–349. http://dx.doi.org/10.1037/0022-0167.42.3.338

Kroenke, K., & Spitzer, R. L. (2002). The PHQ–9: A new depression diagnostic and severity measure. *Psychiatric Annals, 32*, 509–515. http://dx.doi.org/10.3928/0048-5713-20020901-06

Kroenke, K., Spitzer, R. L., & Williams, J. B. (2001). The PHQ–9: Validity of a brief depression severity measure. *Journal of General Internal Medicine, 16*, 606–613. http://dx.doi.org/10.1046/j.1525-1497.2001.016009606.x

Kropp, P. R. (2008). Intimate partner violence risk assessment and management. *Violence and Victims, 23*, 202–220. http://dx.doi.org/10.1891/0886-6708.23.2.202

Kropp, P. R., & Gibas, A. (2010). The Spousal Assault Risk Assessment Guide. In R. K. Otto & K. S. Douglas (Eds.), *Handbook of violence risk assessment* (pp. 227–250). New York, NY: Taylor & Francis.

Kropp, P. R., & Hart, S. D. (2000). The Spousal Assault Risk Assessment (SARA) Guide: Reliability and validity in adult male offenders. *Law and Human Behavior, 24*, 101–118. http://dx.doi.org/10.1023/A:1005430904495

Krupnick, J. L., Sotsky, S. M., Simmens, S., Moyer, J., Elkin, I., Watkins, J., & Pilkonis, P. A. (1996). The role of the therapeutic alliance in psychotherapy and pharmacotherapy outcome: Findings in the National Institute of Mental Health Treatment of Depression Collaborative Research Program. *Journal of Consulting and Clinical Psychology, 64*, 532–539. http://dx.doi.org/10.1037/0022-006X.64.3.532

Kubany, E. S., Leisen, M. B., Kaplan, A. S., Watson, S. B., Haynes, S. N., Owens, J. A., & Burns, K. (2000). Development and preliminary validation of a brief broad-spectrum measure of trauma exposure: The Traumatic Life Events Questionnaire. *Psychological Assessment, 12*, 210–224. http://dx.doi.org/10.1037/1040-3590.12.2.210

Kulka, R. A., Schlenger, W. E., Fairbank, J. A., Hough, R. L., Jordan, B. K., Marmar, C. R., & Weiss, D. S. (1990). *Trauma and the Vietnam War generation: Report of findings from the National Vietnam Veterans Readjustment Study*. Philadelphia, PA: Brunner/Mazel.

LaMotte, A. D., Taft, C. T., Reardon, A. F., & Miller, M. W. (2014). Agreement between veteran and partner reports of intimate partner aggression. *Psychological Assessment, 26*, 1369–1374. http://dx.doi.org/10.1037/pas0000018

LaMotte, A. D., Taft, C. T., Weatherill, R. P., Scott, J. P., & Eckhardt, C. I. (2014). Examining intimate partner aggression assessment among returning veterans and their partners. *Psychological Assessment, 26*, 8–15. http://dx.doi.org/10.1037/a0034579

Larsen, S. E., & Hamberger, L. K. (2015). Men's and women's experience of IPV: Part II. A review of new developments in comparative studies in clinical populations. *Journal of Family Violence, 30*, 1007–1030. http://dx.doi.org/10.1007/s10896-015-9730-x

LaTaillade, J. J., Epstein, N. B., & Werlinich, C. A. (2006). Conjoint treatment of intimate partner violence: A cognitive behavioral approach. *Journal of Cognitive Psychotherapy, 20*, 393–410. http://dx.doi.org/10.1891/jcpiq-v20i4a005

Leisring, P., Dowd, L., & Rosenbaum, A. (1999, July). Characteristics of women mandated to anger management treatment. Paper presented at the 6th International Family Violence Research Conference, Durham, NH.

Levesque, D. A., Gelles, R. J., & Velicer, W. F. (2000). Development and validation of a stages of change measure for men in batterer treatment. *Cognitive Therapy and Research, 24*, 175–199.

Levine, P. A., & Kline, M. (2006). *Trauma through a child's eyes: Awakening the ordinary miracle of healing*. Berkeley, CA: North Atlantic Books.

Lila, M., Herrero, J., & Gracia, E. (2008). Multiple victimization of Spanish adolescents: A multilevel analysis. *Adolescence, 43*, 333–350.

Linehan, M. M. (1993). *Cognitive–behavioral treatment of borderline personality disorder*. New York, NY: Guilford Press.

Linehan, M. M., Armstrong, H. E., Suarez, A., Allmon, D., & Heard, H. L. (1991). Cognitive–behavioral treatment of chronically parasuicidal borderline patients. *Archives of General Psychiatry, 48*, 1060–1064. http://dx.doi.org/10.1001/archpsyc.1991.01810360024003

Lipsky, S., Caetano, R., Field, C. A., & Bazargan, S. (2005). The role of alcohol use and depression in intimate partner violence among Black and Hispanic patients in an urban emergency department. *The American Journal of Drug and Alcohol Abuse, 31*, 225–242. http://dx.doi.org/10.1081/ADA-47923

Lobitz, W. C., & LoPiccolo, J. (1972). New methods in the behavioral treatment of sexual dysfunction. *Journal of Behavior Therapy and Experimental Psychiatry, 3*, 265–271. http://dx.doi.org/10.1016/0005-7916(72)90047-X

Love, A. R., Morland, L. A., Menez, U., Taft, C., MacDonald, A., & Mackintosh, M. A. (2015). "Strength at Home" intervention for male veterans perpetrating intimate partner aggression: Perceived Needs Survey of Therapists and Pilot Effectiveness Study. *Journal of Interpersonal Violence, 30*, 2344–2362. http://dx.doi.org/10.1177/0886260514552445

Magdol, L., Moffitt, T. E., Caspi, A., & Silva, P. A. (1998). Developmental antecedents of partner abuse: A prospective-longitudinal study. *Journal of Abnormal Psychology, 107*, 375–389. http://dx.doi.org/10.1037/0021-843X.107.3.375

Maguire, E., Macdonald, A., Krill, S., Holowka, D., Marx, B., Woodward, H., . . . Taft, C. T. (2015). Examining trauma and posttraumatic stress disorder symptoms in court-mandated intimate partner violence perpetrators. *Psychological Trauma: Theory, Research, Practice, and Policy, 7*, 473–478. http://dx.doi.org/10.1037/a0039253

Maiuro, R. D., Cahn, T. S., & Vitaliano, P. P. (1986). Assertiveness deficits and hostility in domestically violent men. *Violence and Victims, 1*, 279–289.

Maiuro, R. D., & Eberle, J. A. (2008). State standards for domestic violence perpetrator treatment: Current status, trends, and recommendations. *Violence and Victims, 23*, 133–155. http://dx.doi.org/10.1891/0886-6708.23.2.133

Mallinckrodt, B. (1996). Change in working alliance, social support, and psychological symptoms in brief therapy. *Journal of Counseling Psychology, 43*, 448–455. http://dx.doi.org/10.1037/0022-0167.43.4.448

Mankowski, E. S., Haaken, J., & Silvergleid, C. S. (2002). Collateral damage: An analysis of the achievements and unintended consequences of batterer intervention programs and discourse. *Journal of Family Violence, 17*, 167–184. http://dx.doi.org/10.1023/A:1015061517888

Marsh, J. C., Angell, B., Andrews, C. M., & Curry, A. (2012). Client–provider relationship and treatment outcome: A systematic review of substance abuse, child welfare, and mental health services research. *Journal of the Society for Social Work and Research, 3*, 233–267. http://dx.doi.org/10.5243/jsswr.2012.15

Marshall, A. D., & Holtzworth-Munroe, A. (2010). Recognition of wives' emotional expressions: A mechanism in the relationship between psychopathology and intimate partner violence perpetration. *Journal of Family Psychology, 24*, 21–30. http://dx.doi.org/10.1037/a0017952

Marshall, A. D., Robinson, L. R., & Azar, S. T. (2011). Cognitive and emotional contributors to intimate partner violence perpetration following trauma. *Journal of Traumatic Stress, 24*, 586–590. http://dx.doi.org/10.1002/jts.20681

Martin, D. J., Garske, J. P., & Davis, M. K. (2000). Relation of the therapeutic alliance with outcome and other variables: A meta-analytic review. *Journal of Consulting and Clinical Psychology, 68*, 438–450. http://dx.doi.org/10.1037/0022-006X.68.3.438

Maxwell, C. D., Davis, R. C., & Taylor, B. G. (2010). The impact of length of domestic violence treatment on the patterns of subsequent intimate partner violence. *Journal of Experimental Criminology, 6*, 475–497. http://dx.doi.org/10.1007/s11292-010-9106-4

Mbilinyi, L. F., Neighbors, C., Walker, D. D., Roffman, R. A., Zegree, J., Edleson, J., & O'Rourke, A. (2011). A telephone intervention for substance-using adult male perpetrators of intimate partner violence. *Research on Social Work Practice, 21*, 43–56. http://dx.doi.org/10.1177/1049731509359008

McCollum, E. E., & Stith, S. M. (2008). Couples treatment for interpersonal violence: A review of outcome research literature and current clinical practices. *Violence and Victims*, *23*, 187–201. http://dx.doi.org/10.1891/0886-6708.23.2.187

McFall, R. M. (1982). A review and reformulation of the concept of social skills. *Behavioral Assessment*, *4*, 1–33.

McFarlane, J. M., Groff, J. Y., O'Brien, J. A., & Watson, K. (2006). Secondary prevention of intimate partner violence: A randomized controlled trial. *Nursing Research*, *55*, 52–61. http://dx.doi.org/10.1097/00006199-200601000-00007

McFarlane, J., Malecha, A., Gist, J., Watson, K., Batten, E., Hall, I., & Smith, S. (2004). Increasing the safety-promoting behaviors of abused women. *The American Journal of Nursing*, *104*, 40–50. http://dx.doi.org/10.1097/00000446-200403000-00019

Meis, L. A. (2008). *Negative peer influences among partner-violent men: Countertherapeutic talk and participants' responses to group intervention* (Doctoral dissertation). Available from ProQuest Dissertations and Theses database. (UMI No. 3324638)

Miller, M. W., & Resick, P. A. (2007). Internalizing and externalizing subtypes in female sexual assault survivors: Implications for the understanding of complex PTSD. *Behavior Therapy*, *38*, 58–71. http://dx.doi.org/10.1016/j.beth.2006.04.003

Miller, M. W., Wolf, E. J., & Keane, T. M. (2014). Posttraumatic stress disorder in *DSM–5*: New criteria and controversies. *Clinical Psychology: Science and Practice*, *21*, 208–220. http://dx.doi.org/10.1111/cpsp.12070

Miller, W. R., Benefield, R. G., & Tonigan, J. S. (1993). Enhancing motivation for change in problem drinking: A controlled comparison of two therapist styles. *Journal of Consulting and Clinical Psychology*, *61*, 455–461. http://dx.doi.org/10.1037/0022-006X.61.3.455

Miller, W. R., Meyers, R. J., & Tonigan, J. S. (1999). Engaging the unmotivated in treatment for alcohol problems: A comparison of three strategies for intervention through family members. *Journal of Consulting and Clinical Psychology*, *67*, 688–697. http://dx.doi.org/10.1037/0022-006X.67.5.688

Miller, W. R., & Rollnick, S. (2002). *Motivational interviewing: Preparing people to change addictive behavior* (2nd ed.). New York, NY: Guilford Press.

Miller, W. R., & Rollnick, S. (2012). *Motivational interviewing: Helping people change*. New York, NY: Guilford Press.

Miller, W. R., Taylor, C. A., & West, J. (1980). Focused versus broad-spectrum behavior therapy for problem drinkers. *Journal of Consulting and Clinical Psychology*, *48*, 590–601. http://dx.doi.org/10.1037/0022-006X.48.5.590

Monson, C. M., & Fredman, S. J. (2012). *Cognitive–behavioral conjoint therapy for posttraumatic stress disorder: Therapist's manual*. New York, NY: Guilford Press.

Monson, C. M., Fredman, S. J., Adair, K. C., Stevens, S. P., Resick, P. A., Schnurr, P. P., . . . Macdonald, A. (2011). Cognitive–behavioral conjoint therapy for

PTSD: Pilot results from a community sample. *Journal of Traumatic Stress*, *24*, 97–101. http://dx.doi.org/10.1002/jts.20604

Monson, C. M., Fredman, S. J., Macdonald, A., Pukay-Martin, N. D., Resick, P. A., & Schnurr, P. P. (2012). Effect of cognitive-behavioral couple therapy for PTSD: A randomized controlled trial. *JAMA*, *308*, 700–709. http://dx.doi.org/10.1001/jama.2012.9307

Monson, C. M., Resick, P. A., & Rizvi, S. L. (2014). Posttraumatic stress disorder. In D. H. Barlow (Ed.), *Clinical handbook of psychological disorders* (5th ed., pp. 62–113). New York, NY: Guilford Press.

Monson, C. M., Schnurr, P. P., Resick, P. A., Friedman, M. J., Young-Xu, Y., & Stevens, S. P. (2006). Cognitive processing therapy for veterans with military-related posttraumatic stress disorder. *Journal of Consulting and Clinical Psychology*, *74*, 898–907. http://dx.doi.org/10.1037/0022-006X.74.5.898

Monson, C. M., Taft, C. T., & Fredman, S. J. (2009). Military-related PTSD and intimate relationships: From description to theory-driven research and intervention development. *Clinical Psychology Review*, *29*, 707–714. http://dx.doi.org/10.1016/j.cpr.2009.09.002

Mooney, K. A., & Padesky, C. A. (2000). Applying client creativity to recurrent problems: Constructing possibilities and tolerating doubt. *Journal of Cognitive Psychotherapy*, *14*, 149–161.

Moore, T. M., Stuart, G. L., Meehan, J. C., Rhatigan, D. L., Hellmuth, J. C., & Keen, S. M. (2008). Drug abuse and aggression between intimate partners: A meta-analytic review. *Clinical Psychology Review*, *28*, 247–274. http://dx.doi.org/10.1016/j.cpr.2007.05.003

Morrel, T. M., Elliott, J. D., Murphy, C. M., & Taft, C. T. (2003). Cognitive behavioral and supportive group treatments for partner violent men. *Behavior Therapy*, *34*, 77–95. http://dx.doi.org/10.1016/S0005-7894(03)80023-0

Murphy, C. M. (2001). Toward empirically based standards for abuser intervention: The Maryland model. *Journal of Aggression, Maltreatment & Trauma*, *5*, 249–264. http://dx.doi.org/10.1300/J146v05n02_15

Murphy, C. M. (2013). Social information processing and the perpetration of intimate partner violence: It is (and isn't) what you think. *Psychology of Violence*, *3*, 212–217. http://dx.doi.org/10.1037/a0033344

Murphy, C. M., & Baxter, V. A. (1997). Motivating batterers to change in the treatment context. *Journal of Interpersonal Violence*, *12*, 607–619. http://dx.doi.org/10.1177/088626097012004009

Murphy, C. M., & Eckhardt, C. I. (2005). *Treating the abusive partner: An individualized cognitive–behavioral approach*. New York, NY: Guilford Press.

Murphy, C. M., Eckhardt, C. I., Clifford, J. M., LaMotte, A. D., & Meis, L. A. (2015). *Individual versus group cognitive behavioral therapy for partner abusive men*. Unpublished manuscript, Department of Psychology, University of Maryland, Baltimore County, Baltimore.

Murphy, C. M., & Hoover, S. A. (1999). Measuring emotional abuse in dating relationships as a multifactorial construct. *Violence and Victims, 14*, 39–53.

Murphy, C. M., Hoover, S., & Taft, C. T. (1999, November). *The Multidimensional Measure of Emotional Abuse: Factor structure and subscale validity*. Paper presented at the 34th annual convention of the Association for the Advancement of Behavior Therapy, Toronto, Canada.

Murphy, C. M., Linehan, E. L., Reyner, J. C., Musser, P. H., & Taft, C. T. (2012). Moderators of response to motivational interviewing for partner-violent men. *Journal of Family Violence, 27*, 671–680. http://dx.doi.org/10.1007/s10896-012-9460-2

Murphy, C. M., & Maiuro, R. D. (2009). *Motivational interviewing and stages of change in intimate partner violence*. New York, NY: Springer.

Murphy, C. M., Meis, L., Clifford, J., Persampiere, J., & Eckhardt, C. (2008, July). *Individual versus group cognitive behavioral therapy for partner abusive men*. Paper presented at the International Family Violence Research Conference, Portsmouth, NH.

Murphy, C. M., Meis, L. A., & Eckhardt, C. I. (2009). Individualized services and individual therapy for partner abuse perpetrators. In K. D. O'Leary & E. M. Woodin (Eds.), *Psychological and physical aggression in couples: Causes and interventions* (pp. 211–231). Washington, DC: American Psychological Association. http://dx.doi.org/10.1037/11880-010

Murphy, C. M., Musser, P. H., & Maton, K. I. (1998). Coordinated community intervention for domestic abusers: Intervention system involvement and criminal recidivism. *Journal of Family Violence, 13*, 263–284.

Murphy, C. M., & O'Leary, K. D. (1989). Psychological aggression predicts physical aggression in early marriage. *Journal of Consulting and Clinical Psychology, 57*, 579–582. http://dx.doi.org/10.1037/0022-006X.57.5.579

Murphy, C. M., & Scott, E. (1996). *Cognitive–behavioral therapy for domestically assaultive individuals: A treatment manual*. Unpublished manuscript, University of Maryland–Baltimore County.

Murphy, C. M., Taft, C. T., & Eckhardt, C. I. (2007). Anger problem profiles among partner violent men: Differences in clinical presentation and treatment outcome. *Journal of Counseling Psychology, 54*, 189–200. http://dx.doi.org/10.1037/0022-0167.54.2.189

Murphy, C. M., & Ting, L. (2010). The effects of treatment for substance use problems on intimate partner violence: A review of empirical data. *Aggression and Violent Behavior, 15*, 325–333. http://dx.doi.org/10.1016/j.avb.2010.01.006

Musser, P. H., Semiatin, J. N., Taft, C. T., & Murphy, C. M. (2008). Motivational interviewing as a pregroup intervention for partner-violent men. *Violence and Victims, 23*, 539–557. http://dx.doi.org/10.1891/0886-6708.23.5.539

Nadelson, T. (2005). *Trained to kill: Soldiers at war*. Baltimore, MD: Johns Hopkins University Press.

Neidig, P. H., & Friedman, D. H. (1984). *Spouse abuse: A treatment approach for couples*. Champaign, IL: Research Press.

Nelson, B. S., Wangsgaard, S., Yorgason, J., Kessler, M. H., & Carter-Vassol, E. (2002). Single- and dual-trauma couples: Clinical observations of relational characteristics and dynamics. *American Journal of Orthopsychiatry, 72*, 58–69. http://dx.doi.org/10.1037/0002-9432.72.1.58

Nelson, L. A., Yoash-Gantz, R. E., Pickett, T. C., & Campbell, T. A. (2009). Relationship between processing speed and executive functioning performance among OEF/OIF veterans: Implications for postdeployment rehabilitation. *The Journal of Head Trauma Rehabilitation, 24*, 32–40. http://dx.doi.org/10.1097/HTR.0b013e3181957016

Newnham, E. A., & Janca, A. (2014). Childhood adversity and borderline personality disorder: A focus on adolescence. *Current Opinion in Psychiatry, 27*, 68–72. http://dx.doi.org/10.1097/YCO.0000000000000028

Nezu, A. M., Nezu, C. M., & D'Zurilla, T. (2012). *Problem-solving therapy: A treatment manual*. New York, NY: Springer.

Norwood, A., & Murphy, C. (2012). What forms of abuse correlate with PTSD symptoms in partners of men being treated for intimate partner violence? *Psychological Trauma: Theory, Research, Practice, and Policy, 4*, 596–604. http://dx.doi.org/10.1037/a0025232

Novaco, R. W., & Chemtob, C. M. (1998). Anger and trauma: Conceptualization, assessment, and treatment. In V. M. Follette, J. I. Ruzek, & F. R. Abueg (Eds.), *Cognitive–behavioral therapies for trauma* (pp. 162–190). New York, NY: Guilford Press.

O'Donnell, C., Cook, J. M., Thompson, R., Riley, K., & Neria, Y. (2006). Verbal and physical aggression in World War II former prisoners of war: Role of posttraumatic stress disorder and depression. *Journal of Traumatic Stress, 19*, 859–866. http://dx.doi.org/10.1002/jts.20157

O'Farrell, T. J., & Clements, K. (2012). Review of outcome research on marital and family therapy in treatment for alcoholism. *Journal of Marital & Family Therapy, 38*, 122–144. http://dx.doi.org/10.1111/j.1752-0606.2011.00242.x

O'Farrell, T. J., & Murphy, C. M. (1995). Marital violence before and after alcoholism treatment. *Journal of Consulting and Clinical Psychology, 63*, 256–262. http://dx.doi.org/10.1037/0022-006X.63.2.256

O'Farrell, T. J., Murphy, C. M., Stephan, S. H., Fals-Stewart, W., & Murphy, M. (2004). Partner violence before and after couples-based alcoholism treatment for male alcoholic patients: The role of treatment involvement and abstinence. *Journal of Consulting and Clinical Psychology, 72*, 202–217. http://dx.doi.org/10.1037/0022-006X.72.2.202

O'Farrell, T. J., Van Hutton, V., & Murphy, C. M. (1999). Domestic violence before and after alcoholism treatment: A two-year longitudinal study. *Journal of Studies on Alcohol, 60*, 317–321. http://dx.doi.org/10.15288/jsa.1999.60.317

Ogle, R. L., & Miller, W. R. (2004). The effects of alcohol intoxication and gender on the social information processing of hostile provocations involving male and female provocateurs. *Journal of Studies on Alcohol*, *65*, 54–62. http://dx.doi.org/10.15288/jsa.2004.65.54

O'Hare, T. (1996). Court-ordered versus voluntary clients: Problem differences and readiness for change. *Social Work*, *41*, 417–422.

Olatunji, B. O., Ciesielski, B. G., & Tolin, D. F. (2010). Fear and loathing: A meta-analytic review of the specificity of anger in PTSD. *Behavior Therapy*, *41*, 93–105. http://dx.doi.org/10.1016/j.beth.2009.01.004

O'Leary, K. D., Heyman, R. E., & Neidig, P. H. (1999). Treatment of wife abuse: A comparison of gender-specific and conjoint approaches. *Behavior Therapy*, *30*, 475–505. http://dx.doi.org/10.1016/S0005-7894(99)80021-5

Orcutt, H. K., King, L. A., & King, D. W. (2003). Male-perpetrated violence among Vietnam veteran couples: Relationships with veteran's early life characteristics, trauma history, and PTSD symptomatology. *Journal of Traumatic Stress*, *16*, 381–390. http://dx.doi.org/10.1023/A:1024470103325

Orth, U., & Wieland, E. (2006). Anger, hostility, and posttraumatic stress disorder in trauma-exposed adults: A meta-analysis. *Journal of Consulting and Clinical Psychology*, *74*, 698–706. http://dx.doi.org/10.1037/0022-006X.74.4.698

Ozer, E. J., Best, S. R., Lipsey, T. L., & Weiss, D. S. (2003). Predictors of posttraumatic stress disorder and symptoms in adults: A meta-analysis. *Psychological Bulletin*, *129*, 52–73. http://dx.doi.org/10.1037/0033-2909.129.1.52

Palmstierna, T., Haugan, G., Jarwson, S., Rasmussen, K., & Nøttestad, J. A. (2012). Cognitive–behaviour group therapy for men voluntary seeking help for intimate partner violence. *Nordic Journal of Psychiatry*, 66, 360–365. http://dx.doi.org/10.3109/08039488.2012.665080

Parrott, D. J., Drobes, D. J., Saladin, M. E., Coffey, S. F., & Dansky, B. S. (2003). Perpetration of partner violence: Effects of cocaine and alcohol dependence and posttraumatic stress disorder. *Addictive Behaviors*, *28*, 1587–1602. http://dx.doi.org/10.1016/j.addbeh.2003.08.036

Pence, E., & Paymar, M. (1993). *Education groups for men who batter: The Duluth model*. New York, NY: Springer.

Persampiere, J., Poole, G., & Murphy, C. M. (2014). Neuropsychological correlates of anger, hostility, and relationship-relevant distortions in thinking among partner violent men. *Journal of Family Violence*, *29*, 625–641. http://dx.doi.org/10.1007/s10896-014-9614-5

Picard, M., Scarisbrick, D., & Paluck, R. (1991). *H.E.L.P.S.: A brief screening device for traumatic brain injury*. New York, NY: Comprehensive Regional Traumatic Brain Injury Rehabilitation Center.

Pico-Alfonso, M. A., Garcia-Linares, M. I., Celda-Navarro, N., Blasco-Ros, C., Echeburúa, E., & Martinez, M. (2006). The impact of physical, psychological, and sexual intimate male partner violence on women's mental health: Depressive symptoms, posttraumatic stress disorder, state anxiety, and suicide. *Journal of Women's Health, 15*, 599–611. http://dx.doi.org/10.1089/jwh.2006.15.599

Pinto, L. A., Sullivan, E. L., Rosenbaum, A., Wyngarden, N., Umhau, J. C., Miller, M. W., & Taft, C. T. (2010). Biological correlates of intimate partner violence perpetration. *Aggression and Violent Behavior, 15*, 387–398. http://dx.doi.org/10.1016/j.avb.2010.07.001

Pitman, R. K., Orr, S. P., Forgue, D. F., de Jong, J. B., & Claiborn, J. M. (1987). Psychophysiologic assessment of posttraumatic stress disorder imagery in Vietnam combat veterans. *Archives of General Psychiatry, 44*, 970–975. http://dx.doi.org/10.1001/archpsyc.1987.01800230050009

Poston, J. M., & Hanson, W. E. (2010). Meta-analysis of psychological assessment as a therapeutic intervention. *Psychological Assessment, 22*, 203–212. http://dx.doi.org/10.1037/a0018679

Prochaska, J. O., & DiClemente, C. C. (1982). Transtheoretical therapy: Toward a more integrative model of change. *Psychotherapy: Theory, Research & Practice, 19*, 276–288. http://dx.doi.org/10.1037/h0088437

Prochaska, J. O., & DiClemente, C. C. (1992). The transtheoretical approach. In J. C. Norcross & M. R. Goldfried (Eds.), *Handbook of psychotherapy integration* (pp. 300–334). New York, NY: Basic Books.

Prochaska, J. O., Johnson, S., & Lee, P. (2009). The transtheoretical model of behavior change. In S. A. Shumaker, J. K. Ockene, & K. A. Riekert (Eds.), *The handbook of health behavior change* (3rd ed., pp. 59–83). New York, NY: Springer.

Ptacek, J. (1988). Why do men batter their wives? In K. Yllö & M. Bograd (Eds.), *Feminist perspectives on wife abuse* (pp. 133–157). Thousand Oaks, CA: Sage.

Raudenbush, S. W., Bryk, A. S., Cheong, Y. F., & Congdon, R. T. (2004). HLM6: Hierarchical linear and nonlinear modeling [Computer software]. Chicago, IL: Scientific Software International.

Raver, C. C., Jones, S. M., Li-Grining, C., Zhai, F., Bub, K., & Pressler, E. (2011). CSRP's Impact on low-income preschoolers' preacademic skills: Self-regulation as a mediating mechanism. *Child Development, 82*, 362–378. http://dx.doi.org/10.1111/j.1467-8624.2010.01561.x

Reitzel-Jaffe, D., & Wolfe, D. A. (2001). Predictors of relationship abuse among young men. *Journal of Interpersonal Violence, 16*, 99–115. http://dx.doi.org/10.1177/088626001016002001

Renshaw, K. D., Rodrigues, C. S., & Jones, D. H. (2008). Psychological symptoms and marital satisfaction in spouses of Operation Iraqi Freedom veterans: Relationships with spouses' perceptions of veterans' experiences and symptoms. *Journal of Family Psychology, 22*, 586–594. http://dx.doi.org/10.1037/0893-3200.22.3.586

Resick, P. A., Galovski, T. E., Uhlmansiek, M. O., Scher, C. D., Clum, G. A., & Young-Xu, Y. (2008). A randomized clinical trial to dismantle components of cognitive processing therapy for posttraumatic stress disorder in female victims of interpersonal violence. *Journal of Consulting and Clinical Psychology, 76,* 243–258. http://dx.doi.org/10.1037/0022-006X.76.2.243

Resick, P. A., & Schnicke, M. K. (1992). Cognitive processing therapy for sexual assault victims. *Journal of Consulting and Clinical Psychology, 60,* 748–756. http://dx.doi.org/10.1037/0022-006X.60.5.748

Rhodes, K. V., Houry, D., Cerulli, C., Straus, H., Kaslow, N. J., & McNutt, L. A. (2009). Intimate partner violence and comorbid mental health conditions among urban male patients. *Annals of Family Medicine, 7,* 47–55. http://dx.doi.org/10.1370/afm.936

Rollnick, S., & Miller, W. R. (1995). What is motivational interviewing? *Behavioural and Cognitive Psychotherapy, 23,* 325–334. http://dx.doi.org/10.1017/S135246580001643X

Rondeau, G., Brodeur, N., Brochu, S., & Lemire, G. (2001). Dropout and completion of treatment among spouse abusers. *Violence and Victims, 16,* 127–143.

Rosenbaum, A. (2010). Rethinking batterer intervention. *PsycCRITIQUES, 55*(22). http://dx.doi.org/10.1037/a0019588

Rosenbaum, A., & Leisring, P. A. (2003). Beyond power and control: Towards an understanding of partner abusive men. *Journal of Comparative Family Studies, 34,* 7–22.

Rosenbaum, A., & O'Leary, K. D. (1981). Marital violence: Characteristics of abusive couples. *Journal of Consulting and Clinical Psychology, 49,* 63–71. http://dx.doi.org/10.1037/0022-006X.49.1.63

Rosenberg, M. S. (2003). Voices from the group: Domestic violence offenders' experience of intervention. *Journal of Aggression, Maltreatment & Trauma, 7,* 305–317. http://dx.doi.org/10.1300/J146v07n01_13

Safran, J. D., & Muran, J. C. (1996). The resolution of ruptures in the therapeutic alliance. *Journal of Consulting and Clinical Psychology, 64,* 447–458. http://dx.doi.org/10.1037/0022-006X.64.3.447

Saunders, J. B., Aasland, O. G., Babor, T. F., de la Fuente, J. R., & Grant, M. (1993). Development of the Alcohol Use Disorders Identification Test (AUDIT): WHO collaborative project on early detection of persons with harmful alcohol consumption II. *Addiction, 88,* 791–804. http://dx.doi.org/10.1111/j.1360-0443.1993.tb02093.x

Savarese, V. W., Suvak, M. K., King, L. A., & King, D. W. (2001). Relationships among alcohol use, hyperarousal, and marital abuse and violence in Vietnam veterans. *Journal of Traumatic Stress, 14,* 717–732. http://dx.doi.org/10.1023/A:1013038021175

Scalia, J. (1994). Psychoanalytic insights and the prevention of pseudosuccess in the cognitive-behavioral treatment of batterers. *Journal of Interpersonal Violence, 9,* 548–555. http://dx.doi.org/10.1177/088626094009004008

Schacht, R. L., Dimidjian, S., George, W. H., & Berns, S. B. (2009). Domestic violence assessment procedures among couple therapists. *Journal of Marital & Family Therapy, 35,* 47–59. http://dx.doi.org/10.1111/j.1752-0606.2008.00095.x

Schmutte, G. T., Leonard, K. E., & Taylor, S. P. (1979). Alcohol and expectations of attack. *Psychological Reports, 45*, 163–167. http://dx.doi.org/10.2466/pr0.1979.45.1.163

Schnur, J. B., & Montgomery, G. H. (2010). A systematic review of therapeutic alliance, group cohesion, empathy, and goal consensus/collaboration in psychotherapeutic interventions in cancer: Uncommon factors? *Clinical Psychology Review, 30*, 238–247. http://dx.doi.org/10.1016/j.cpr.2009.11.005

Schumacher, J. A., Feldbau-Kohn, S., Slep, A. M. S., & Heyman, R. E. (2001). Risk factors for male-to-female partner physical abuse. *Aggression and Violent Behavior, 6*, 281–352. http://dx.doi.org/10.1016/S1359-1789(00)00027-6

Schumacher, J. A., & Leonard, K. E. (2005). Husbands' and wives' marital adjustment, verbal aggression, and physical aggression as longitudinal predictors of physical aggression in early marriage. *Journal of Consulting and Clinical Psychology, 73*, 28–37. http://dx.doi.org/10.1037/0022-006X.73.1.28

Schumm, J. A., O'Farrell, T. J., Kahler, C. W., Murphy, M. M., & Muchowski, P. (2014). A randomized clinical trial of behavioral couples therapy versus individually based treatment for women with alcohol dependence. *Journal of Consulting and Clinical Psychology, 82*, 993–1004. http://dx.doi.org/10.1037/a0037497

Schumm, J. A., O'Farrell, T. J., Murphy, C. M., & Fals-Stewart, W. (2009). Partner violence before and after couples-based alcoholism treatment for female alcoholic patients. *Journal of Consulting and Clinical Psychology, 77*, 1136–1146. http://dx.doi.org/10.1037/a0017389

Schwartz, J. P., Waldo, M., & Daniel, D. (2005). Gender-role conflict and self-esteem: Factors associated with partner abuse in court-referred men. *Psychology of Men & Masculinity, 6*, 109–113. http://dx.doi.org/10.1037/1524-9220.6.2.109

Scott, K. L. (2004). Stage of change as a predictor of attrition among men in a batterer treatment program. *Journal of Family Violence, 19*, 37–47. http://dx.doi.org/10.1023/B:JOFV.0000011581.01231.1e

Scott, K., King, C., McGinn, H., & Hosseini, N. (2011). Effects of motivational enhancement on immediate outcomes of batterer intervention. *Journal of Family Violence, 26*, 139–149. http://dx.doi.org/10.1007/s10896-010-9353-1

Semiatin, J. (2012). *Trauma exposure, PTSD, and treatment response for partner violent men* (Unpublished doctoral dissertation). University of Maryland–Baltimore County.

Semiatin, J. N., Murphy, C. M., & Elliott, J. D. (2013). Observed behavior during group treatment for partner-violent men: Acceptance of responsibility and promotion of change. *Psychology of Violence, 3*, 126–139. http://dx.doi.org/10.1037/a0029846

Simpson, L. E., Atkins, D. C., Gattis, K. S., & Christensen, A. (2008). Low-level relationship aggression and couple therapy outcomes. *Journal of Family Psychology, 22*, 102–111. http://dx.doi.org/10.1037/0893-3200.22.1.102

Simpson, L. E., Doss, B. D., Wheeler, J., & Christensen, A. (2007). Relationship violence among couples seeking therapy: Common couple violence or battering? *Journal of Marital & Family Therapy*, *33*, 270–283. http://dx.doi.org/10.1111/j.1752-0606.2007.00021.x

Singer, J. D., & Willett, J. B. (2003). *Applied longitudinal data analysis: Modeling change and event occurrence*. New York, NY: Oxford University Press.

Sippel, L. M., & Marshall, A. D. (2011). Posttraumatic stress disorder symptoms, intimate partner violence perpetration, and the mediating role of shame processing bias. *Journal of Anxiety Disorders*, *25*, 903–910. http://dx.doi.org/10.1016/j.janxdis.2011.05.002

Skinner, H. A. (1982). The Drug Abuse Screening Test. *Addictive Behaviors*, *7*, 363–371. http://dx.doi.org/10.1016/0306-4603(82)90005-3

Slotter, E. B., & Finkel, E. J. (2011). I^3 theory: Instigating, impelling, and inhibiting factors in aggression. In P. R. Shaver & M. Mikulincer (Eds.), *Human aggression and violence: Causes, manifestations, and consequences* (pp. 35–52). Washington, DC: American Psychological Association. http://dx.doi.org/10.1037/12346-002

Smith, M. E. (2007). Self-deception among men who are mandated to attend a batterer intervention program. *Perspectives in Psychiatric Care*, *43*, 193–203. http://dx.doi.org/10.1111/j.1744-6163.2007.00134.x

Solomon, Z., Dekel, R., & Mikulincer, M. (2008). Complex trauma of war captivity: A prospective study of attachment and post-traumatic stress disorder. *Psychological Medicine*, *38*, 1427–1434. http://dx.doi.org/10.1017/S0033291708002808

Sonkin, D. J., & Dutton, D. (2003). Treating assaultive men from an attachment perspective. *Journal of Aggression, Maltreatment & Trauma*, *7*, 105–133. http://dx.doi.org/10.1300/J146v07n01_06

Spielberger, C. D. (1989). *State–Trait Anxiety Inventory: Bibliography* (2nd ed.). Palo Alto, CA: Consulting Psychologists Press.

Steele, C. M., & Josephs, R. A. (1990). Alcohol myopia: Its prized and dangerous effects. *American Psychologist*, *45*, 921–933. http://dx.doi.org/10.1037/0003-066X.45.8.921

Stith, S. M., Green, N. M., Smith, D. B., & Ward, D. B. (2008). Marital satisfaction and marital discord as risk markers for intimate partner violence: A meta-analytic review. *Journal of Family Violence*, *23*, 149–160. http://dx.doi.org/10.1007/s10896-007-9137-4

Stith, S. M., & McCollum, E. E. (2011). Conjoint treatment of couples who have experienced intimate partner violence. *Aggression and Violent Behavior*, *16*, 312–318. http://dx.doi.org/10.1016/j.avb.2011.04.012

Stith, S. M., McCollum, E. E., Amanor-Boadu, Y., & Smith, D. (2012). Systemic perspectives on intimate partner violence treatment. *Journal of Marital & Family Therapy*, *38*, 220–240. http://dx.doi.org/10.1111/j.1752-0606.2011.00245.x

Stith, S. M., Rosen, K. H., McCollum, E. E., & Thomsen, C. J. (2004). Treating intimate partner violence within intact couple relationships: Outcomes of multicouple versus individual couple therapy. *Journal of Marital & Family Therapy*, *30*, 305–318. http://dx.doi.org/10.1111/j.1752-0606.2004.tb01242.x

Stith, S. M., Rosen, K. H., Middleton, K. A., Busch, A. L., Lundeberg, K., & Carlton, R. P. (2000). The intergenerational transmission of spouse abuse: A meta-analysis. *Journal of Marriage and Family, 62,* 640–654. http://dx.doi.org/10.1111/j.1741-3737.2000.00640.x

Stith, S. M., Smith, D. B., Penn, C. E., Ward, D. B., & Tritt, D. (2004). Intimate partner physical abuse perpetration and victimization risk factors: A meta-analytic review. *Aggression and Violent Behavior, 10,* 65–98. http://dx.doi.org/10.1016/j.avb.2003.09.001

Straus, M. A. (2008). Dominance and symmetry in partner violence by male and female university students in 32 nations. *Children and Youth Services Review, 30,* 252–275. http://dx.doi.org/10.1016/j.childyouth.2007.10.004

Straus, M., Gelles, R., & Steinmetz, S. K. (1980). *Behind closed doors: A survey of family violence in America.* Garden City, NY: Doubleday.

Straus, M. A., Hamby, S. L., Boney-McCoy, S., & Sugarman, D. B. (1996). The revised Conflict Tactics Scales (CTS2): Development and preliminary psychometric data. *Journal of Family Issues, 17,* 283–316. http://dx.doi.org/10.1177/019251396017003001

Street, A. E., & Arias, I. (2001). Psychological abuse and posttraumatic stress disorder in battered women: Examining the roles of shame and guilt. *Violence and Victims, 16,* 65–78.

Stuart, G. L., Ramsey, S. E., Moore, T. M., Kahler, C. W., Farrell, L. E., Recupero, P. R., & Brown, R. A. (2002). Marital violence victimization and perpetration among women substance abusers: A descriptive study. *Violence Against Women, 8,* 934–952. http://dx.doi.org/10.1177/107780102400447078

Stuewig, J., Tangney, J. P., Heigel, C., Harty, L., & McCloskey, L. (2010). Shaming, blaming, and maiming: Functional links among the moral emotions, externalization of blame, and aggression. *Journal of Research in Personality, 44,* 91–102. http://dx.doi.org/10.1016/j.jrp.2009.12.005

Swan, S. C., Gambone, L. J., Fields, A. M., Sullivan, T. P., & Snow, D. L. (2005). Women who use violence in intimate relationships: The role of anger, victimization, and symptoms of posttraumatic stress and depression. *Violence and Victims, 20,* 267–285. http://dx.doi.org/10.1891/vivi.20.3.267

Taft, C. T., Howard, J., Monson, C. M., Walling, S. M., Resick, P. A., & Murphy, C. M. (2014). "Strength at Home" intervention to prevent conflict and violence in military couples: Pilot findings. *Partner Abuse, 5,* 41–57. http://dx.doi.org/10.1891/1946-6560.5.1.41

Taft, C. T., Kachadourian, L. K., Suvak, M. K., Pinto, L. A., Miller, M. M., Knight, J. A., & Marx, B. P. (2012). Examining impelling and disinhibiting factors for intimate partner violence in veterans. *Journal of Family Psychology, 26,* 285–289. http://dx.doi.org/10.1037/a0027424

Taft, C. T., Macdonald, A., Creech, S. K., Monson, C. M., & Murphy, C. M. (2015). A randomized controlled clinical trial of the Strength at Home Men's

Program for partner violence in military veterans. *The Journal of Clinical Psychiatry*. Advance online publication. http://www.ncbi.nlm.nih.gov/pubmed/26613288

Taft, C. T., Macdonald, A., Monson, C. M., Walling, S. M., Resick, P. A., & Murphy, C. M. (2013). "Strength at Home" group intervention for military populations engaging in intimate partner violence: Pilot findings. *Journal of Family Violence, 28*, 225–231. http://dx.doi.org/10.1007/s10896-013-9496-y

Taft, C. T., Monson, C. M., Schumm, J. A., Watkins, L. E., Panuzio, J., & Resick, P. A. (2009). Posttraumatic stress disorder symptoms, relationship adjustment, and relationship aggression in a sample of female flood victims. *Journal of Family Violence, 24*, 389–396. http://dx.doi.org/10.1007/s10896-009-9241-8

Taft, C. T., & Murphy, C. M. (2007). The working alliance in intervention for partner violence perpetrators: Recent research and theory. *Journal of Family Violence, 22*, 11–18. http://dx.doi.org/10.1007/s10896-006-9053-z

Taft, C. T., Murphy, C. M., Elliott, J. D., & Morrel, T. M. (2001). Attendance-enhancing procedures in group counseling for domestic abusers. *Journal of Counseling Psychology, 48*, 51–60. http://dx.doi.org/10.1037/0022-0167.48.1.51

Taft, C. T., Murphy, C. M., King, D. W., Musser, P. H., & DeDeyn, J. M. (2003). Process and treatment adherence factors in group cognitive–behavioral therapy for partner violent men. *Journal of Consulting and Clinical Psychology, 71*, 812–820. http://dx.doi.org/10.1037/0022-006X.71.4.812

Taft, C. T., Pless, A. P., Stalans, L. J., Koenen, K. C., King, L. A., & King, D. W. (2005). Risk factors for partner violence among a national sample of combat veterans. *Journal of Consulting and Clinical Psychology, 73*, 151–159. http://dx.doi.org/10.1037/0022-006X.73.1.151

Taft, C. T., Schumm, J. A., Marshall, A. D., Panuzio, J., & Holtzworth-Munroe, A. (2008). Family-of-origin maltreatment, posttraumatic stress disorder symptoms, social information processing deficits, and relationship abuse perpetration. *Journal of Abnormal Psychology, 117*, 637–646. http://dx.doi.org/10.1037/0021-843X.117.3.637

Taft, C. T., Street, A. E., Marshall, A. D., Dowdall, D. J., & Riggs, D. S. (2007). Posttraumatic stress disorder, anger, and partner abuse among Vietnam combat veterans. *Journal of Family Psychology, 21*, 270–277. http://dx.doi.org/10.1037/0893-3200.21.2.270

Taft, C. T., Vogt, D. S., Marshall, A. D., Panuzio, J., & Niles, B. L. (2007). Aggression among combat veterans: Relationships with combat exposure and symptoms of posttraumatic stress disorder, dysphoria, and anxiety. *Journal of Traumatic Stress, 20*, 135–145. http://dx.doi.org/10.1002/jts.20197

Taft, C. T., Walling, S. M., Howard, J. M., & Monson, C. (2011). Trauma, PTSD, and partner violence in military families. In S. M. Wadsworth & D. Riggs (Eds.), *Risk and resilience in U.S. military families* (pp. 195–212). New York, NY: Springer. http://dx.doi.org/10.1007/978-1-4419-7064-0_10

Taft, C. T., Watkins, L. E., Stafford, J., Street, A. E., & Monson, C. M. (2011). Posttraumatic stress disorder and intimate relationship problems: A meta-analysis.

Journal of Consulting and Clinical Psychology, 79, 22–33. http://dx.doi.org/10.1037/a0022196

Taft, C. T., Weatherill, R. P., Scott, J. P., Thomas, S. A., Kang, H. K., & Eckhardt, C. I. (2015). Social information processing in anger expression and partner violence in returning U.S. veterans. *Journal of Traumatic Stress, 28,* 314–321. http://dx.doi.org/10.1002/jts.22017

Tangney, J. P., & Dearing, R. L. (2002). *Shame and guilt.* New York, NY: Guilford Press. http://dx.doi.org/10.4135/9781412950664.n388

Taylor, S. (2004). Efficacy and outcome predictors for three PTSD treatments: Exposure therapy, EMDR, and relaxation training. In S. Taylor (Ed.), *Advances in the treatment of posttraumatic stress disorder: Cognitive–behavioral perspectives* (pp. 13–37). New York, NY: Springer.

Taylor, S. P., & Leonard, K. E. (1983). Alcohol and human physical aggression. In R. G. Geen & E. I. Donnerstein (Eds.), *Aggression: Theoretical and empirical reviews: Vol. 2. Issues in research* (pp. 77–101). San Diego, CA: Academic Press.

Teten, A. L., Schumacher, J. A., Bailey, S. D., & Kent, T. A. (2009). Male-to-female sexual aggression among Iraq, Afghanistan, and Vietnam veterans: Co-occurring substance abuse and intimate partner aggression. *Journal of Traumatic Stress, 22,* 307–311. http://dx.doi.org/10.1002/jts.20422

Thomaes, S., Bushman, B. J., Stegge, H., & Olthof, T. (2008). Trumping shame by blasts of noise: Narcissism, self-esteem, shame, and aggression in young adolescents. *Child Development, 79,* 1792–1801. http://dx.doi.org/10.1111/j.1467-8624.2008.01226.x

Thomaes, S., Stegge, H., Olthof, T., Bushman, B. J., & Nezlek, J. B. (2011). Turning shame inside-out: "Humiliated fury" in young adolescents. *Emotion, 11,* 786–793. http://dx.doi.org/10.1037/a0023403

Thomas, M. D., Bennett, L. W., & Stoops, C. (2013). The treatment needs of substance abusing batterers: A comparison of men who batter their female partners. *Journal of Family Violence, 28,* 121–129. http://dx.doi.org/10.1007/s10896-012-9479-4

Thompson, H. (2012). Screening, assessment, and intervention for intimate partner violence in integrated care. In R. Curtis & E. Christian (Eds.), *Integrated care: Applying theory to practice* (pp. 227–241). New York, NY: Routledge.

Thompson, M. P., Basile, K. C., Hertz, M. F., Sitterle, D., & Centers for Disease Control and Prevention. (2006). Measuring intimate partner violence victimization and perpetration: A compendium of assessment tools. In *Measuring intimate partner violence victimization and perpetration: A compendium of assessment tools.* Retrieved from http://www.endvawnow.org/uploads/browser/files/IPV%20Compendium.pdf

Ting, L., Jordan-Green, L., Murphy, C. M., & Pitts, S. C. (2009). Substance use problems, treatment engagement, and outcomes in partner violent men. *Research on Social Work Practice, 19,* 395–406. http://dx.doi.org/10.1177/1049731508329418

Tjaden, P., & Thoennes, N. (2000). Prevalence and consequences of male-to-female and female-to-male intimate partner violence as measured by the National Violence Against Women Survey. *Violence Against Women*, 6, 142–161. http://dx.doi.org/10.1177/10778010022181769

Twentyman, C. T., & Zimering, R. T. (1979). Behavioral training of social skills: A critical review. *Progress in Behavior Modification*, *7*, 319–400. http://dx.doi.org/10.1016/B978-0-12-535607-7.50012-8

Vetere, A., & Cooper, J. (2001). Working systemically with family violence: Risk, responsibility and collaboration. *Journal of Family Therapy*, *23*, 378–396. http://dx.doi.org/10.1111/1467-6427.00191

Vogt, D., Vaughn, R., Glickman, M. E., Schultz, M., Drainoni, M. L., Elwy, R., & Eisen, S. (2011). Gender differences in combat-related stressors and their association with postdeployment mental health in a nationally representative sample of U.S. OEF/OIF veterans. *Journal of Abnormal Psychology*, *120*, 797–806. http://dx.doi.org/10.1037/a0023452

Wareham, J., Boots, D. P., & Chavez, J. M. (2009). A test of social learning and intergenerational transmission among batterers. *Journal of Criminal Justice*, *37*, 163–173. http://dx.doi.org/10.1016/j.jcrimjus.2009.02.011

Weathers, F. W., Blake, D. D., Schnurr, P. P., Kaloupek, D. G., Marx, B. P., & Keane, T. M. (2013a). *The Clinician-Administered PTSD Scale for* DSM–5 *(CAPS-5)*. Retrieved from U.S. Department of Veterans Affairs website: http://www.ptsd.va.gov/professional/assessment/adult-int/caps.asp

Weathers, F. W., Blake, D. D., Schnurr, P. P., Kaloupek, D. G., Marx, B. P., & Keane, T. M. (2013b). *The Life Events Checklist for* DSM–5 *(LEC-5)*. Retrieved from U.S. Department of Veterans Affairs website: http://www.ptsd.va.gov/professional/assessment/te-measures/life_events_checklist.asp

Weathers, F. W., Litz, B. T., Keane, T. M., Palmieri, P. A., Marx, B. P., & Schnurr, P. P. (2013). *The PTSD Checklist for* DSM–5 *(PCL-5)*. Retrieved from U.S. Department of Veterans Affairs website: http://www.ptsd.va.gov/professional/assessment/adult-sr/ptsd-checklist.asp

Weisz, A. N., Tolman, R. M., & Saunders, D. G. (2000). Assessing the risk of severe domestic violence: The importance of survivors' predictions. *Journal of Interpersonal Violence*, *15*, 75–90. http://dx.doi.org/10.1177/088626000015001006

Werrbach, G. B., Grotevant, H. D., & Cooper, C. R. (1990). Gender differences in adolescents' identity development in the domain of sex role concepts. *Sex Roles*, *23*, 349–362. http://dx.doi.org/10.1007/BF00289225

Westphal, M., Olfson, M., Bravova, M., Gameroff, M. J., Gross, R., Wickramaratne, P., . . . Neria, Y. (2013). Borderline personality disorder, exposure to interpersonal trauma, and psychiatric comorbidity in urban primary care patients. *Psychiatry: Interpersonal and Biological Processes*, *76*, 365–380. http://dx.doi.org/10.1521/psyc.2013.76.4.365

Whitaker, D. J., Haileyesus, T., Swahn, M., & Saltzman, L. S. (2007). Differences in frequency of violence and reported injury between relationships with reciprocal and nonreciprocal intimate partner violence. *American Journal of Public Health, 97*, 941–947. http://dx.doi.org/10.2105/AJPH.2005.079020

Whitfield, C. L., Anda, R. F., Dube, S. R., & Felitti, V. J. (2003). Violent childhood experiences and the risk of intimate partner violence in adults: Assessment in a large health maintenance organization. *Journal of Interpersonal Violence, 18*, 166–185. http://dx.doi.org/10.1177/0886260502238733

Widom, C. S. (1989). Does violence beget violence? A critical examination of the literature. *Psychological Bulletin, 106*, 3–28. http://dx.doi.org/10.1037/0033-2909.106.1.3

Williams, K. R., & Grant, S. R. (2006). Empirically examining the risk of intimate partner violence: The revised Domestic Violence Screening Instrument (DVSI–R). *Public Health Reports, 121*, 400–408.

Williams, K. R., & Houghton, A. B. (2004). Assessing the risk of domestic violence reoffending: A validation study. *Law and Human Behavior, 28*, 437–455. http://dx.doi.org/10.1023/B:LAHU.0000039334.59297.f0

Wilson, J. P., & Krauss, G. E. (1983). *Posttraumatic stress disorders (PTSD): Collected papers*. Cleveland, OH: Cleveland State University Press.

Wood, S. L., & Sommers, M. S. (2011). Consequences of intimate partner violence on child witnesses: A systematic review of the literature. *Journal of Child and Adolescent Psychiatric Nursing, 24*, 223–236. http://dx.doi.org/10.1111/j.1744-6171.2011.00302.x

World Health Organization. (1992). *Classification of mental and behavioural disorders: Clinical descriptions and diagnostic guidelines, 10th revision (ICD–10)*. Geneva, Switzerland: Author.

Wright, B. K., Kelsall, H. L., Sim, M. R., Clarke, D. M., & Creamer, M. C. (2013). Support mechanisms and vulnerabilities in relation to PTSD in veterans of the Gulf War, Iraq War, and Afghanistan deployments: A systematic review. *Journal of Traumatic Stress, 26*, 310–318.

Yalom, I. D. (1995). *The theory and practice of group psychotherapy* (4th ed.). New York, NY: Basic Books.

Zeman, J., & Shipman, K. L. (1996). Children's expression of negative affect: Reasons and methods. *Developmental Psychology, 32*, 842–849. http://dx.doi.org/10.1037/0012-1649.32.5.842

INDEX

ABOUT THE AUTHORS

Casey T. Taft, PhD, is a staff psychologist at the National Center for PTSD in the Veterans Affairs Boston Healthcare System, and professor of psychiatry at Boston University School of Medicine. Dr. Taft received his PhD in clinical psychology from the University of Maryland, Baltimore County. He was the 2006 Young Professional Award winner from the International Society for Traumatic Stress Studies, and the 2009 Linda Saltzman Memorial Intimate Partner Violence Researcher Award winner. He has served or is currently serving as principal investigator on funded grants focusing on understanding and preventing intimate partner violence through the National Institute of Mental Health, the Department of Veterans Affairs, the Centers for Disease Control, the Department of Defense, and the Blue Shield of California Foundation. Dr. Taft has published over 100 empirical papers and book chapters, chaired an American Psychological Association task force on trauma in the military, and consulted with the United Nations on preventing violence and abuse globally.

Christopher M. Murphy, PhD, is professor and chair of psychology at the University of Maryland, Baltimore County, and clinical supervisor for the New Behaviors Program for intimate partner violence at HopeWorks, a community-based nonprofit agency in Howard County, Maryland. Dr. Murphy received his PhD in clinical psychology from Stony Brook University. He received the 2015 Linda Saltzman Memorial Intimate Partner Violence Researcher Award from the Institute on Violence, Abuse, and Trauma. His research, which has been supported by the National Institute of Mental Health and the National Institute on Alcohol Abuse and Alcoholism, focuses on the efficacy of cognitive behavioral and motivational interventions for individuals who engage in partner violence, the identification of personal and contextual factors that inhibit treatment response in this population, the role of alcohol and drug use in partner violence and its treatment, and the forms and effects of emotional relationship abuse.

Suzannah K. Creech, PhD, is a research psychologist in the Treatment Core at the VHA VISN 17 Center of Excellence for Research on Returning War Veterans and the Central Texas Veterans Healthcare System, and an assistant professor (research) in the Department of Psychiatry at the Alpert Medical School of Brown University. Dr. Creech received her PhD in clinical psychology from Texas A&M University. She also completed an advanced fellowship in PTSD treatment at the Brown Psychology Training Consortium and another fellowship in clinical research at the VA Boston Health Care System. She has spent her career working with veterans and service members recovering from exposure to trauma. Dr. Creech's recent work has focused on family and relationship functioning in women veterans who deployed to Iraq and Afghanistan.